# RUNNING OUT OF CONTROL

# RUNNING OUT OF CONTROL

## DILEMMAS OF GLOBALIZATION

### R. Alan Hedley

Kumarian
Press, Inc.

*Dedicated to*

*Our grandchildren's children.*

*Running Out of Control: Dilemmas of Globalization*

Published 2002 in the United States of America by Kumarian Press, Inc.,
1294 Blue Hills Avenue, Bloomfield, Connecticut 06002 USA.

Copyediting and design by Nicholas A. Kosar.
Proofreading by Beth Richards. Index by Robert Swanson.
The text of this book is set in Adobe Sabon 10.5/14.

Printed in the United States of America on acid-free paper by
Thomson-Shore, Inc.
Text printed with vegetable oil-based ink.

∞ The paper used in this publication meets the minimum requirements
of the American National Standard for Information Sciences—Permanence of
Paper for Printed Library Materials, ANSI Z39.48–1984.

Library of Congress Cataloging-in-Publication Data
  Hedley, R. Alan.
    Running out of control : dilemmas of globalization / R. Alan Hedley.
      p.      cm.
    Includes bibliographical references and index.
    ISBN 1-56549-152-1 (hardcover : alk. paper) — ISBN 1-56549-151-3 (pbk.:
alk. paper)
      1. Globalization.  I. Title.
    JZ1318 .H43 2002
    303.48'2—dc21                                    2002006238

    11  10  09  08  07  06  05  04  03  02        10  9  8  7  6  5  4  3  2  1

First Printing 2002

# CONTENTS

# TABLES, FIGURES, AND BOXES

## BOXES

# ABBREVIATIONS

| | |
|---|---|
| AOL | America Online |
| CIS | Commonwealth of Independent States (former Soviet Union) |
| CAD | Computer-aided design |
| CAE | Computer-aided engineering |
| CAM | Computer-aided manufacturing |
| CFCs | Chlorofluorocarbons |
| CIM | Computer-integrated manufacturing |
| $CO_2$ | Carbon dioxide |
| CPU | Central processing unit |
| DARPA | Defense Advanced Research Projects Agency |
| EPA | Environmental Protection Agency |
| EU | European Union |
| FDI | Foreign direct investment |
| GDP | Gross domestic product |
| GM | General Motors |
| GNP | Gross national product |
| GPI | Genuine Progress Indicator |
| HDI | Human Development Index |
| HTML | Hypertext Markup Language |
| IPCC | Inter-Governmental Panel on Climate Change |
| ICT | Information and communications technology |
| IRS | Internal Revenue Service |
| ITU | International Telecommunication Union |
| LAN | Local area network |
| MAI | Multilateral Agreement on Investment |
| NASA | National Aeronautics and Space Administration |
| NGO | Non-governmental organization |
| NIPC | National Infrastructure Protection Center |
| NPP | Net primary productivity |
| OECD | Organisation for Economic Co-operation and Development |
| OPEC | Organization of Petroleum Exporting Countries |
| PPP | Purchasing power parity |
| TNC | Transnational corporation |
| TRIPS | Trade Related Intellectual Property Rights |
| UN | United Nations |

| WAN | Wide area network |
| WHO | World Health Organization |
| WINS | Wireless Integrated Network Sensors project |
| WTO | World Trade Organization |
| Y2K | Year 2000 |

# PREFACE

*I read the news today, oh boy.*
                    —The Beatles, 1967

**THE IDEA FOR THIS BOOK** originated in 1999 when I was preparing a course on industrialization, a course I had not taught for several years. I began by trying to put the effects of industrialization into contemporary perspective as we neared the end of the twentieth century—not just what industrialization has achieved, but also problems it has created. By the time I stood in front of the class in January 2000, I announced that I was going to write a book called *Apocalypse When?* I then explained that industrialization, both in its direct effects and the fact that it has been introduced very unevenly into the world, is largely responsible for the following global problems, each of which puts humankind at severe risk:

- the unanticipated and increasingly harmful effects of technology

- worsening environmental degradation and loss of biodiversity

- the widening gap between the developed and developing countries

- increasing cultural conflict

- human population growth

I told the class that my generation was not leaving them with as many opportunities in this world as we had inherited from the generation before us, and that if we didn't begin *immediately* and *collectively* as a species to solve these problems, future generations would be even worse off. This introduction to the course sparked some lively and informative discussion as we grappled with these issues, as well as eliciting additional problems that the students themselves raised (increasing epidemic diseases and urbanization).

When classes ended, I began to investigate in detail the effects of the new information and communications technology revolution with which we are presently engaged, and how it has facilitated an increasingly globalized world. By virtually eliminating space and time barriers, this microelectronic revolution has increased both the magnitude and speed of human impacts—on each other and on the environment in which we live. An equally important feature of this revolution is that we are increasingly connected to each other through interdependent electronic networks. An illustration of what these qualitative changes in magnitude, speed, and interdependence can mean in terms of individual behavior was dramatically brought to our attention in May 2000 when a single Filipino student almost instantaneously infected millions of computer systems worldwide with his "love bug" virus. I use this example to open the book.

As I continued to research and write, I received valuable input from my students in courses on globalization and social change. In discussing issues crucial to the continuing evolution of our species, I noticed that these students seemed to be taking these matters far more seriously than students I had taught a generation earlier. Moreover, in small but significant ways, these students were also modifying their daily behavior in light of the new reality they now must confront. I discuss some of the options that are available in Chapter 5.

A highly significant event in terms of the immense problems we face occurred on September 11, 2001, when the entire world witnessed how truly vulnerable those supported by complex, interdependent infrastructures are to deliberate attack, calamitous accident, or natural catastrophe. As the terrorist attacks on New York and Washington, D.C., revealed how a few dissidents could successfully cripple a superpower, so also did the 1986 accidental nuclear explosion at Chernobyl reveal the devastating cascading effects of technological malfunction, and violent earthquakes in Los Angeles (1994) and Kobe (1995) revealed the frailty of human works in relation to the might of nature. These events variously highlight the acute vulnerability of interdependent human systems, be they metropolitan centers, industrial facilities, or transportation and communication networks.

In the days following September 11, the media were filled with countless unsubstantiated threats and rumors: Was the Nimda virus that destroyed more than 8 million computer networks linked to the terrorist attacks? Would more deadly and highly contagious smallpox and plague viruses follow the mailing of anthrax bacteria to highly placed officials? Would something big happen next week? Did the terrorists have nuclear capability? Were the nation's bridges the next target? Could terrorists bring down the Internet? How vulnerable to attack are slaughterhouses and the meat packing industry? Could bioterrorism be used against the agricultural sector? What about the 850,000 industrial facilities that routinely use hazardous chemicals? How likely is an attack on America's nuclear power plants? Could hackers launch an electronic attack on the nation's power grid? Or hack into the systems that direct planes, causing mid-air collisions and crashes? Or command a dam's computer system to open floodgates?

September 11, 2001, marked a profound change in national consciousness as all developed countries began to institute emergency measures to guard against a wide-ranging host of possible terrorist attacks. Identified as extremely vulnerable are interdependent national and international electronic networks that provide essential services such as telecommunications, water supply systems, transportation, electrical power, gas and oil storage and delivery, banking and finance, government operations, and emergency services. These networks, originally established to increase scale, access, speed, efficiency, and predictability—or in a word, *control*—are themselves now at severe risk, as they can be accessed by anyone with a computer, sufficient skill, and the motivation to wreak havoc on these integrated systems that support modern globalization.

Consequently, the book I began in 1999 has taken on new urgency. Today, not only is there a *possibility* that these interdependent networks could be deliberately compromised, there is also a *distinct probability*. Is it possible to make these systems completely fail-safe? The concerted expert opinion, as you will read, is that this objective is simply not attainable. In the long run, from whatever cause, system breakdown is inevitable. How then may we achieve some semblance of security in a post–September 11 world? The answer to this question must involve our attempt to extend security to *all* peoples of the world. In other words, it is in our enlightened self-interest to bridge the many divides that separate us: in income, health, education, and access to the earth's diminishing resources. Only by acting *collectively* do our grandchildren's children have any hope of inheriting a world in which close to 10 billion people (two-thirds more in 2060 than in 1999) may live reasonably satisfying lives with far fewer natural resources than we now enjoy.

# ACKNOWLEDGMENTS

**AN AUTHOR IS A SCAVENGER,** always on the lookout for new, interesting, and challenging ideas. There are standard places to search for them: books, journals, and now, the Internet. I acknowledge these people in the Bibliography. As well, personal contacts represent a potential source of good ideas: colleagues, students, friends, family—even total strangers. It is this group I wish to acknowledge here. Whether the contribution involved reading and critiquing the entire manuscript (Robert Hagedorn), or sections of it (Carren Learning Dujela, Gene Racicot, Martha McMahon, Vivian Berda, and Anna Winnett), answering specific technical questions (Eric Manning and Lanjing Li), alerting me about possible good sources (Cecilia Benoit and David Gartrell), or responding to my various thoughts on the subject (my students), I benefited immensely from your ideas. Thank you!

Another group of people provided me with much appreciated moral support and inspiration along the way. David Turpin was instrumental in getting me started on this venture. Akira Nakamura, Subbiah Arunachalam, Athreya Venkatesh, Fatimah Daud, Adolphine Yawa Aggor, and Thark Bahadur Shah not only provided their support, they also served as an important target audience for my writing. Also, Zheng Wu offered his encouragement on a very timely daily basis. Last, but certainly not least, are my two grandsons, Nikolas and Alex. As I wrote, I continually thought of them and their generation, wondering what kind of life we would be leaving for *their* children. In dedicating this book to our grandchildren's children, I hope to instill within all of us our own personal link to the future that will guide our everyday behavior in more sustainable ways.

In a class all by herself is my wife Darby Carswell. Not only did she do all of the above, she did much, much more. It is impossible to express in words my deep gratitude to her for all that she has done in helping me to achieve my goal.

As principal investigator of a research project on "Crises and Contingencies Management," Professor Akira Nakamura of Meiji University supplied very welcome funding for the preparation of this book. I am indebted to him also for his wise counsel.

Given the topic of this book, I decided it would be appropriate to have it published by "a forward-looking, scholarly press that promotes active international engagement and an awareness of global connectedness." I was not mistaken in my choice of Kumarian Press. From my first contact with Editor-in-Chief Linda Beyus, I have received tremendous encouragement, expert professional advice, and friendly associations. I sincerely hope that our partnership will continue long into the future. Finally, I would like to thank the anonymous reviewer for the helpful comments on my manuscript.

# 1

---

# UNDERSTANDING GLOBALIZATION

*I'll put a girdle round about the earth*
*In forty minutes.*
> —Puck in Shakespeare's *A Midsummer Night's Dream*

**ON MAY 4, 2000,** the so called "love bug" virus, a self-propagating computer worm, infected government, business, and personal computers around the world (CNN 2000a). Spreading like lightning via Microsoft Outlook e-mail systems and attacking all Windows-based computers, the virus destroyed HTML and script files by overwriting them with its own code, and then inserted itself into all system e-mail addresses, ready to repeat its devastation on all those listed (Virus Bulletin 2000). The virus was activated when unsuspecting e-mailers opened a "LOVE-LETTER-FOR-YOU.TXT" file, or twenty-two known variants, including "Virus ALERT!!!" warnings (Computer Associates 2000). In just twenty-four hours, the love bug had wreaked havoc worldwide, immobilizing most communication and information systems it infiltrated and costing billions of dollars in damage and lost productivity. The alleged perpetrator was a twenty-two-year-old male college student in the Philippines (CNN 2000b).

This sensational news event serves as a useful illustration of what this book is about. First, it is about revolutionary changes in how the world is structured. Increasingly, the forces of production, distribution/transmission, and consumption of goods and services are globally organized, having been managed originally at local, regional, and then national levels. Second, it is about control. Human history may be characterized as a series of varied attempts to improve our odds against nature and to gain control over our individual and collective destinies. Over the millennia, through the development and application of various strategic technologies, we have managed to expand human control to include the total

**Figure 1.1    Minimal Requirements for Achieving Effective System Control**

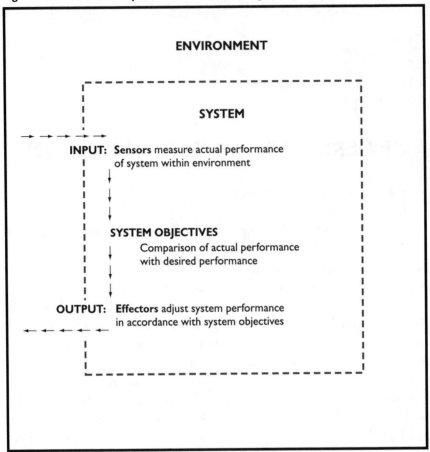

global environment (and beyond). In this book, employing a "systems theory" perspective, I examine how human control systems are evolving as a result of globalization.

A system such as the Filipino love bug computer virus is a set of inter-related elements which interacts dynamically with its environment. In the case of the love bug, this system is linked to its environment—the Internet—which is composed of millions of linked computers. An environment comprises those elements outside the system whose attributes affect the system, and also whose attributes are affected by the behavior of the system (Hall and Fagen 1968). What is considered to be a system as distinct from its environment depends upon the level of analysis (discussed in Chapter 2) and the problem at hand. Figure 1.1 graphically represents the minimal requirements for attaining system control. First, a system must be able to measure in some way what is happening in its environment. The system assesses this information in relation to the objectives it wants to achieve and then adusts its performance accordingly (it writes the code necessary to transmit the love bug virus). I will say more about systems theory as we go along.

The love bug event is important because it points to the vulnerability of interdependent, networked systems. The Filipino student successfully accomplished his mission largely because Microsoft operating systems dominate information and communications technology (ZDNet 1999), and therefore represent a single, albeit complex, set of systems to decode and reprogram. Because of the pervasiveness of Microsoft products throughout all electronic information and communications systems, and because most of these systems are interlinked through the Internet, and because most of the work in industrially developed nations now involves computers, the potential to bring about maximal damage and disruption is astronomical (Hedley 2000).

The love bug incident reveals an interesting paradox about control in the global age. On the one hand, interconnected real-time global networks are created to increase predictability and control. Yet on the other hand, their very structure makes them highly susceptible to massively disrupting chain reactions which are threats to control. Consequently, the price for the greater access, speed, and efficiency of interdependent versus independent systems is higher environmental risk. More generally, as I demonstrate throughout this book, as a result of decreasing system diversity in a world in which we have virtually eliminated the insulating effects of time and space, global interdependence poses a serious challenge to all human activity.

Although it is true that the world has been globalized since European colonizers discovered new territories in the fifteenth and sixteenth centuries, it is only within the past few decades that transportation, communication, and information networks have been created such that more and more of our activities are taking place within a global environment, as the love bug so aptly demonstrated. Consequently, we are dealing with a set of problems relatively novel in human experience.

Let me now highlight the main features of this book. In the remainder of Chapter 1, I first define the very complex, multidimensional concept of globalization, and then empirically assess how extensively it is apparent throughout the world. As you will note, to date globalization is neither a universal nor a uniform phenomenon, being restricted largely to select activities and people in the developed countries. I then outline the forces responsible for producing globalization (principally technological innovations in transportation, communication, and information processing harnessed by capitalist enterprise), and also examine what may be characterized as counterforces to globalization—the hitherto disenfranchised and excluded vast majority of the world's population.

In Chapter 2, I introduce six theories of social change that attempt to explain and account for our present circumstance: two development theories that predict overall global convergence in social structure and process; two underdevelopment theories that argue against convergence, focusing instead on differences in global development patterns; and two technological development theories that concentrate on how technology represents a structural challenge to global development. In concluding Chapter 2, I discuss various methods and strategies for researching social change.

In Chapter 3, I analyze changes in control systems within the context of globalization, focusing primarily on those who establish and maintain these systems. For comparative purposes, I generally describe how control has changed over the course of human history, but concentrate specifically on changes to control introduced during the latter half of the twentieth century. In my examination of control, I deal with each of the four dimensions of globalization identified in Chapter 1: technological, economic, political, and sociocultural. Here, I make the case that although our ability to devise increasingly complex systems of control has expanded tremendously the physical and mental capacities of the human species, our attempts to establish integrated and uniform global control are introducing hitherto unanticipated and unintended uncertainties for human existence.

In Chapter 4, I examine the encroachment of human systems on the global ecological environment over time in terms of habitat loss and fragmentation, pollution, biotic changes, and exploitation of wild living resources. The global eco-environment is extremely important because it represents the ultimate set of constraints or limits beyond which human activity is impossible. I identify what some of these constraints are and how close we are to reaching them.

Finally, in Chapter 5, I summarize all the issues of control I have raised throughout the book. In terms of the theories presented in Chapter 2, I incorporate these control issues into a broad discussion of the following structural problems of globalization: the interdependence and standardization of integrated electronic controls systems; the inability to control adequately the activities of transnational corporations (and other border-straddling organizations); global instability produced by highly unequal resource and income distributions; increasing human demand fueled by cumulative technology, capitalist enterprise, rising aspirations, and population growth; and the ecological limits to human extraction, production, consumption, and pollution. In the latter half of Chapter 5, I describe some promising approaches and strategies that various individuals and organizations have initiated to deal with these problems.

## WHAT IS GLOBALIZATION?

Albert Einstein (1936) once observed that the categories are not inherent in the phenomena. In other words, concepts such as "globalization" and "information and communications technology revolution" are human constructs we have developed in order to understand better the complexities of what we believe is happening in the world. Theories are simplified models of reality, and the first step in theory construction is categorization or classification. Over the past few decades, researchers and social commentators have coined the term "globalization" in order to focus on what they believe are interrelated processes which are having tremendous impacts on our lives in the late twentieth and early twenty-first centuries. Consequently, there is no one correct definition of globalization; it has many different meanings and interpretations, depending upon who is discussing it and in what context. However, there are elements of agreement as to what globalization means.

The derivation of the term "globalization" implies that it involves worldwide processes that are relatively novel and still unfolding. These multidimensional processes are being experienced unevenly throughout the world and in different sectors of social life. *Globalization is a complex set of human forces involving the production, distribution/transmission, and consumption of technical, economic, political, and sociocultural goods and services which are administratively and technologically integrated on a worldwide basis.* This definition highlights the point that globalization comprises technological, economic, political (including military), and sociocultural dimensions. Together these interrelated dimensions make up the (human) global system which operates within the broader global ecological environment.

Concerning the four dimensions of globalization, as I have already mentioned, innovations in transportation, communication, and information processing within the past three or four decades have permitted the creation of a technological infrastructure that facilitates the other dimensions of globalization. While technology may be seen as the facilitating means to modern globalization, the primary motivation has been economic—the harnessing of natural and human resources and the establishing of markets and investments worldwide by capitalist enterprise to achieve greater corporate control. In part, to counter the forces of technologically enhanced global capitalism, and to represent civic interests, governments and nongovernmental organizations have also globalized through the formation of international alliances. However, these coalitions have been insufficient to moderate the effects of another important dimension of globalization—the worldwide cultural overlay of Western values, norms, institutions, and practices. Because globalization was initiated predominantly by corporations and countries in the Western world, inevitably, what is produced, transmitted, and consumed is monocultural. Thus, globalization as a multidimensional concept involves a worldwide technological infrastructure in which Western-style capitalism predominates.

Finally, if technology facilitates globalization, the ecological biosphere within which we all live represents its outside limits. Certainly during the past few decades, mounting evidence on a variety of fronts such as climate change, pollution, ozone depletion, cumulative environmental degradation, and population growth indicates we are nearing these limits. Consequently, globalization also involves a critical tension between our technological ability to modify the natural environment and the ultimate ecological constraints beyond which human existence is impossible.

In the following section, I describe the various forces instrumental in producing our globalized world.

## FORCES OF GLOBALIZATION

The world has always been a large place, but in some senses it has become much smaller than it was. It measures 25,000 miles in circumference (*Britannica* 1999). As recently as the late nineteenth century, the great science fiction writer Jules Verne wrote the then unbelievable novel, *Around the World in Eighty Days*. Today, not only can we physically circumnavigate the world in one day, we can electronically orbit the planet in just eight seconds (Phillips 1996)—three hundred times faster than

Shakespeare's magical Puck. Globalization is both feasible and viable now because of technological innovations in transportation, communication, and information processing during the latter part of the twentieth century. In fact, many experts claim that these interrelated innovations constitute the basis for a new technological revolution every bit as significant as the industrial revolution some 250 years earlier.

A major impetus for this recent revolution was World War II, itself a global phenomenon. Government-sponsored research centers produced myriad inventions and discoveries that were applied to the war effort. Some of these, most notably the work in nuclear fission, rocketry, and jet engines, contributed directly to the arsenal of the warring nations, whereas others such as materials development (plastic, superalloys, aluminum, and synthetics) made more indirect contributions. A third area of concentration involved the development of reliable, high-speed support systems, and it was in this context that the computer and telecommunications industries were created and set the stage for the information and communications technology (ICT) revolution that was to follow.

The fact that these technological innovations were organizationally sponsored highlights a second underlying force of globalization. In the years following World War II, organizations in the private, public, and civil sectors all harnessed these innovations to suit their purposes. In the private sector, corporations employed these innovations to secure competitive advantage by becoming transnational in their operations. In the public sector, governments entered into international alliances in attempts to create a stable world order out of the chaos produced by the War. And in reaction to these moves on the part of organizations in the private and public sectors, ordinary citizens—civil society—formed international non-governmental organizations of their own in order to achieve what they believed were important development objectives. Consequently, technologically enhanced organizations of all types were also instrumental in ushering in the global age.

Finally, on an individual basis, people all over the world also helped to bring about globalization. They enthusiastically adopted the numerous technological innovations in transportation, communication, and information processing to reach out and touch others, both physically and electronically, all around the globe.

Following is a discussion of each of these three main forces of globalization.

## Technological Forces

**Transportation**    Notable innovations in transportation during the past fifty years include the launching of container ships for shipping raw materials and finished manufactured goods worldwide, the introduction of commercial jets, and the debut of space travel. With regard to container ships, Herman (1983:135) states that "the impact of containerization on the shipping industry can rightly be compared to the impact which steamships had on the field when they were first introduced over a hundred

---

## BOX 1.1

## FEDEX: A GLOBAL CORPORATION

At 11:45 a.m. on June 11, 2000, I shipped a paper by FedEx from my office in Victoria, Canada, to a colleague in Madras, India. From Victoria, the paper went to Vancouver (4:16 p.m.) and Memphis, Tennessee (6:14 p.m.), FedEx headquarters and central routing hub. My paper left Memphis on 06/12/00 at 2:46 a.m. bound for the European hub city of Paris (8:18 p.m.), and then on to Dubai in the Persian Gulf (2:17 p.m., 06/13/00), and Bombay, India (3:00 a.m., 06/14/00), where it had to wait for commercial customs release (11:00 a.m.). My paper arrived in Madras (9:08 a.m., 06/15/00) and was finally delivered to my Indian colleague (11:30 a.m.).

All of this information I obtained from entering my FedEx tracking number at the FedEx Web site (www.fedex.com). My paper was merely one of millions of shipments that FedEx handles and tracks every day.

According to a July 11, 2000, FedEx Corporation press release posted on its Web site:

FedEx Express, a $15 billion subsidiary of FedEx Corp., connects areas that generate 90% of the world's gross domestic product in 24–48 hours with door-to-door, customs cleared service and a money back guarantee. The company's unmatched air route authorities and infrastructure make it the world's largest express transportation company, providing fast, reliable and time-definite transportation of more than 3.3 million items to 210 countries each working day. FedEx employs approximately 145,000 employees and has more than 43,000 drop-off locations, 663 aircraft and 44,500 vehicles in its integrated global network. The company maintains electronic connections with more than 2.5 million customers via FedEx Powership®, FedEx Ship®, and FedEx InternetShip®.

years ago." A container ship has specially designed holds, hatches, and cranes which enable it to take whole truck trailers on board without loading and unloading their contents. This reduces ship time in port (from 65 to 25 percent annually), cuts stevedoring costs, and virtually eliminates pilferage. It also permits the construction of larger, faster (from fifteen to twenty-five knots), more fuel-efficient vessels which reduces total operating expenses. For example, Herman (1983:135) cites comparative statistics on the North Atlantic route for 1970: "fifty containerships provided a tonnage greater by approximately one-third than the one hundred and seventy vessels which operated there only one-half decade before." And given that "over 80 per cent of world trade by volume is carried by ship" (Herman 1983:3), the inducements offered by containerization are substantial.

The idea of container ships emerged in 1951 when a shipping company "took a converted truck body as deck cargo from Miami to Puerto Rico" (Gilman 1983:8). Pearson and Fossey (1983:220) report that only 106 container ships were built worldwide prior to the 1960s; however, in the 1960s, 478 were constructed, and in the following decade 1,931 more container ships were launched.

While container ships are important for the efficient and speedy transportation of goods, jet aircraft are invaluable for transporting people and time-sensitive cargo quickly around the globe. The first commercial jet airline service was introduced in Britain in 1952 (Woytinsky and Woytinski 1955:500). By 1962, "the difference in speed between the fastest piston-engined transport and a jet was 240 miles an hour, a differential almost as great as all the speed increases made by commercial airplanes between 1918 and 1953" (Serling 1982:100). In effect, the world became smaller and more accessible. Recent figures on worldwide air traffic demonstrate this point. According to the International Civil Aviation Organization (ICAO 2001), in 1999 world airlines carried some 1.6 billion people and 28.2 million metric tons of air cargo (see Box 1.1).

The concept of globalization received a major boost on October 4, 1957, when the Soviet Union successfully launched Sputnik I, the first-ever space satellite. About the size of a basketball and weighing 183 pounds, it took just ninety-eight minutes to orbit the planet (NASA 2000). Subsequent space flights provided the first photographs of the Earth as a globe. No longer was it necessary only to conceptualize it in this fashion; now we could actually *see* it as a spherical whole. Space flight literally produced a new world view of planet Earth. Our world definitely became smaller.

**Communication and Information Processing**    While technological innovations in transportation reduced the constraints of time and space, advances in communications and information processing technology have virtually eliminated these formerly circumscribing barriers, thus accounting for the claims of a new ICT revolution.

Naisbitt (1982) discusses how developments in information and communications technology have collapsed what he calls the "information float"—the time it takes for a sender of information first to collect and process information, and then to transmit it through some communication channel to a receiver, who also must process it. Whereas the information float was a factor that could not be ignored before the 1970s, today it is trivial. Naisbitt (1982:23) explains:

One way to think about the foreshortening of the information float is to think about when the world changed from trading goods and services to standardized currencies. Just imagine how that speeded up transactions. Now, with the use of electrons to send money around the world at the speed of light, we have almost completely collapsed the . . . information float. The shift from money to electronics is as basic as when we went from barter to money.

At the very core of this transformation was the creation of the electronic microchip:

In the microchip, combining millions of components operating in billionths of seconds in a space the size of the wing of a fly, human beings built a machine that overcame all the conventional limits of mechanical time and space. Made essentially of the silicon in sand—one of the most common substances in earth—microchips find their value not in their substance but in their intellectual content: their design or software. (Gilder 1989:12)

Business applications of the microchip took place between 1969 and 1971 at Intel Corporation, which "developed all the key components of the personal computer—the working memory, the software memory, and the microprocessor CPU" (Gilder 1989:92). Thus was born the first stage of the ICT microelectronic revolution.

Another stage came into being in 1970 when scientists at Corning Glass Works announced that they had "created a medium [optical fiber] that could transport unprecedented amounts of information on laser beams for commercially viable distances" (Diebold 1990:132), thus providing the first revolutionary medium for what is now known as the information highway—the Internet. In parallel with this discovery, work was also proceeding on wireless and satellite connectivity (Bell Labs 1999).

Coincident with these developments, another momentous event in the creation of the ICT revolution occurred in 1969. In order to withstand the possibility of a nuclear military attack, the U.S. Department of Defense's Advanced Research Projects Agency created a centerless network of supercomputers at major universities and research centers, such that if one computer was struck, the others could still function independently[1] (Flower 1997; Kahn 1999). Called ARPANET, this electronic network was the forerunner of the Internet which was formally established in 1989. "Widespread development of LANS [local area networks], PCs [personal computers] and workstations in the 1980s, [as well as the growing use of e-mail], allowed the nascent Internet to flourish" (Leiner et al. 2000).

All of these developments, taking place at approximately the same time, together formed the foundation for a globalized world little constrained by time and space. And, given recent leading edge developments in transportation, communication, and information processing, there is every reason to expect this trajectory of innovation to continue. In fact, as a result of these innovations the distinction among these terms is becoming blurred. Consider, for example, the relatively new practice of telecommuting—the partial or complete substitution of telecommunications services for transportation to a conventional workplace. In reality, it is a creative and innovative blend of all three of these processes. According to a 2001 survey of the U.S. labor force, 28.8 million workers were transporting themselves both physically and electronically to work (International Telework Association 2001); worldwide, the number of teleworkers is projected to rise to 137 million by 2003 (Edwards 2001). Other creative blends of transportation, communication, and information processing include teleconferencing, teleshopping, virtual education, virtual surgery, and space satellites.

Although I have provided specific dates when these various technological innovations were recorded in history, in actual fact they took years to come to fruition. The years following World War II (particularly given the breakup of European colonial empires and the Cold War tensions between capitalism and communism) represented an era of economic reconstruction and scientific enterprise and application. However, as Table 1.1 indicates, a global ICT infrastructure is by no means in place for the vast majority of the world. Most people living in low and middle income

Table 1.1    Transportation, Communication, and Information Indicators

| INDICATORS | INCOME OF COUNTRIES | | | |
|---|---|---|---|---|
| | Low | Middle | High | World |
| Population (millions, 1999) | 2417 | 2667 | 891 | 5975 |
| Percent population | 40.5 | 44.6 | 15 | 100 |
| Kilograms of oil equivalent consumption per capita (1997) | 563 | 1368 | 5369 | 1692 |
| Air passengers carried (millions, 1998) | 54 | 292 | 1121 | 1467 |
| Percent air passengers | 3.7 | 19.9 | 76.4 | 100 |
| Radios per 1000 people (1997) | 157 | 359 | 1286 | 418 |
| TV sets per 1000 people (1998) | 76 | 257 | 661 | 247 |
| Telephone main lines/1000 (1998) | 23 | 109 | 567 | 146 |
| Mobile telephones/1000 (1998) | 2 | 31 | 265 | 55 |
| Personal computers/1000 (1998) | 3 | 23 | 311 | 71 |
| Internet hosts/10,000 (Jan./00) | 0.4 | 10 | 777 | 120 |

*Source*: Adapted from World Bank, 2001:275, 293, 309, 311.
*Note*: According to the World Bank (2001:271): "Economies are classified into three categories according to income. . . . The GNP per capita cutoff levels are as follows: low-income, $755 or less in 1999; middle-income, $756–9,265; and high-income, $9,266 or more."

countries (85 percent of the world's population) are on the other side of what has been termed the digital divide. Substantial proportions of people have yet even to acquire electricity or access a telephone. The World Resources Institute (2000) contends that "as much as 80 percent of the world's population has never made a phone call." In addition, it estimates that there are more telephones in New York City than in all of rural Asia, and more Internet accounts in the city of London than in the continent of Africa. Although the Internet connected approximately 513 million people in 2001 (Nua Internet Surveys), that represents only 8.4 percent of the world's population. In other words, while many significant technological innovations have indeed been achieved since World War II, they have yet to be diffused globally.

**Table 1.2    Foreign Direct Investment Stock by Country (billions of US$)**

| COUNTRY | 1900[a] | 1930[a] | 1960[a] | 1971 | 1980 | 1990 | 1999[b] |
|---|---|---|---|---|---|---|---|
| United States | 0.5 | 14.7 | 31.8 | 82.8 | 220.2 | 430.5 | 1,131.5 |
| United Kingdom | 12.1 | 18.2 | 13.2 | 23.1 | 80.4 | 229.3 | 664.1 |
| Germany | 4.8 | 1.1 | 0.6 | 7.0 | 43.1 | 151.6 | 420.9 |
| Netherlands | 1.1 | 2.3 | 1.7 | 3.5 | 42.1 | 109.0 | 306.4 |
| France | 5.2 | 3.5 | 2.2 | 9.2 | 23.6 | 110.1 | 298.0 |
| Japan | neg[c] | neg | neg | 4.3 | 19.6 | 201.4 | 292.8 |
| Switzerland | neg | neg | neg | 6.5 | 21.5 | 66.1 | 199.5 |
| Canada | neg | 1.3 | 3.0 | 5.7 | 23.8 | 84.8 | 178.3 |
| Italy | neg | neg | neg | NA[d] | 7.3 | 57.3 | 168.4 |
| Belgium & Luxembourg | neg | neg | neg | NA | 6.0 | 40.6 | 159.5 |
| Sweden | neg | 0.5 | 0.5 | 3.3 | 3.7 | 49.5 | 105.0 |
| Others | neg | neg | neg | 13.5 | 31.9 | 186.2 | 834.9 |
| Total[e] | 23.8 | 41.6 | 53.8 | 159.2 | 523.2 | 1,716.4 | 4,759.3 |

*Sources*: Data for 1970–71 adapted from Buckley, 1985:200. Data for 1980–1999 from UNCTAD, 2000:300–5.
*Notes*:
a. Includes foreign portfolio (individual) investment and foreign direct (TNC) investment.
b. Estimates.
c. Negligible.
d. Not available.
e. World total, excluding Comecon countries, except for 1998.

## Organizational Forces

**Transnational Corporations**    A transnational corporation (TNC) is "any enterprise that undertakes foreign direct investment, owns or controls income-gathering assets in more than one country, produces goods or services outside its country of origin, or engages in international production" (Biersteker 1978:xii). Variously termed multinational corporations or multinational enterprises, transnational corporations are formal business organizations that have spatially dispersed operations in at least two countries. One of the most transnational of all major TNCs (see Table

1.3) is Nestlé, the Swiss food giant: 84 percent of its total assets, 99 percent of its sales, and 97 percent of its workforce are foreign-based (UNCTAD 1999:78).

Although TNCs were in existence prior to the twentieth century (colonial trading companies such as the East India Company, the Hudson Bay Company, and the Virginia Company of London were precursors of the modern TNC), it is only since the 1960s that they have become a major force on the world scene (World Bank 1987:45). Table 1.2 corroborates this fact by listing the foreign direct investment (FDI) stock of corporations at various intervals during the twentieth century.[2] In 1900, only European corporations were major transnational players, but by 1930 American TNCs had begun to make their presence felt. The year 1960 is pivotal because it marks the new global era in corporate transnationalization. For each of the decades from 1960 to the present, world FDI stock has more than tripled, whereas it only doubled during the entire first half of the twentieth century.

The phenomenal increase in transnational corporate activity during the last four decades may be accounted for in large part by the technological innovations in transportation, communication, and information processing I have just discussed. They permitted corporations to establish profitable worldwide operations and still maintain effective and timely control. Not since before World War II and the Great Depression which preceded it had the corporate sector much opportunity to demonstrate its economic clout. It was in this mood that it eagerly embraced all technological innovations that would give it competitive advantage. Consequently the threefold increase in foreign direct investment between 1960 and 1971 by technologically enhanced, transnationalizing corporations reveals another manifestation of the new global age. Table 1.2 indicates that TNCs from just eleven countries accounted for 82 percent of all foreign direct investment in 1999. American TNCs comprised almost one-quarter of the total foreign investment, and corporations in the Triad (United States, European Union, and Japan) were responsible for nearly 80 percent of world FDI stock (UNCTAD 2000:300). Clearly, TNCs mainly operate out of and invest in the developed countries of the global economy.

The magnitude of foreign direct investment flow in the world is illustrated by the fact that worldwide sales of foreign affiliates in 1999 were $13.6 trillion. This figure is almost twice as high as world exports of goods and services valued at $6.9 trillion (UNCTAD 2000:4). This means that global networks of transnational corporations have replaced in im-

Table 1.3    Annual Revenues of Leading Corporations and Gross National Products of Selected Countries 1998–99 (billions of US$)

| Nation/Corporation | GNP/ Revenues | Nation/Corporation | GNP/ Revenues |
|---|---|---|---|
| United States (1) | $7,921.3 | Israel (36) | $95.2 |
| Japan (2) | 4,089.9 | Nippon Telegraph & Telephone (13) | 93.6 |
| Germany (3) | 2,122.7 | International Business Machines (16) | 87.5 |
| France (4) | 1,466.2 | BP Amoco (17) | 83.4 |
| United Kingdom (5) | 1,263.8 | Volkswagen (19) | 80.1 |
| General Motors (1) | 176.6 | Malaysia (39) | 79.8 |
| Denmark (23) | 176.4 | Hitachi (23) | 71.9 |
| Wal-Mart Stores (2) | 166.8 | Chile (42) | 71.3 |
| Exxon Mobil (3) | 163.9 | Matsushita (24) | 65.6 |
| Ford Motor (4) | 162.6 | Philip Morris (29) | 61.8 |
| DaimlerChrysler (5) | 160.0 | Sony (30) | 60.1 |
| Norway (25) | 152.1 | Boeing (32) | 58.0 |
| Greece (31) | 122.9 | New Zealand (46) | 55.8 |
| South Africa (32) | 119.0 | Honda Motor (34) | 54.8 |
| Mitsui (6) | 118.6 | Nissan Motor (36) | 53.7 |
| Mitsubishi (7) | 117.8 | Czech Republic (48) | 51.8 |
| Toyota Motor (8) | 115.7 | Toshiba (38) | 51.6 |
| General Electric (9) | 111.6 | Bank of America (39) | 51.4 |
| Iran (33) | 109.6 | Nestlé (41) | 50.0 |
| Royal Dutch/Shell Group (11) | 105.4 | Hungary (51) | 45.6 |

Sources: For annual revenues of corporations, Fortune, 2000:F1–F2; for GNP, World Bank, 2000:230–31.

Notes: Gross national product (GNP) measures the total value of goods and services produced by citizens (resident and nonresident) of a particular nation. The numbers in parentheses refer to the overall rank of a nation or corporation in terms of either GNP or revenues.

portance traditional import-export practices of the past in terms of delivering goods and services to markets worldwide. In 1999, some 63,000 TNCs controlled 690,000 foreign affiliates around the globe (UNCTAD 2000:9). These two sets of facts underline the central and growing importance of TNCs in structuring international economic relations.

The rise of modern transnational corporations and the power they hold are reflected in Table 1.3 which compares the annual revenues of some of the world's largest global companies with the gross national products (the annual total value of goods and services produced by resident and nonresident citizens of a particular country) of selected countries. For example, General Motors, the leading corporation in revenues in 1999, had the twenty-third largest economy in the world ($176.6 billion), edging out Denmark at $176.4 billion, and surpassing by far the combined national output of New Zealand, Hungary, and the Czech Republic. These statistics would appear to give some truth to the old saying that "what's good for General Motors is good for the country" (Wilson 1952). Of the one hundred largest economies in the world, nearly half (forty-nine) are transnational corporations (*Fortune* 2000:F1–F2; World Bank 2000:230–31).

Of the five hundred largest corporations in the world, more than one-quarter (128) are in the financial sector (banks, insurance, and securities) (*Fortune* 2000:F15–F21). A major reason for this is that most of the services and products financial firms provide can be traded electronically, and consequently these organizations have taken great advantage of the new global ICT infrastructure. As the editors of *Fortune* (2000:F15) state: "Money went global long before 'globalization' became a buzzword. That's why banks have the most entries on the [Global 500] list, as well as the highest revenues and profits." Other firms well represented in the Global 500 are those instrumental in the move toward globalization: modern transportation (aerospace, airlines, and courier services), communication (telecommunications, network communications, and mass media), and information processing (computers, computer services, and electronics). Of these corporations, those in the mass media have been extremely influential in promoting a global perspective in that they transmit content as well as providing infrastructure (see Box 1.2). I deal more fully in Chapter 3 with the types of global perspectives these corporations are communicating.

**International Government Alliances**    Whereas transnational corporations constitute a major impetus for globalization in the private sector, international government alliances comprise a growing force in the public sector. By far the most important of these alliances in terms of promoting globalization is the United Nations. Established in 1945 following World War II, the UN now represents nearly every country in the world (UN 2000a). To become a member state of the UN, a country must agree to the

## BOX 1.2

## THE MASS MEDIA GIANTS OF THE GLOBAL 500

Much of what we watch, read, listen to, and are entertained by is produced by just five global corporations—AOL Time Warner, the Walt Disney Company, Viacom, Seagram, and News Corporation. These mass media giants are among the five hundred largest corporations in the world; their combined revenues in 2000 were over $108 billion (*Fortune* 2001:152, F17). They own movie studios, theaters and video stores, television and cable networks, radio stations, publishing houses, newspapers and magazines, recording studios, theme parks, resorts, cruise lines, professional sport franchises, and malls, stores and on-line merchandising all over the world. They exert a tremendous influence on our lives. As AOL Time Warner's Web site proclaims: "AOL Time Warner is helping transform the global information and entertainment landscape." News Corporation is no less modest: "Virtually every minute of the day, in every time zone on the planet, people are watching, reading and interacting with our products. In the course of 24 hours News Corporation reaches nearly half a billion people in more than 70 countries." Viacom claims to have a "global reach" of 100 countries, and "appeals to audiences in every demographic category across virtually all media." Seagram with the world's largest music company operates out of sixty-three countries around the world, and Disney has international attractions throughout the Americas, Europe, and the Asia-Pacific region.

For more information about these media behemoths, check out their Web sites at www.aoltimewarner.com, disney.go.com, www.viacom.com, www.seagram.com, and www.newscorp.com.

terms of the UN Charter which mandate a global perspective:

- to maintain international peace and security;
- to develop friendly relations among nations;
- to cooperate in solving international problems and promoting respect for human rights;
- to be a centre for harmonizing the actions of nations (UN 2000a).

Although it may be observed that the UN Charter is often honored in the breach, nevertheless the United Nations does serve as a global harmonizing force as it works toward achieving peace, establishing justice, human rights, and international law, providing humanitarian assistance, and promoting sustainable development. The UN "cannot force action by any State, but its recommendations are an important indication of world opinion and represent the moral authority of the community of nations" (UN 2000a). In accomplishing its mission, the United Nations is assisted by other international agencies with whom it has entered into contractual agreement, most of which are responsible for monitoring, maintaining, and regulating an increasingly complex global infrastructure. These include the Food and Agricultural Organization, World Health Organization, World Bank, International Labour Organization, International Civil Aviation Organization, International Telecommunication Union, and World Meteorological Organization. Some of these agencies actually predate the United Nations.

A newly formed international alliance is the World Trade Organization (WTO). Although it was established in 1995, the WTO has its roots in the international multilateral trading system originally conceived following World War II (the General Agreement on Tariffs and Trade) (WTO 2000). As of October 2000, the WTO was a 139 member-state alliance whose "main function is to ensure that [global] trade flows as smoothly, predictably and freely as possible." Member states negotiate trade agreements, which in turn are ratified in their own countries. These agreements form the legal foundation for international trade and commerce. Early agreements led to tariff reductions, while later accords have expanded to include global electronic commerce, telecommunications, and financial services.

Another very important international alliance is the Organisation for Economic Co-operation and Development (OECD). Also originating in the post-war years, the OECD now comprises twenty-nine member countries, mostly in Europe and North America (including Mexico), although other countries (Turkey, Japan, Australia, New Zealand, and Korea) are represented (OECD 2000a). Committed to the principles of a market economy and pluralistic democracy, the OECD is primarily a research and policy advocacy organization. While concentrating much of its energy on activities within member countries, it is also concerned with global economic and social development in that what happens in the world at large has impact on all countries. Among the various themes the OECD pursues are agriculture and food, biotechnology, energy, environment, health, education, governance, information society, electronic commerce, trade, international migration and development, and future studies (OECD 2000b). The research that the OECD conducts (much of it published) forms the foundation for the policies it advocates.

In addition to the United Nations, the WTO, and the OECD, many regional alliances have formed since World War II to promote various political, economic, military, sociocultural, scientific, and other agendas. The European Union is perhaps the best known and most comprehensive of these regional blocs. The idea of a European Union first came about in a speech by Winston Churchill in 1946 when he proposed a "United States of Europe" (Eurotimes 2000a). In 1957, the first real manifestation of this idea was born with the formation of a six-nation European Economic Community. Today, the European Union is comprised of fifteen member states which simultaneously "assert national interests while fostering intergovernmental co-operation and diplomatic ties" (Eurotimes 2000b). Other less integrated regional blocs include the Association of South-East Asian Nations, Mercosur, the North American Free Trade Association, the Organization of American States, and the Southern African Development Community. There are many such international alliances in existence. Although not global in membership, they usually promote perspectives more global than those of individual nation-states.

**Nongovernmental Organizations**    International nongovernmental organizations (NGOs) represent the so-called "people's voice" in reaction to the two formally organized private and public sectors, and are a growing force of globalization. NGOs are voluntary organizations of people who coalesce, physically and/or electronically, around some issue or concern involving various facets of development. Although NGOs have existed in some form since human beings first formed societies, it is only since World War II that they have made their presence felt on the international stage. For example, at the beginning of the twentieth century, there were just 176 international NGOs worldwide. However, by 1993, the Commission on Global Governance listed 28,900 (cited in UNDP 1999:26), and the number is growing monthly. International "NGOs have been effective advocates for human development, maintaining pressure on national governments, international agencies and corporations to live up to commitments and to protect human rights and environmental standards" (UNDP 1999:35). Box 1.3 provides a recent dramatic example of just how effective they can be.

## BOX 1.3

## MAI-NOT!

In 1995, the Organisation for Economic Co-operation and Development (OECD), an international government alliance of the richest twenty-nine countries in the world, began negotiations on a draft Multilateral Agreement on Investment (MAI) (OECD 1995). In response to "the dramatic growth and transformation of foreign direct investment (FDI) which has been spurred by widespread liberalisation and increasing competition for foreign capital," the objectives of the Multilateral Agreement on Investment were "to raise the level of existing liberalisation" [of FDI] based on a 'top-down' approach," to provide "investment protection . . . with effective dispute settlement procedures," and "to apply these commitments to all parties to the MAI at all levels of government" (OECD 1995). Details of the actual terms of the MAI may be examined at the OECD Web site. The intention of the MAI was to increase even more foreign direct investment by transnational corporations through the removal of "investment barriers, discriminatory treatment and uncertainties." Implementation of the MAI was set for May 1997.

According to one nongovernmental organization, Public Citizen (1998a), founded by Ralph Nader in 1971, "no draft text of the MAI had ever been accessible to the public" until February 1997. However, when a draft was finally leaked, NGOs all over the world launched a global "MAI-Not!" campaign in the attempt to postpone, revise, or even withdraw the MAI. Their main objections were that the MAI would give transnational corporations inordinate powers to conduct business and make investments in any country in which the MAI was in effect.

By October 1997, with the assistance of e-mail and hastily set up Web sites, over six hundred NGOs in more than seventy countries from all geographical regions and representing hundreds of thousands of people had formed a coalition to sign a "Joint NGO Statement." The introduction to this joint statement follows:

As a coalition of development, human rights, labour, environment and consumer groups from around the world, with representation in over 70 countries, we consider the draft Multilateral Agreement on Investment (MAI) to be a damaging agreement which should not proceed in its current form, if at all.

There is an obvious need for multilateral regulation of investments in view of the scale of social and environmental disruption created by the increasing mobility of capital. However, the intention of the MAI is not to regulate investments but to regulate governments. As such, the MAI is unacceptable.

MAI negotiations began in the OECD in the Spring of 1995, more than two years ago, and are claimed to be substantially complete by the OECD. Such negotiations have been conducted without the benefit of participation from non-OECD countries and civil society, including non-governmental organizations representing the interests of workers, consumers, farmers or organizations concerned with the environment, development and human rights.

As a result, the draft MAI is completely unbalanced. It elevates the rights of investors far above those of governments, local communities, citizens, workers and the environment. The MAI will severely undermine even the meagre progress made towards sustainable development since the Rio Earth Summit in 1992 (Public Citizen 1998b).

As a result of this Joint NGO Statement, protest actions by individual NGOs, and the resulting worldwide public outcry, the Chair of the Negotiating Group on MAI recommended that OECD governments postpone signing the MAI Treaty in April 1998 as planned (Corporate Watch 1998).

In October 1998, just one week before OECD countries were scheduled to resume talks on the MAI, and only one year after the Joint NGO Statement, "France [the home country of the OECD] declared that it was pulling out indefinitely from negotiations. . . . It is widely perceived that the French withdrawal has signaled the end of the MAI—at least at the OECD" (Council of Canadians 1998).

Originally working mainly on the grass-roots level, NGOs have taken advantage of the emerging ICT revolution to form networks of similarly minded NGOs all over the world. One such NGO network is Idealist (2000), the Internet arm of Action Without Borders. It is a searchable (by topic and location) directory of all 20,000 nonprofit sites on the World Wide Web which are located in 150 countries. According to its mission statement:

Action Without Borders is independent of any government, political ideology or religious creed. Its work is guided by the common desire of its members and supporters to find practical solutions to social and environmental problems, in a spirit of generosity and mutual respect. (Idealist 2000)

A more politically and geographically focused international NGO network is the Third World Network (2000) based in Malaysia. It conducts research, publishes books and magazines, serves as a clearing-house, and provides a voice, both on the Internet and at international gatherings, which is broadly representative of Southern interests and perspectives. Other NGO networks include the American Council for Voluntary International Action (InterAction 2000), a coalition of more than 165 non-profit American organizations, the Canadian International Institute for Sustainable Development (IISDnet 2000), the British World Humanity Action Trust (WHAT 2000), and the French-based NGO-NET (2000) which provides support to grass-roots NGOs, mainly in Africa.

It is important to note that these Internet-based NGO networks provide links to Web sites that contain information about grass-roots NGOs, regardless of whether or not they are connected to the Web. Given the real lack of an adequate ICT infrastructure in the developing regions of the world (see Table 1.1), particularly in sub-Saharan Africa, it would not be feasible to do otherwise. Provided that there is *some* Internet connection, information can be passed along. For example, in a recent lecture tour of India on "Women and Development," I was able to provide members of the audience the actual names, addresses, and phone numbers of some local NGOs about whom they had no knowledge. In other words, not all people need to have direct access to the Internet in order to benefit from it. Because of this, international NGO networks have become effective global clearing-houses of information on all aspects of development throughout the world.

**Environmental Movement**    The environmental movement is comprised of many grass-roots and international NGOs, as well as scientific organizations, all over the world. What makes it unique in establishing the case for globalization is the growing realization that our planet and everything on it comprise a very complex, interdependent, living whole. This means that when humans modify their environment in certain ways—such as urbanization, agriculture, forestry, mining and so forth—other consequences, both foreseen and unforeseen, are bound to follow. Approxi-

mately thirty years ago, the concept of biological diversity or biodiversity—
"the total variability of life on Earth"—was coined, largely in an attempt
to focus research on the extent to which human beings are contributing
toward environmental degradation, and whether some of the evident trends
are reversible (Heywood and Baste 1995). It was also at this time that the
concept of sustainable development originated (Fisher 1993).

Why is biodiversity important? Aside from being important for the
particular natural systems under siege and for providing needed resources
such as food, water, shelter, and medicine for human survival, there is a
more comprehensive set of reasons relating to globalization as a worldview.

The sheer diversity of life is of inestimable value. It provides a foundation for the
continued existence of a healthy planet and our own well-being. Many biologists
now believe that ecosystems rich in diversity gain greater resilience and are therefore able to recover more readily from stresses such as drought or human-induced
degradation. When ecosystems are diverse, there is a range of pathways for primary production and ecological processes such as nutrient cycling, so that if one
is damaged or destroyed, an alternative pathway may be used and the ecosystem
can continue functioning at its normal level. If biological diversity is greatly diminished, the functioning of ecosystems is put at risk (Biodiversity Unit 1993).

Contributing to the concept of Earth as an interconnected organism,
the American National Aeronautics and Space Administration (NASA),
in conjunction with Japan and the European Space Agency, has launched
a series of satellites that have established "an international Earth-observing capability" involving "a global-scale examination of the Earth to study
the interaction of all the environmental factors—air, water, land, biota—
that make up the Earth system" (NASA 1996). NASA reports that "scientists have been observing the Earth from space for more than 30 years,
making measurements of the atmosphere, the oceans, the polar regions
and land masses" (NASA 1996).

Consequently, the environmental movement has been instrumental in
altering people's perceptions of the world in which they live. Instead of
focusing only on the particular geographical location in which they live,
human beings are now coming to realize that their actions may have consequences for the world at large and for the quality of life they and subsequent generations will enjoy.

## Individual Forces

**Physical Migration**    As well as technological innovations and transnational organizations and alliances, individual people also comprise a globalizing force in that the human population, aided largely by improvements in transportation, has become increasingly mobile in a variety of ways.

Mass movements of people around the globe is a post-war phenomenon. During World War II, international travel was restricted, and during the Great Depression before it, the world economy rarely permitted it. With respect to emigration, the most permanent form of human migration, it is only since the war that vast numbers of people have emigrated, mostly from poor to rich countries.[3] The major receiving countries have been the United States, Germany, Canada, and Australia (World Bank 2000:38), such that their populations have become increasingly diverse. The World Bank (2000:37–40) reports that in recent years between two and three million people emigrate annually, with the consequence that now more than 130 million are living outside the countries in which they were born. To these figures must be added international refugees, and as conflicts and natural disasters have risen, so has forced migration. In 1975, the world's international refugees numbered 2.5 million, but just twenty years later, that total had multiplied almost ten times to 23 million (World Bank 2000:38).

Less permanent forms of migration include international guest workers (mostly to Europe and the United States), exchange students, and tourists. The demand for guest workers, mainly from North Africa, South Asia, and Mexico, is partly a function of the global economy, but increasingly it is tied to the demographic profile of the industrially developed countries. As a whole, the total fertility rate in the high income countries is below replacement level (1.7 births per woman ), and the population is aging (World Bank 2000:243), which could lead to eventual labor shortages. To the extent that these trends continue, demand for foreign labor could increase substantially during the twenty-first century.

Study abroad and foreign exchange are also relatively recent occurrences in terms of the numbers involved and variety of programs offered. For example, at my own mid-size university, there are currently 118 student and faculty exchange agreements with other universities in 27 different countries (UVic International 2000). In 1998–99 in the United States, almost half a million foreign students enrolled in colleges and universities, three times more than in the mid-1970s (Open Doors 1999a). In turn, nearly 114,000 American students studied abroad during 1997–98, a 15 percent increase over the previous year (Open Doors 1999b). Worldwide, Switzerland has the greatest percentage (15.9 percent) of foreign students at the tertiary level, followed by Australia (12.6 percent), Austria (11.5 percent), and the United Kingdom (10.8 percent) (OECD 2000c). Clearly, the option to complete at least part of a degree program in another country has become increasingly viable.

International tourism has also expanded enormously during the past fifty years. According to the World Tourism Organization (2000), "Between 1950 and 1999 the number of international arrivals has shown an evolution from a mere 25 million international arrivals to the current 664 million, corresponding to an average annual growth rate of 7 per cent." Not only has the number of tourists increased, so too have their destinations. In 1950, almost all of the 25 million tourists went to just fifteen countries; however, in 1999, more than seventy countries hosted at least one million international visitors. Air transport was the most common means of travel (43.7 percent), followed by road (41.4 percent), sea (7.8 percent), and rail (7.0 percent), and France, Spain, the United States, Italy, and China were the most popular destinations. (See Box 1.4 to find out who accompanies these international travelers.)

Not only is international tourism a significant force of globalization, it also contributes in a huge way to the global economy:

In 1998, international tourism and international fare receipts (receipts related to passenger transport of residents of other countries) accounted for roughly 8 per cent of total export earnings on goods and services worldwide. Total international tourism receipts, including those generated by international fares, amounted to an estimated US$532 billion, surpassing all other international trade categories (World Tourism Organization 2000).

In other words, international tourism generates more revenue than international trade in either automotive products ($525 billion), chemicals ($503 billion), food ($443 billion), computer and office equipment ($399 billion), fuels ($344 billion), textiles and clothing ($331 billion), or telecommunications equipment ($283 billion). And considering that international tourism is on an annual growth trajectory of 7 percent, it will only become a more important contributor to the world gross domestic product.

**Electronic Migration**    Not only are people physically traversing the globe in increasing numbers, they are also orbiting it electronically at a skyrock-

## BOX 1.4

## MICROBES FLY THE GLOBAL SKIES

A report in my local newspaper (*Times Colonist* 10/13/00:A1) warned of "a big year for flu" because so many people from all over the world attended the Olympics in Australia, which "had an especially prolonged flu season this year." A check at FluNet, maintained by the World Health Organization (WHO) (http://oms2.b3e.jussie.fr/FluNet/f_recent_activity.html) confirmed that there had been a "regional outbreak" of influenza in Australia between September 10 and October 14, 2000.

A search at the WHO site led me to the *WHO Report on Global Surveillance of Epidemic-prone Infectious Diseases* (www.who.int/emc-documents/surveillance/whocdscsrisr2001c.html) which states: "In the modern world, with increased globalization, and rapid air travel, there is a need for international coordination and collaboration. Everyone has a stake in preventing epidemics." The *Report* focuses on nine infectious diseases (including influenza) all of which have "high epidemic potential."

More recently, with outbreaks of hoof and mouth and mad cow diseases in Europe, especially Britain, customs officers and disease control experts in all countries are taking special precautions to prevent the global spread of these highly infectious diseases via international travelers. These measures include prohibiting passengers from carrying any agricultural products with them, mandatory notification of any farm contact, requiring antibiotic foot baths for the shoe soles of all deplaning passengers, placing additional inspectors and dog teams at airports, and public education programs (www.naturalhealthyliving.com/article 1007.html).

The Centers for Disease Control and Prevention headquartered in Atlanta in the United States maintain a comprehensive "Travelers' Health" Web site (www.cdc.gov/travel).

eting rate. The International Telecommunication Union (ITU 2000) reports that international telephone calls in 1999 reached a new high of 100 billion minutes, climbing an average of 10 billion minutes per year since 1995. According to the ITU, "the world market for telecommunications (services and equipment) doubled between 1990 and 1999," and is being driven now by the burgeoning mobile cellular communications market. "At the end of 1999, there were more than 450 million subscribers around the world, up from just 11 million in 1990, . . . a compound annual growth rate of more than 50 per cent per year" (ITU 2000). The ITU estimates that mobile cellular subscribers will actually exceed conventional fixed-line users during this decade.

Also contributing to the rapid growth of electronic migration is the use of the Internet in general and for e-mail in particular. As I have already reported, Nua Internet Surveys (2001) estimated that 513 million people had accessed the Internet at least once during the three months before August 2001, and this figure is projected to rise to more than 765 million by 2005 (CommerceNet 2000). In January 2002, the Internet Software Consortium counted more than 147 million host sites on the Internet, almost 38 million more than it enumerated twelve months earlier. Quite clearly, all forms of electronic communication are growing exponentially.

## OVERVIEW OF FORCES OF GLOBALIZATION

The years following World War II, but especially those from the late-1960s onward, represented a period of rapid and massive technological, organizational, and individual change. Spurred largely by innovations in transportation, communication, and information processing, first organizations and then individuals increasingly began to take on global perspectives. Although most attention has centered on the rise of technologically enhanced transnational corporations during this period, international alliances and nongovernmental organizations have also made major contributions to globalization. And indeed, ordinary people themselves have also participated in expanding global activities.

However, as I have mentioned, the entire world is currently far from globalized. Although technological innovations have been implemented, they are restricted by and large to the developed countries (see Table 1.1); and although foreign direct investment has mushroomed, it is mainly limited to these same countries (see Table 1.2); and although many people have engaged in global migration, again, the overwhelming majority are from the developed regions of the world (see Table 1.1). Only international government alliances and particularly nongovernmental organizations can claim that their activities are global in scope. The global age has arrived only for the privileged few organizations and individuals who have implemented, managed, and prospered from the global infrastructure. The vast majority of both organizations and individuals in the world have yet to reap the benefits of globalization, and, in fact, there are major obstacles to achieving a truly global world. It is to these constraints that I now turn.

## COUNTERFORCES TO GLOBALIZATION

On at least three levels, huge proportions of humanity are put at risk by the forces of globalization, and consequently, there are growing signs that many people are actively resisting the global age. On the most general level, examine how the world is divided by region. In describing various regions of the world, certain terms come to be adopted, first by official agencies such as the United Nations and national governments, and then more generally by scholars, journalists, and others interested in making sense out of international relations and development. For example, in 1980 Willy Brandt coined the terms "North" and "South" in his *Report of the Independent Commission on International Development Issues* (Brandt Report 1980). In this report is a map of the world with a bold line dividing it into two parts—North and South. In this chapter, I have used the terms "developed" and "developing" countries which are categories created by the United Nations to classify all countries in the world. This classification scheme mirrors the North-South dichotomy. These terms are often used as convenient labels to divide the world into two camps—rich and poor. The fact that the global ICT revolution is presently taking place largely in the rich, developed North is generating backlash in the poor, developing South. Many fear that it could broaden the already enormous development gap between North and South (South Commission 1990).

Paralleling and exacerbating this development gap is a cultural gap which has widened as a result of globalization. On the one side are predominant Western cultural perspectives and values, including Christianity and the global use of English. [4] On the other side are non-Western cultural perspectives and values, including religions other than Christianity and non-European languages. Individual countries and cultural groups within the South are voicing concerns that the forces of globalization could threaten their ethnic, religious, and linguistic heritage and ways of living (Hedley 2000:595–97).

Finally, within the developed countries, there is what might be termed a growing class disparity. Studies of the distribution of income and wealth over the last three decades of the twentieth century reveal increasing inequality and polarity (Morris and Western 1999; Keister and Moller 2000). It is claimed that global restructuring has caused at least part of this disparity. Consequently, workers and citizens who are not part of the vanguard of the global era, although they are the overwhelming majority, are increasingly disaffected by the promises of globalization.

On each of these three levels of analysis—regional, cultural, and class—it is the larger of the two categories that is at risk from the forces of globalization. Thus, from the perspective of the South, or the non-Western, or the masses, globalization is not viewed with enthusiasm, and consequently active opposition to it could result. These constitute the counterforces to globalization.

## Regional

**North and South**    The concept of development does not have a long history. It dates back to the industrial revolution 250 years ago which first produced global differences among the peoples of the world in terms of socioeconomic development. The most profound result of this revolution was a huge gain in human productivity, which in turn significantly raised individual income (Hedley 1992:63–97). Firebaugh (2000:324), in a careful review of studies of world income inequality over time, notes that by 1820, "per capita income in Western Europe (the world's richest region at the time) was roughly three times greater than per capita income in Africa." Moreover, the advantages of industrialization have been cumulative: today, "per capita income is almost 14 times greater in Western Europe than it is in Africa, [and] the gap is even larger for individual nations. Average incomes in the richest and the poorest nations now differ by a factor of about 30" (Firebaugh 2000:324). According to the World Bank (2000:14):

The average per capita income of the poorest and middle thirds of all countries has lost ground steadily over the last several decades compared with the average income of the richest third. Average per capita GDP of the middle third has dropped from 12.5 to 11.4 percent of the richest third and that of the poorest third from 3.1 to 1.9 percent.[5]

Income inequality between North and South does not reveal the whole story. Each year the United Nations Development Programme publishes a *Human Development Report* in which it ranks all countries on a Human Development Index (HDI). "The HDI reflects achievements in the most basic human capabilities—leading a long life, being knowledgeable and enjoying a decent standard of living" (UNDP 1999:127). Although the UN acknowledges that the HDI is crude in terms of measuring such a complex phenomenon as human development, it is limited in what data are available for most countries. To date, the HDI is the best instrument available. Table 1.4 presents the average HDI values for various world regions, including the developing and developed (industrialized) countries considered as a whole. What is immediately apparent is that there are two global realities: one in which the vast majority of the world's population live relatively short lives under comparatively austere educational and economic circumstances; and the other in which a select minority enjoy much longer lives, almost universal education at all levels, and a high standard of living. This disparity is even more stark when one compares the countries scoring highest and lowest on the Human Development Index: on average, Canadians live over twice as long as citizens of Sierra Leone (79.1 years v. 37.9 years), have more than four times the educational enrollment (100 percent v. 24 percent), and make over fifty times more annual income ($23,582 v. $458) (UNDP 2000:157, 160). Certainly there must be different interpretations in these two countries (and in the North and South) of Articles 3, 25, and 26 of the United Nations *Universal Declaration of Human Rights* which was adopted by the General Assembly in 1948:

Article 3   Everyone has the right to life, liberty and security of person.

Article 25   Everyone has the right to a standard of living adequate for the health and well-being of himself and of his family, including food, clothing, housing, and medical care and necessary social services . . . .

Article 26   Everyone has the right to education . . . .

## Cultural

**Ethnic, Religious, and Linguistic Diversity**   Recent research attention has focused on globalization and the effects of information and commu-

Table 1.4  Average Life Expectancy, Education, Income, and Human Development Index, 1998

| World Regions | Life Expectancy at Birth (Years) | Education Enrollment[a] (%) | Real GDP per capita (PPP$)[b] | Human Development Index[c] |
|---|---|---|---|---|
| All developing countries | 64.7 | 60 | 3,270 | 0.642 |
| Least developed countries[d] | 51.9 | 37 | 1,064 | 0.435 |
| Sub-Saharan Africa | 48.9 | 42 | 1,607 | 0.464 |
| Arab States | 66.0 | 60 | 4,140 | 0.635 |
| East Asia (including China) | 70.2 | 73 | 3,564 | 0.716 |
| Southeast Asia & Pacific | 66.3 | 66 | 3,234 | 0.691 |
| South Asia (including India) | 63.0 | 52 | 2,112 | 0.560 |
| Latin America & Caribbean | 69.7 | 74 | 6,510 | 0.758 |
| Eastern Europe & the CIS[e] | 68.9 | 76 | 6,200 | 0.777 |
| Industrialized countries | 77.8 | 92 | 21,790 | 0.908 |
| World | 66.9 | 64 | 6,526 | 0.712 |

*Source*: Adapted from UNDP, 2000:160.
*Notes*:
a. Combined first, second, and third-level gross enrollment ratio.
b. PPP (purchasing power parity) rates allow a standard comparison of real price levels between regions, just as conventional price indexes allow comparison of real values over time; otherwise, normal exchange rates may over- or undervalue purchasing power.
c. The HDI is computed as an average of life expectancy, educational enrollment, and purchasing power parity. For further details, see UNDP 2000:269.
d. Forty-three countries, mainly in Africa, identified by the UN as most in need of development assistance.
e. Commonwealth of Independent States. The entire group of countries comprises the former Soviet bloc.

nications technology on cultural diversity. One emerging global scenario, variously labeled cultural imperialism, McWorld, global monoculture, and McDonaldization, is that all cultures are becoming increasingly homogenized as a result of Western, predominantly American, influences (Hedley 2000:595–97). Although this scenario was posited much earlier in the form of modernization theory, it has gained renewed credence due to the capability of modern information and communication technological systems to superimpose Western transnational corporate consumer culture (including values) on most endemic cultures of the world. Throughout all major and not so major urban centers on Earth, one is confronted with the superstructure of McDonald's, Coke, Nike, Levi's, Calvin Klein, Marlboro, Revlon, Barbie, Disney, 711, Hilton, Hollywood, and the Hard Rock Café. This sociocultural superstructure is supported by a complex technological infrastructure, including MTV, CNN, AOL Time Warner, the Internet, and Visa/MasterCard.

With regard to this infrastructure, it is important to note that not only does it provide purely technical support, it also comprises a significant aspect of the global cultural superstructure itself. For example, concerning the media, Parenti (1993:23) states that "the media may not always be able to tell us what to think, but they are strikingly successful in telling us what to think about." In other words, given that these media are themselves Western-based, they construct a social-cultural world from a predominantly Western perspective.

The same is true of the Internet. Analysis of the Internet, the worldwide network of personal computers connected to host computers, indicates that it is overwhelmingly American-based, English-speaking, and Western-focused. In January 2002, approximately 72 percent of the estimated 147 million Internet host computers were in the United States, 78 percent in English-speaking nations, and 89 percent of the Internet operated out of Western countries (Internet Software Consortium 2002).[6]

Unlike earlier technologies, information and communication technology is essentially cultural. Even though computer software commands computers in binary code, the software originates in words, the effective currency of culture. According to Einstein (1954:336 [1941]): "The mental development of the individual and his way of forming concepts depend to a high degree upon language. This makes us realize to what extent the same language means the same mentality." And Gilder (1989:328) further adds that we are now reaching the stage where "the distinction between hardware and software will all but vanish."

Although earlier technologies incorporated aspects of culture in their designs in the form of standards and regulations, these were more limited in scope. But information and communication technology, by its very nature, is cultural. "The notion that information and communication are, in fact, culturally neutral is the greatest myth of our time" (Mowlana 1996:179). Consequently, given that "about 80 per cent of the world market in packaged software is produced by American firms" (Keniston 1998)—one linguistic cultural entity—and that "hardware designs increasingly embody software concepts" (Gilder 1989:329), cultural convergence on a massive scale could well be the result.

Cultural diversity within and among countries is threatened as a result of globalization and the introduction of global information and communication systems. As a final illustration of this phenomenon, note what is happening to the world's living languages. According to Leuprecht (1998), linguistic diversity probably reached its apex about 15,000 years ago, when "a world population five hundred times less than it is today is supposed to have spoken some 10,000 languages." Since this time, as a result of the ravages of colonization, nationalism, and now, globalization, it is estimated that there are a total of 6,703 living languages in existence (*Ethnologue* 1996). However, within this century alone, linguists predict that half will become extinct. Electronic mass media, international trade and foreign direct investment, global consumerism and pop culture, tourism, and the Internet are all putting extreme pressure on endangered languages and the cultural groups they represent.

## Class

**Elites and Masses**    In a widely cited book, former U.S. Secretary of Labor Robert Reich (1992) attempts to map the emerging occupational structure of the new global information and communication economy. He proposes a new occupational classification system comprised of three major categories which better reflect the work being done in the global era: 1) routine production services, 2) in-person services, and 3) symbolic-analytic services. "Routine production services entail the kinds of repetitive tasks performed by the old foot soldiers of American capitalism in the high-volume enterprise. They are done over and over—one step in a sequence of steps for producing finished products tradeable in world commerce" (p. 174). As well as traditional semiskilled factory workers, routine production services include low- and mid-level supervisors and managers, data-entry and processing clerks, and other similar positions in both the traditional and modern sectors of the economy that are performed in standardized fashion. Using the American labor force as an illustrative case, Reich gauges that routine production services account for approximately 25 percent of all workers.

"In-person services . . . also entail simple and repetitive tasks. . . . The big difference between in-person servers and routine producers is that *these* services must be provided person-to-person, and thus are not sold

Figure 1.2    **Graphic Representation and Summary of Book**

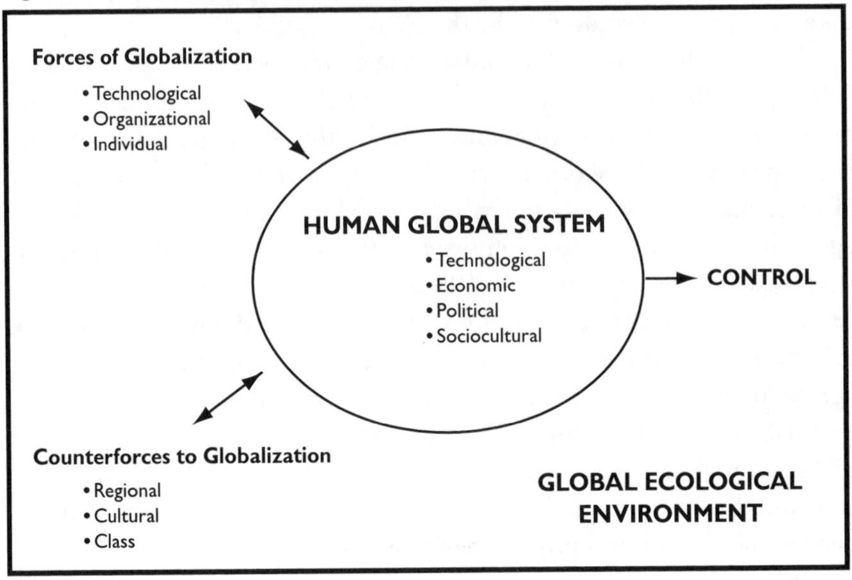

**Forces of Globalization**
- Technological
- Organizational
- Individual

**HUMAN GLOBAL SYSTEM**
- Technological
- Economic
- Political
- Sociocultural

**CONTROL**

**Counterforces to Globalization**
- Regional
- Cultural
- Class

**GLOBAL ECOLOGICAL
ENVIRONMENT**

worldwide" (p. 176). In-person services include the vast army of low-level service workers in such areas as retail sales, offices, hotels and restaurants, hospitals and nursing homes, real estate, transportation, and security and protection. Reich estimates that in-person services comprise 30 percent of all workers. Together, routine production and in-person services make up over half of the labor force. To these two categories Reich adds a miscellaneous category of workers in the natural resources sector (5 percent) and government employees (15 percent) who are "sheltered from global competition" for a grand total of 80 percent of all jobs.

Symbolic-analytic services comprise the remaining 20 percent, and also according to Reich, represent the wave of the future. Symbolic analysts are problem identifiers, problem solvers, and strategic-brokers who engage in "the manipulation of symbols—data, words, oral and visual representations" (p.177). Included in this category are high-level scientists, engineers, corporate executives and bankers, consultants, professionals, and creative media artists. Symbolic-analytic services and talents are not constrained by national borders; they are traded in the global marketplace, and herein lies the key to their rising elite status and income.

Because symbolic-analytic services are in high demand in the global economy, and because they can be dispensed via global information and communication networks, the fortunes of symbolic analysts have been rising meteorically. In contrast, routine producers in developed countries are increasingly competing with millions and millions of lower paid routine producers in developing countries, with the consequence that their incomes have stagnated or even fallen during recent decades. In-person servers have experienced a similar fate owing to the excess of supply over demand for their relatively unskilled services.

These developments underlie at least in part the growing disparity and polarity in income and wealth in developed countries during the past thirty years (Morris and Western 1999; Keister and Moller 2000). According to Morris and Western (1999:645), "immigration . . . , trade with developing countries, foreign investment, and outsourcing are all thought to lower demand for low-wage . . . workers. As a result, wages fall at the bottom of the earnings distribution and inequality rises." Consequently, for the mass of ordinary workers in developed countries, globalism does not offer the advantages that it does for the elite symbolic analysts. In fact, "a significant number of [these ordinary] workers . . . [are] earning less than their counterparts in the 1960s" (Morris and Western 1999:625).

## CONCLUSION

Figure 1.2 summarizes in graphical form the discussion to date. I opened the chapter with the story of the love bug virus to illustrate that globalization is having worldwide impacts on structures of control within society. Analysis of control within the context of the human global system (which in turn operates within the broader global ecological environment) comprises the substance of this book. After providing a definition of the multidimensional concept of globalization, I described the major forces that brought it about, and when this occurred. Prompted largely by technological and organizational developments following World War II, there is now in place a global infrastructure of production, distribution/transmission, and consumption. With regard to the forces of globalization listed in Figure 1.2, note that not only do I have an arrow pointing to their effects in bringing about globalism, I have also reversed the arrow, indicating that globalization in turn spurs additional technological, organizational, and individual developments.

As an illustration of the vastly changed world in which we now live and with which we must cope, examine the list in Box 1.5. In this chapter alone I have mentioned sixty-nine innovations that were not present in your grandparents' day (c. 1950), many of which have altered radically

## BOX 1.5

## WHEN I WAS YOUR AGE . . .

How many times did you hear this while growing up? Think of your grandparents at the age you are now, and attempt to reconstruct their society, noting how different it was from your society today. To demonstrate this difference, search through this chapter for words, inventions, and concepts that are familiar to you, but which were unknown in your grandparents' day (c. 1950). The list below reveals just some of the startling developments we have experienced in only two generations.

| | |
|---|---|
| aerospace | Microsoft |
| AOL | mobile cellular communications |
| biodiversity | NASA |
| biotechnology | NGOs |
| commercial jets | North & South |
| computer virus | on-line merchandising |
| computer worm | optical fiber |
| container ships | outsourcing |
| digital divide | personal computer |
| download | software |
| Earth-observing capability | space satellite |
| electronic commerce | space travel |
| electronic microchip | Sputnik |
| electronic migration | supercomputer |
| e-mail | superconductors |
| environmental movement | surfing |
| European Union | sustainable development |
| FedEx | telecommuting |
| global consumerism | teleconferencing |
| global ICT infrastructure | teleshopping |
| globalization | terabytes |
| global village | transnational corporation |
| hackers | Triad |
| host computers | virtual education |
| HTML | virtual library |
| Human Development Index | virtual surgery |

| | |
|---|---|
| ICT revolution | Visa/MasterCard |
| information highway | Web server |
| information society | Web sites |
| Internet | wireless telephony |
| laptop computer | workstations |
| laser beams | World Bank |
| local area networks | World Trade Organization |
| McDonald's | World Wide Web |
| microprocessor CPU | |

the ways we live. I have tried to present the most important developments to give you a flavor of the uniqueness of this era, but the list is by no means exhaustive. It is, however, indicative of the excitement, the challenge, and the problems we face.

The global technological and organizational infrastructure has been established primarily by corporations, governments, and individuals in rich developed countries for their own benefit. As I mentioned, the overwhelming majority of the world's population has yet to be connected to this infrastructure. Figure 1.2 reveals that on three levels of analysis, the globally unconnected represent counterforces to globalization. Here too, I have drawn the arrow in both directions to reveal the negatively reinforcing processes in operation. To date, globalization is an exclusionary force, denying active participation to particular regions, cultures, and classes. In turn, this is causing backlash. For many nations, cultures, institutions, organizations, and individuals in the world, modern globalism constitutes an elitist, Northern-based, Western-focused, technologically supported form of economic and cultural imperialism. In order to turn this vicious circle into a virtuous circle, the President of the World Bank (Wolfensohn 1997:6) has issued a *Challenge of Inclusion* "to reduce . . . disparities across and within countries, to bring more people into the economic mainstream, [and] to promote equitable access to the benefits of development regardless of nationality, race, or gender." Whether this challenge becomes reality remains to be seen; however, until it does, the world as a whole cannot truly be characterized as globalized.

# CHAPTER SUMMARY

1.1 It is the central thesis of this book that globalization has impacts on all facets of how we live. In order to demonstrate this thesis, I examine how the forces of globalization are revising the ways in which we can control our life chances in an increasingly interconnected world.

1.2 Globalization as a complex set of forces involves the production, distribution/transmission, and consumption of technical, economic, political, sociocultural goods and services which are administratively and technologically integrated on a worldwide basis.

1.3 Innovations in technology constitute a major force of globalization. Following World War II, developments in transportation (such as the introduction of container ships, commercial jets, and space travel) and communication and information processing (such as the creation of the electronic microchip, personal computer, optical fiber, and the Internet) substantially reduced the constraints of time and space, virtually making the world a smaller place.

1.4 Although a global transportation, information, and communication infrastructure is now in place, most of the world's population (approximately 85 percent) do not have access to it.

1.5 Developments in transportation, information, and communication have permitted organizations to restructure on a global basis. Most visible have been transnational corporations which tripled their foreign direct investments in each decade since 1960. Governments have also formed international alliances and agreements, the most important of these being the establishment of the United Nations in 1945. In response to global developments in the private and public sectors, nongovernmental organizations (NGOs) have also formed on an international basis to represent and advocate for ordinary people's issues and concerns.

1.6 One increasingly significant issue for NGOs and scientists alike is the impact of humans on their environment. The environmental movement is a globalizing force in that it has established the increasingly common perception that our planet and everything that it comprises constitute a very complex, interdependent, living whole.

1.7 Ordinary people have also taken advantage of developments in transportation, communication, and information processing to traverse the globe in increasing numbers, both physically (as emigrants, refugees, guest workers, exchange scholars, and tourists) and electronically (in the form of fixed-line and mobile telephones, e-mail, and the Internet).

1.8 A counterforce to globalization is the huge and growing development gap between South and North which has produced two global realities: one, the South, in which the vast majority of the world's population live relatively short lives under comparatively austere educational and economic circumstances; and the other, the North, in which a select minority enjoy much longer lives, almost universal education at all levels, and a high standard of living.

1.9 Another counterforce is the negative reaction of most endemic cultures of the world to the superimposition of Western—mainly American—cultural values and practices (including the predominant use of English) on their traditional diverse ways of life.

1.10 A third counterforce, occurring as a result of global restructuring, is the growing inequality and polarity within developed countries which is causing resentment among ordinary workers and citizens who are increasingly disaffected by the promises of globalization.

# 2

## STUDYING SOCIAL CHANGE

*The more things change, the more they remain the same.*[1]
—Alphonse Karr, *Les Guêpes*

*Change is eternal. Nothing ever changes.*
—Immanuel Wallerstein, *The Modern World-System*

**HOW MAY WE EXPLAIN GLOBALISM** as an emergent form of social organization in the late twentieth century? What will be the relative impacts of the forces and counterforces of globalization that I described in Chapter 1? What are the effects of globalization on control? What are likely future patterns of global development? In order to answer questions like these, social scientists employ two complementary strategies—theory and research. Theory, which consists of a set of interrelated propositions or general statements of relationship, provides a focus for discerning and examining complex phenomena so that we can make sense of the myriad changes occurring around us. Without this focus, we would be employed in mindless recording without knowing what is important and not important. Theories provide lenses to "see," permitting us to assemble similar pieces of information or data into the same category, and thus afford us the ability to generalize and predict.

Different theories, like the different lenses of the microscope and telescope, offer different vantage points or ways of seeing the world. For example, what one theorist may see as evidence of social change, another may very well interpret as indicating stability. One is not right and the other wrong. Depending upon what each is seeking to explain, and given the logical considerations involved in the two theories and the units and levels of analysis employed, each may be making valid, if somewhat different, points about the world. Recall Einstein's (1936) observation that the categories are not inherent in the phenomena; rather categories are constructed by human observers, or theorists, to simplify the vast complexity they are witnessing. In order to provide a broad and hopefully balanced theoretical overview of the many changes described in Chapter 1, I present six theories of social change which involve a variety of theoretical orientations or perspectives.

Research is the means by which social scientists test the validity of their theories—or, put another way, determine whether particular theoretical propositions actually explain empirical circumstance. For each concept or variable in a theoretical proposition, researchers construct corresponding empirical indicators, such that it becomes possible through measurement to assess how well theories explain or account for changes that have occurred. Research results allow researchers to refine and modify theories so that they better match the reality they are purported to explain. In this fashion, theory and research are reciprocal components of the same process—attempting to understand, explain, and predict changes in social structure and social behavior. Over the past several decades, researchers have devised various procedures and strategies to measure change. I describe some of these procedures following my discussion of the six theories of social change.

## THEORIES OF SOCIAL CHANGE

Before discussing change, let us consider some basic and fundamental limiting conditions or universal constants. First, all members of the human species have the same basic physiological needs and constraints. We all need food, water, and shelter in order to survive. Although there is a tremendous range over which these resources are actually distributed among the world's people, the fact remains there are minimal requirements for human survival. Also, we all have physiological limits we cannot exceed. For example, although we have increased our life expectancy as a species, we have not increased our life span—"the maximum age that human beings could reach under optimum conditions" (Haupt and Kane 1980:9).[2] And although we have invented airplanes and submarines, we ourselves can neither fly in the air nor live in the oceans. In these regards, from our earliest beginnings humankind has experienced no change.

Second, as a species we are bound by the limiting conditions of the planet we inhabit. Again, while we can artificially insulate ourselves from the elements, we must nevertheless accept whatever the forces of nature dispense, be this feast or famine. Here too, at least until the prospect of interstellar travel actually materializes, we continue to be bound by the same basic ground rules as our early ancestors.

If we now look at the changes we *have* implemented, very generally most of them were instituted to improve humankind's odds against nature, or as was more usual, a select portion of humankind. The impetus for many of these changes has been control—control over our individual and collective (however this is defined) destinies. Very closely tied to the striving for control is the pursuit of the possible. In part, the history of social change can also be interpreted as an attempt to reduce the distance between the actual and the ideal, or, as Moore (1963:19) states it: "Anything less than total control of human biology and the nonhuman environment leaves ample opportunities for strain and innovation."

To lay bare the conditions under which we are all constrained and to specify the human agenda that universally motivates us is important. However, sociologists are more intrigued about unravelling the myriad differences that now characterize us and explaining how they came about. In our earliest history, the limiting conditions more narrowly constrained our behavior and aspirations, thus minimizing individual and group differences. However, over time as we have adapted individually and socially to our environment, these differences have become disproportionately apparent. The explanation of these differences directly involves us in the study of varying types and patterns of social change.

In considering types of social change, I restrict my examination to those that are humanly induced as opposed to naturally occurring, and to those that have implications for large social systems—such as nations and regions of the world—rather than individuals. Thus, although earthquakes, floods, and tornados can produce substantial changes for those experiencing them, these changes fall outside the purview of this analysis. However, if changes in the atmosphere, land, and water occur as a result of human agency, they are included. Similarly, whereas the decision of a family to limit the number of children it will have results in a changed pattern of life for this family, only when this same decision is made by a significant proportion of families, and thus has implications for societies at large, are the resulting structural changes included for analysis.

With these caveats in mind, let us now examine two theories of social change that attempt to explain the overall global development pattern of various countries and regions in the world (development theories), two theories that focus more on differences in global development patterns (underdevelopment theories), and two more that concentrate on how technology itself represents a structural challenge to human development (technological development theories).

## Development Theories

In the aftermath of World War II and the breakup of the European colonies, and with the formation of the United Nations, interest turned to the development prospects of what were then called the "underdeveloped" countries of the world. Was it possible to reduce the gross disparities among nations and people, and if so, how? Many North American and European scholars, relying heavily on the historical founders of sociology, adopted an evolutionary functionalist perspective in their view of development, suggesting that it is unilinear and in large part technologically determined. According to **modernization theory**, the developed capitalist countries represent the highest stage of societal evolution which was reached through the very complex process of industrialization. Industrialization involves not only factories and machinery; in addition, it comprises a complementary social philosophy and set of institutions. Modernization theorists maintained that the path to modernization of the underdeveloped countries lay in their adoption of Western values, techniques, and institutional structures, which meant that they must at the same time reject their own supposedly incompatible social institutions and lifestyles (Armer and Katsillis 1992). Only then could they become modern and enjoy the higher standard of living associated with modernity.

In 1960, four American labor economists (Kerr et al. 1964 [1960]) proposed a more technologically deterministic version of modernization theory. According to **convergence theory**, there is a "logic of industrialization," such that uniformities (that is to say, convergence) appear in social structures and social processes regardless of where in the world or in what cultural context industrialization is introduced. In the words of these proponents of convergence theory:

Industrialization came into a most varied world; a world with many cultures, at many stages of development from the primitiveness of quasi-animal life to high levels of civilization. It was a world marked by great diversity; in terms of the contrast between the least and most civilized societies; a world more diverse than at any other time during the history of mankind on this planet. Into the midst of this disparity of systems there intruded a new and vastly superior technique of production; a technique which by its very nature was bound to spur imitation, since the more modern was always the superior. This technique knew no geo-graphical limits; recognized no elites or ideologies. Once unleashed on the world, the new technique kept spreading and kept advancing (Kerr et al. 1964:223).

Because the results of technology or a technique of production can be precisely measured in terms of quantity and quality of output, it is possible to determine which technology is superior in accomplishing specific objectives, and consequently the superior technology becomes widely adopted. Such was the fate of specialized and mechanized factory production as it was initiated first in Europe and North America, and then later in Japan, the Soviet Union, India, Latin America, and East Asia.

The central tenet of convergence theory is that upon the introduction of technologically superior factory production, structural adaptations are made that in turn have repercussions on other aspects of society until eventually all industrialized societies, no matter how dissimilar they were initially, converge in certain patterns of social organization and behavior. Some of the direct or first-order consequences include "an open and mobile society that assigns occupations on universalistic grounds, an educational system that serves the needs of industry, a hierarchically differentiated and disciplined work force, a consensual web of rules regulating industrial social life, and increasing governmental involvement in industrial relations" (Form 1979:4). Other more far-ranging or second-order consequences include trends toward urbanization, bureaucratization, secularization, smaller nuclear families, greater female labor force participation, and more societal and international interdependence. In other words, industrialization as a process provokes both immediate and widespread social changes such that all nations, East and West, North and South, in adapting to this process themselves become more homogenized.

Not only do social structures and processes become adapted to industrialization, there are also manifest changes in human personality and behavior. As an illustration of the changes that occur, consider an often cited study of working men in six developing countries[3] (Inkeles and Smith 1974). The researchers attempted to discover whether the nature of the work these men performed—whether industrial or nonindustrial—influenced what they valued and how they behaved in society. The researchers found in *all* countries that experienced factory hands, more than traditional urban or nonindustrial workers, more than rural-urban migrants, more than cultivators of the land, scored highly on an "overall modernity" scale. With respect to values, a modern man was more likely to:

- be open to new experience and accept change;

- be oriented toward the present and future rather than the past;

- be concerned with being on time and planning in advance;

- believe in self-determination and reject fatalism;

- be independent of traditional authority figures;

- believe in the efficacy of education, science, and technology;

- be ambitious for self and children;

- be tolerant of social differences; and

- be interested in civic and community affairs and broader social issues.

Behaviorally, the experienced factory worker was more apt to

- read a newspaper every day;

- discuss politics with his wife;

- join voluntary organizations;

- communicate with officials about public issues;

- vote; and

- be knowledgeable about political, community, and social issues.

Although the proponents of both modernization and convergence theory state that the overwhelming impetus of industrialization is toward uniformity, they do acknowledge that there are some differences in its adoption worldwide. This diversity arises from a number of sources, principally the ideological predispositions of indigenous elites, existing cultural traditions, key resources and central industries, and the actual period (for example, early or late) in which industrialization is introduced, as well as its rate of introduction (Kerr et al. 1964:223–26). However, the overall thrust of modernization and convergence theory is that if traditional societies become more like modern (that is to say, Western) societies, their chances for so-called civilized development are greater. Given the technological and organizational forces of globalization described in Chapter 1, the proponents of this theoretical perspective predict a trend toward greater global convergence in the twenty-first century.

Modernization and convergence theory have been heavily criticized for being both ethno- and Euro-centric, and biased in favor of dominant capitalist interests. In fact, studies of industrialization in non-Western countries have found that the actual process of industrialization as well as its broader ramifications differ in marked respects from the so-called universal Western model (Dore 1973). In addition, given the growing realization of the often devastating impacts of economic industrial development on global ecosystems, many experts have concluded that the supposedly modern and vastly superior development path taken by the West is not ecologically sustainable (Brundtland Commission 1987).

## Underdevelopment Theories

In the forefront of the critics of modernization and convergence theory were advocates of **dependency theory**, a global perspective that emerged in Latin America during the 1960s (Cardoso and Faletto 1979 [1969]). Rather than predicting convergence, dependency theorists argued that the current global economic and political structure, originally established by the rich developed nations on terms favorable to them, sustains the rift between developed and developing countries.

. . . the dependency approach viewed the global system as consisting of a "core" of advanced industrial countries connected both economically and politically to a larger "periphery" of poor nations. The structure of the global system was conceptualized primarily in terms of trade and capital flows reinforced by political domination. The principal concern was with the consequences of these ties for social, political, and economic change in the countries of the periphery (Evans 1992:773).

With regard to international trade, dependency theorists pointed out that one of the legacies of European colonization was the creation of limited product economies in developing countries to provide raw resources, including minerals and semi-finished manufactured goods (such as textiles), not grown or produced in Europe (Murdoch 1980:202–70). Not only did this measure produce imbalanced economies, but also because of regional specialization in the resources produced, it placed many developing countries in direct competition with each other, thus driving down the prices of their exports. Moreover, the terms of trade historically established by the "core" countries placed a higher relative value on what they

**Figure 2.1    The Colonial Dual Economy**

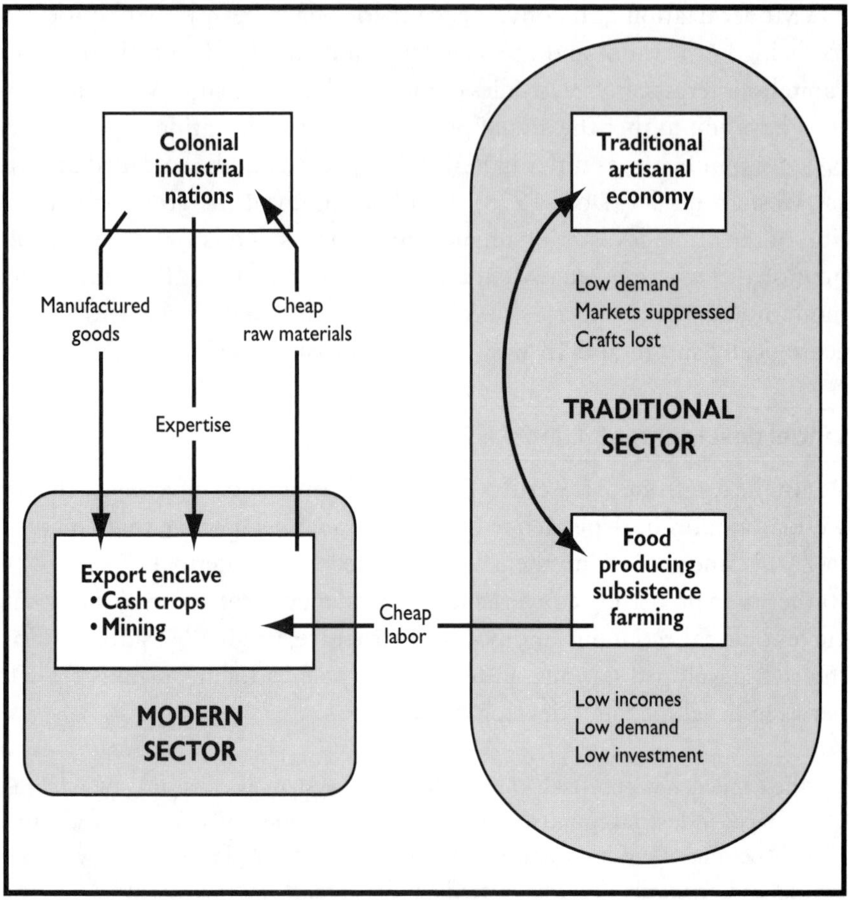

*Source*: Murdoch, William W. *The Poverty of Nations: The Political Economy of Hunger and Population*, p. 225, 1980. Reprinted by permission of the Johns Hopkins University Press.

produced (manufactured goods) than on what the "periphery" countries produced (raw materials), thus causing "an invisible transfer of resources from the poor to the rich nations" (Murdoch 1980:251). Figure 2.1 graphically represents how the European powers essentially recreated the core-peripheral structure of the global economy within the countries they colonized.

A similar dependency effect exists with regard to foreign investment in peripheral countries. In a study of foreign investment in these countries from 1940 to 1990, Kentor (1998:1042) found that although there are short-term positive effects, the overall result is that "peripheral countries with relatively high dependence on foreign capital exhibit slower economic growth than . . . less dependent peripheral countries." Rather than contributing to the long-term economic growth of these countries, foreign capital investment forces peripheral economies to adjust to core interests, thus retarding growth.

A theoretical extension of dependency theory is **world-systems analysis.** Devised initially by Immanuel Wallerstein (1974), world-systems analysis is more comprehensive than dependency theory in analyzing national and regional development as a product of the total global system. According to this perspective, the world-system is a hierarchy comprised of core, semiperipheral, and peripheral nations "in which upward or downward mobility is conditioned by the resources and obstacles that characterize the international system" (Gereffi 1994:214). In his historical analysis of the contemporary capitalist world-system, Wallerstein locates its origins in sixteenth-century Europe which first employed a capitalist mode of production, and which eventually evolved into the present-day truly global system of production, distribution/ transmission, and consumption. While earlier world empires connected various parts of the world using both economic and political means, the capitalist world-system is unique in that it is able to assert even broader control exclusively through the deployment of an integrated global division of labor. Wallerstein (1974:348) explains: ". . . capitalism as an economic mode is based on the fact that . . . economic factors operate within an arena larger than that which any political entity can totally control. This gives capitalists a freedom of maneuver that is structurally based." Consequently, the capitalist world-system expanded in lock-step with the technology available to it for effective global communication and control.

Unlike modernization and convergence theory, dependency and world-systems theory are predicated on the basis of unequal exchanges among nations within the global system: "the on-going process of a world-economy tends to expand the economic and social gaps among its varying areas in the very process of its development" (Wallerstein 1974:350). In contrast to the developing countries today, the developed countries did not have to deal with countries more developed than they were when they first began to industrialize. This fact constitutes the major difference between the two sets of countries. The core occupies a central position of global power because it developed first, and therefore was able to establish the basic rules of global trade and investment. These rules compound the development gap between core and periphery.

Although dependency and world-systems theory can offer general explanations for periphery-core mobility, they cannot predict specific cases (such as the rapid economic growth of the newly industrializing countries of East Asia during the 1980s).[4] Consequently, while a country's position within the core-(semiperiphery)-periphery global system is a necessary condition to predict its future socioeconomic development, it is not sufficient. In addition, mobility (in either direction) depends on what transpires economically, politically, and culturally *within* individual nation states, as well as on the *particular* relationships of various peripheral, semipheripheral, and core nations to each other (Evans and Stephens 1988).

Prior to the emergence of dependency and world-system theory, most development research focused almost exclusively on the national level, thus neglecting the impacts of the global system. It is to the credit of these new theories that they emphasize the importance of the global context in which individual nations operate. However, adoption of a dependency or world-systems perspective does not preclude additional research at the national level, and in fact, recent research has adopted this two-pronged approach. In addition, researchers are now paying close attention not only to a country's position within the global system, but also to the types of relationships established. Although it is still not possible to predict individual cases other than on a probabilistic basis (Reichenbach 1964:74–114), theories of national development within the global context have become increasingly comprehensive and refined over time, and one hopes, increasingly reflective of what is actually being played out on the world stage.

## A Systems-Theory Perspective on Theories of Development and Underdevelopment

While development and underdevelopment theories predict radically different outcomes for global development, they are similar with respect to their description of how certain features of the human global system have evolved. Central to this evolution is the transformation of the world from many diverse nations, each developing more or less independently, to one overall structure of integrated global development. In turn, this transformation also dictates increases in scale, complexity, and centralization.

For development theories, global development is predicated on the actions of the developed countries. Because they have attained, in the terms of this perspective, the highest stage of societal evolution, other countries in the world attempt to emulate them in all aspects of social structure and process. The predicted result, therefore, is a less diverse, convergent world in which all nations are joined together in a common system of production, distribution, and consumption.

Theories of underdevelopment also predict one world-system, but with different characteristics. Beginning similarly from a fragmented world of independently operating nation states, dependency and world-systems theorists describe the formation of an integrated capitalist global system based on unequal exchanges. Although slightly more diverse than the convergence model, the dependency model, by its very name, emphasizes the linked interdependence between core and periphery.

From a systems-theory perspective, both development and underdevelopment theories portray the evolution of global development in similar terms: several hundred years ago, the structure of the world consisted of many different, relatively small and simple, independent systems, not coordinated in any organized fashion. By contrast, the contemporary world structure consists of one extremely large (that is, global), highly complex, integrated system, with all of its subsystems or system elements joined together by one interdependent electronic network (the connecting backbone of this network is the Internet).

This integrated, interdependent human global system represents a new threshold in human activity, for at no time during the history of humankind (with the possible exception of our very earliest beginnings as a species) have all human beings been elements of the *same* interconnected system. This feature is important because, again from a systems-theory perspective, there is a norm of "requisite variety" that states: "the variety within a system must be at least as great as the environmental variety against which it is attempting to regulate itself" (Buckley 1968:495). In other words, variety within a system, organization, or society is essential for its survival and ongoing evolution. Based on the principle that if elements within a system are different rather than similar, the system itself will be more resilient to threat or attack. The norm of requisite variety applies equally to *all* systems. For example, in natural systems, "a classic example is the danger of monoculture with genetically similar or identical plants: a single disease or parasite invasion can be sufficient to destroy all crops. If there is variety, on the other hand, there will always be some crops that survive the invasion" (Heylighen 1991).

With regard to the human global system, the fact that there is just one common network (the Internet) that provides links to all computers in the world renders the entire global system vulnerable. Incursions against the system can originate in a number of ways—either inside or outside the system, deliberately or by accident, or from human or natural sources. For example, the love bug virus discussed in Chapter 1 was perpetrated deliberately by a lone individual operating by and large outside the system he was trying to infect. The fact that his actions reverberated throughout the entire human global system bears testimony to just how vulnerable one interlinked global electronic network actually is.

Consequently, from a systems theory perspective, even though the contemporary human global system was put in place precisely to increase control over human activity, it is also considerably more at risk than the previous institutional arrangement it replaced. In other words, *many independent* systems are more impervious to attack from a particular source than is *one interdependent*, albeit large, system. I discuss the implications of this structural vulnerability more fully in Chapter 3. Now, however, let us examine some theories of technological development, in that technological innovation is an important driver of social change.

## Technological Development Theories

Integrated transnational corporations traversing real-time electronic networks that span the global economy have produced what one writer terms a "borderless world" (Ohmae 1991). These technologically enhanced corporations also operate in the non-nationally controlled interstices of the planet—oceans, seabeds, airwaves, sky, and space. Existing in a sort of parallel world, they are responsible only to amorphous groups of shareholders. Gill and Law (1988:364–65) state that there is a "growing lack of congruence between the 'world economy,' with its tendencies to promote ever-greater levels of economic integration, and an 'international political system' comprised of many rival states." William F. Ogburn, were he alive today, would call this an example of **cultural lag**.

Ogburn conceived the theory of cultural lag by observing the uneven pace of development within society and the corresponding unequal rates of change that produced "maladjustment" and "strain." Through a variety of systematic empirical investigations, he developed the thesis that changes in material culture, "the applications of scientific discovery and the material products of technology" (1964:79 [1956]), occur at a faster rate than changes in the nonmaterial, adaptive culture (that is, values, norms, social institutions, and so forth), thereby causing maladjustment in the nonmaterial culture, or cultural lag. For example, referring to the illustration in the paragraph above, corporations through their application of transportation, communication, and information technology "are interlinked across national boundaries in ways that leave them not fully under the control of a single corporate office against whom national regulations can be applied" (UNCTC 1990:22). In other words, by becoming transnational via "the material products of technology," corporations have created a cultural lag for the political and legal institutions whose role it is to regulate them (Hedley 1999).

According to Ogburn, the material culture changes at a faster rate than the nonmaterial culture, thus producing cultural lag, because of three principal factors. First, science and technology as opposed to the arts, religion, and ritual, for example, are cumulative enterprises that build upon knowledge acquired through previous generations. Consequently, "the number of patents, discoveries in applied science, and inventions has been increasing in something like an exponential curve" (1964:92 [1957]). Second, there is resistance to change or "cultural inertia" in the nonmaterial culture operating in the form of vested interests preserving the status quo; predispositions toward familiar routines, habits, custom, and tradition; social pressures to conform; and anxiety regarding uncertainty and change that provokes a conservative reaction (1922:143–96). And third, Ogburn notes that although changes in the nonmaterial culture could conceivably precede changes in the material, it is unlikely because of the very high degree of planning, prediction, and control this would entail (1922:211–13).

One important conclusion that Ogburn drew from his work on cultural lag is that with ever-increasing technological accumulation and change, our major adjustment as a species is to the technological environment we have created rather than to the nonhuman environment and biological limitations that have previously served as our major constraints. His words ring with remarkable clarity today:

Unlike the natural environment, the technological environment is a huge mass in rapid motion. It is no wonder then that our society with its numerous institutions and organizations has an almost impossible task in adjusting to this whirling technological environment. It should be no surprise to sociologists that the various forms and shapes which our social institutions take and the many shifts in their function are the result of adjustments—not to a changing natural environment, not to a changing biological heritage—but adaptations to a changing technology (Ogburn 1964:85 [1956]).

In a similar vein, Jacques Ellul (1973 [1964]) conceived of **technological system theory** by analyzing the milieus or environments in which human beings exist. According to Ellul, the relationship of people to their environment is crucial for their survival. A milieu provides the means for existence, "but at the same time, the milieu is *what puts one in danger.* Hence, a milieu both makes living possible and also *forces change,* obliges us to transform who we are because of problems arising from the milieu itself"(1981:60, italics in original). Here, Ellul introduces the notion of how humans have evolved over time.

He states that historically humankind has moved successively from living predominantly in a natural environment during the hunting and gathering era, to a largely social environment as a result of the agricultural revolution, and finally to a technological environment (produced by the industrial revolution) which is best manifested by a megalopolis with its complex infrastructure. In a natural environment, nature provides sustenance, but also major perils such as floods and drought. In a social environment (such as an agricultural community), nature is mediated by the prevailing system of social organization, which among other things is responsible for the division of labor, distribution of resources, and protection of the community. Major problems in a social environment involve the allocation of authority and external threat.

In a technological environment, which is nested in a social environment, which in turn is situated in nature, the bases for survival are technological, as are major threats to existence. In employing the term "technology" or "technique," Ellul means far more than machines: "*technique is the totality of methods rationally arrived at and having absolute efficiency . . . in every field of human activity*" (1973:xxv, italics in original). Thus, a technological society comprises an environment in which "the ever-expanding and irreversible rule of technique is extended to all domains of life" (Merton 1973:vi). Consequently, the bases for survival in a technological society include not only metropolitan infrastructures and urban residences, but also interdependent systems of "rational" rules and organizations established to oversee all societal functions. This technological environment also presents major threats to existence, not just from infrastructural breakdown, but from the fact that "no human activity is possible except as it is mediated and censored by the technical medium" (Ellul 1973:418).

Ellul's analysis of contemporary technological society strikes a chord similar to Max Weber's observation that "cumulative technological rationalization" erodes idiosyncratic individual freedom (Gerth and Mills 1958:51). Although Weber was convinced of the technological superiority of bureaucracy as an organizational mechanism to accomplish explicitly defined complex goals, his prognosis for a bureaucratized society was considerably less glowing. Ellul (1980:325 [1977]) echoes his concerns:

The human being who acts and thinks today is not situated as an independent subject with respect to a technological object. He is inside the technological system, he is himself modified by the technological factor. The human being who uses technology today is by that very fact the human being who serves it. And conversely, only the human being who serves technology is truly able to use it.

According to Ellul (1980:316–19), "technique" proceeds without plan. Although human beings might think that "technological growth is based on an *a priori* consent by man," Ellul argues that it occurs "only to utilize . . . technological capacity." In other words, technology feeds on itself, until eventually "the universality of the technological environment produces the image of a Nature." Consequently, for Ellul (and Ogburn and Weber), technique (or technology or bureaucratization) produces within human beings an estrangement from themselves.

In addition to his general comments on the dangers involved in living in a technological environment, Ellul (1990) offers specific observations about the relationship of technique to control. With regard to major technological innovations, he states that at the outset we have very little idea of what we are getting ourselves involved in; our ability to predict is extremely limited. Consider, for example, the invention of the automobile in the late nineteenth century, and then consider its many effects a century later. Not only was this invention responsible for creating the fortunes of most major industries in the twentieth century (for example, auto manufacturers, petroleum, steel, rubber, financing and insurance), it changed the whole design of subsequent urban development and, consequently, even the patterning of social relations. And these are just *some* of its main effects. It would have been impossible for *anyone* to make these predictions a hundred years earlier. As a result, Ellul states, "All technical progress has three kinds of effects: the desired, the foreseen, and the unforeseen" (p. 61).

Moreover, because technological innovations are cumulative, they also become more numerous, complex and powerful. From this observation,

Ellul concludes that "the greater the technical progress, the larger the number of unpredictable effects" (p. 70). A corollary of this conclusion is "the more technique advances, the more serious the risk and the greater its probability" (p. 98). Consequently, as a result of the potentially severe dangers inherent in cumulative technological innovation, and our inability to predict and control them, Ellul cautions that we should incorporate "foresight" into our ideas of technical progress; that is, we should "develop attitudes and institutions and instruction based on the constant possibility of a serious accident . . . [in that] the worst [case scenario] has become much more probable" (p. 98). Returning to the example of the automobile, another of its effects has been massive emissions of carbon dioxide into the atmosphere, which in turn is contributing to global warming. Because "unpredictability is one of the general features of technical progress" (p. 60), application of "foresight" or "the precautionary principle" should constitute an integral feature of all technological innovations. I discuss the precautionary principle more fully in Chapter 4.

## OVERVIEW OF THEORIES OF SOCIAL CHANGE

What sense can we make of these theories in explaining and understanding globalization? First, let us consider the theories of development (modernization and convergence) and underdevelopment (dependency and world-systems), as they appear to contradict each other. Is it possible to predict both development and underdevelopment at the same time? Can the data I presented in Chapter 1 help in evaluating these competing claims?

With regard to the empirical outcome of global development to date, the bulk of evidence supports dependency and world-systems theory. Both these theories state that the global system is comprised of a small core of rich industrialized nations and a much larger constellation of dependent peripheral satellites. The section on "Forces of Globalization" in Chapter 1 bears out this claim:

- Overwhelmingly, the technological innovations associated with transportation, communication, and information processing are restricted to high-income core nations, which comprise just 15 percent of the world's population (see Table 1.1).

- In 1998, TNCs from just eleven core countries were responsible for 82 percent of all foreign direct investments made (see Table 1.2). However, in 1990, FDI made in these same eleven countries was 89 percent of the total; in 1980, 94 percent of the total; and in the first half of the twentieth century, virtually all FDI emanated from these 11 countries. Consequently, since the 1970s, foreign direct investment, although still very concentrated, has gradually expanded to include TNCs from a greater number of countries.

- Of the leading TNCs in the world in terms of annual revenues, all of them are based in the Triad core—the United States, Japan, and Europe (see Table 1.3).

- All of the global government alliances discussed in Chapter 1, including the United Nations, are controlled in some way by core nations. With respect to the United Nations, core control is exercised through the all-powerful Security Council in which five countries are permanent members, four of these being core countries (United States, France, Russian Federation, United Kingdom).[5] In order that any substantive matter appearing before the Security Council may be approved, all five permanent members must concur. "This is the rule of 'great Power unanimity,' often referred to as the 'veto' power" (UN 2000b).

- Although all of the international nongovernmental organizations mentioned in Chapter 1 are concerned with issues designed to achieve overall global development goals, most of them are headquartered and managed in core countries. This fact could deprive developing peripheral countries full opportunity to initiate and direct their own development policies based on their own cultural experience (South Commission 1990).

- Concerning the use of the world's resources, the *Human Development Report* (UNDP 1998:2) notes: "Globally, the 20% of world's people in the highest-income countries account for 86% of total private consumption expenditures—the poorest 20% a minuscule 1.3%." Broken down, these figures reveal that the richest fifth consume 58 percent of total energy, 84 percent of all paper, and own 87 percent of the world's vehicle fleet. The corresponding figures for the poorest fifth are less than 4 percent, 1.1 percent, and less than 1 percent.

- Finally, Table 1.4 reveals that the per capita gross domestic product (GDP) of people living in core countries ($21,790) is almost seven times greater than the per capita GDP ($3,270) of those living in peripheral countries.

Consequently, both dependency and world-systems theory are relatively valid portrayals of global development during the latter half of the twentieth century. However, world-systems analysis goes beyond description. It locates the origins of the contemporary "capitalist world-system" in sixteenth-century Europe (coinciding with European colonial expansion), and provides an explanation for its emergence. In addition, it identifies the capitalist world-economy as the first truly *global* world-system in human history. Thus, world-systems analysis provides a theoretical rationale and empirically documents globalization as a sociological phenomenon.

What is the evidence in Chapter 1 for modernization and convergence theory? Are there global trends toward modernization (that is, Westernization) and convergence? The section on "Forces of Globalization" points more to global *expansion* of Western institutions than to global *convergence*. However, in "Counterforces to Globalization," I did note one strong trend toward convergence: the systematic superimposition of Western institutions, languages, goods, and values on non-Western peoples, achieved largely via the electronic mass media. As well as the media putting pressure on indigenous cultures, so too do international trade and foreign direct investment, global consumerism and pop culture, international tourism, and the Internet exert reinforcing effects. However, these pressures, rather than being manifestations of global cultural convergence, might arguably be simply more evidence of the unequal exchange relationships operating between core and periphery. In any event, as far as explaining and understanding globalization in the late twentieth century, the data in Chapter 1 provide substantially more support for theories of underdevelopment than development.[6]

A notable postscript to this discussion involves convergence of a different kind: convergence among *people* as opposed to convergence of cultures. Throughout the world, growing numbers of people are joining together in nongovernmental organizations to promote *their* visions of development (Fisher 1998). Encompassing issues such as human rights and civil liberties, empowerment and government accountability, financial cooperatives and technical assistance, poverty alleviation and community development, community health and disease prevention, agricultural and environmental sustainability, and education and technical training, there is a burgeoning movement of social activists who are challenging conventional top-down policymakers. Aided substantially by all forms of communication technology, they represent new voices at the "global agenda" table. (I discuss this phenomenon more fully in Chapters 3 and 5.)

A development theory consonant with these people-centered objectives is offered by Nobel laureate Amartya Sen (1999), who proposes that expanding human freedoms represents the "principal means" of development, as well as its "primary end." According to Sen, the granting of political freedoms, economic facilities, social opportunities, transparency guarantees, and protective security—that is, "instrumental freedoms"—transforms institutional mechanisms, drives overall societal development, enriches human life, and, ultimately, enshrines freedom as an intrinsic human value. And given that Sen originally wrote this book at the invitation of the President of the World Bank (Sen 1999:xiii), this "freedom" or "people-centered perspective" could well claim substantially more attention than it has in past decades.

Now let us assess how helpful the technological development theories are in understanding and explaining globalization. What do the data in Chapter 1 say? With respect to the theory of cultural lag, the evidence is clear that changes in material culture (applications of transportation, communication, and information processing technology for the creation of a technical global infrastructure) have preceded those in the nonmaterial culture (an institutionalized global political and legal structure to regulate and control this infrastructure and its attendant problems). Indeed, such a structure has yet to materialize, as the opening illustration to the section on technological development theories reveals. This means we are currently experiencing a global cultural lag. Consequently, Ogburn's theory is useful in pointing out how the processes of globalization are actually developing. Wallerstein (1974:349) agrees: "the size of a world-economy is a function of the state of technology, and in particular of the possibilities of transport and communication within its bounds." In other words, although Wallerstein locates the origin of the contemporary capitalist world-system in the sixteenth century, it was not until the late twentieth century that technologies were developed sufficiently to operate this global system in real time. Hopefully, during the present century, a corresponding global nonmaterial culture will develop such that many of the problems of globalization discussed in Chapter 1 may be resolved.

Finally, let us examine globalization in terms of Ellul's conception of technological systems. Globalism, as defined, certainly qualifies as a

# BOX 2.1

# THE TECHNOLOGICAL SYSTEM VERSUS THE NATURAL SYSTEM?

There is little scientific doubt that increasing atmospheric concentrations of carbon dioxide produced from humans burning fossil fuels are causing global warming. The UN Inter-Government Panel on Climate Change (IPCC 2001) concludes: "The atmospheric concentration of carbon dioxide $(CO_2)$ has increased by 31% since 1750," when the industrial revolution began. In addition, the IPCC states: "The current rate of increase is unprecedented during at least the past 20,000 years." These increasing concentrations of $CO_2$ have caused the global average surface temperature to rise by about 0.6 degrees Celsius during the twentieth century, which in turn has produced a massive reduction in snow and ice cover, causing the global average sea level to rise between 0.1 to 0.2 meters. Each of these trends has been particularly pronounced during the past three decades, and is overwhelmingly attributable to human activities.

Depending on a range of realistic projections of $CO_2$ concentrations during the twenty-first century—$CO_2$ emissions will drop below 1990 levels either "within a few decades" or in "about two centuries"—the IPCC estimates that the average global surface temperature will increase between 1.4 and 5.8° C, with a corresponding rise of the global sea level between 0.09 and 0.88 meters. However, given that "some 80% of the world's land mass stands at less than one metre above the sea" (*Economist* 2000), the high-end projection could not sustain human life as we now know it.

Since the industrially developed countries are responsible for producing the majority of $CO_2$ emissions—"the United States, with just 4 percent of the world's population, emits . . . 23 percent of the global total" (MacKeen 2000)—an agreement was reached in 1997 in Kyoto, Japan, that the developed countries would reduce their $CO_2$ emissions and other greenhouse gases to 5.2 percent below 1990 levels by 2012.

In November 2000, an international conference on global warming was held in The Hague, Netherlands, for the explicit purpose of devising binding measures to implement the Kyoto Protocol, which itself dates back to a convention signed in 1992 at the Earth Summit in Rio de

Janeiro, Brazil (MSNBC 2000).

The Hague climate conference ended in failure. Participating nations failed to reach agreement. Consequently, yet another conference must be held to deal with the devastating effects of technologically driven human activity on the global environment.

What went wrong? Given the projected outcomes, how is it not possible for reasonable people to reach accord that will place their actions within the known constraints of the global environment in which they live?

- Some take issue with the facts, stating that factors other than greater concentrations of greenhouse gases could be responsible for global warming (Amos 2000; Whitehouse 2000).
- Some are lobbyists for "carbon" industries (such as automobiles, petroleum, and coal) (Global Climate Coalition 2000).
- Some don't believe the problem is as serious as it has been stated: "industry and technology will ultimately solve this problem" (Morgan 2000).
- Some favor voluntary controls and industry-led initiatives (Business Environmental Leadership Council 2000).
- Some believe that they will lose national competitive advantage (MSNBC 2000).

In March 2001, newly elected U.S. President George W. Bush announced that the United States had no intention of ratifying the Kyoto Protocol (Pianin 2001). In making this decision, and reneging on one of his campaign pledges, Bush argued that implementation of the Kyoto agreement could harm the U.S. economy.

technological system, which means that for those of us living within this system, globalism provides for our existence and puts us in danger at the same time. With regard to our existence, "the world's our oyster"— provided we can pay for it. The technical forces of globalization can provide us virtually anything in the world any time we want it. And herein lies the danger. The promises of the technological system make us oblivious to its perils.

According to Ellul (1980:317), technology transforms "wants" into "needs":

. . . basic needs (food, protection against bad weather and danger) are met, on the one hand, and turned into an infinity of secondary needs, on the other hand, thanks to modern products and processes. These secondary needs are tacked on to older and essential desires, dreams, tendencies, but they swiftly become "natural" and necessary.

However, although the natural environment may be able to satisfy our basic needs as a species, it certainly cannot satisfy indefinitely our accumulating wants, which are continually fueled by technology (Piel 1992). Because of our belief in and reliance on the power of technology, we are lulled into a false sense of security. "The genius of technique is to produce the most reassuring and innocent ordinariness" (Ellul 1990:19). For an actual example of what Ellul is talking about, see Box 2.1 which illustrates how we (certainly in the North) have become dependent upon a global technological system that could ultimately lead to our demise as a species. Ellul's plea (1980:318) is that we develop an *independent* "intellectual, moral, or spiritual reference point for judging and criticizing technology" such that we can arrive at an appraisal and course of action in the best interests of *humanity*.

Consequently, as far as providing insight on globalization—where, when, and why it originated, who initiated it, what drove it, how it is sustained, and what some of its future impacts may be—all of the theories of social change shed some light. However, the theories of underdevelopment and technological development provide the most comprehensive bases for understanding. Together they permit us to see that globalization is a phenomenon that originated in Europe several hundred years ago as a result of the overthrow of the feudal agrarian system by capitalist enterprise. Capitalists in the global core, assisted hugely by continual technological innovations in transportation, communication, and information processing, established a worldwide, hierarchical, industrial, and geographic division of labor that is even more firmly entrenched today. However, according to mounting evidence (such as the love bug virus, regulatory control of TNCs, and $CO_2$ emissions), there are signs that the increasingly complex and interdependent global network of technical systems that sustains worldwide capitalism also represents a threat to its continuing survival. I examine this claim more fully in the following chapter, but first let us consider in more detail the empirical bases for such claims. In other words, what are the processes by which researchers come to these conclusions?

## RESEARCHING SOCIAL CHANGE

The quotations that open Chapter 2 highlight the difficulty in studying social change: "The more things change, the more they remain the same." "Change is eternal. Nothing ever changes." How are these seeming paradoxes illuminating? Consider the main theme of this book: control in a globalizing world. I chose "control" because it represents a basic problem that human beings have had to confront from their earliest beginnings—that is, "nothing ever changes." But at the same time, the overall thesis of this book is that globalization is influencing all aspects of our lives, including control—that is, "change is eternal." In other words, whether an empirical circumstance represents change or not depends to a large extent on why we want to know and the particular questions we ask. Consider the following illustration.

During the course of our lives, each of us experiences many changes as we pass through various stages of the life cycle. The physiological changes in our bodies are accompanied by different social roles and responsibilities, or, as Shakespeare put it, "one man in his time plays many parts, his acts being seven ages." As we pass from infancy through childhood and finally reach adult status, we are bombarded with novel experiences and ideas; we are in a process of constant change. Yet, even as we marvel at the changes we are experiencing as individuals, we increasingly become aware that "in *every* society, *every* individual has an age role and a sex [gender] role" (Lenski and Lenski 1982:49, italics added). In other words, what is novel for us is commonplace within society. "Social relationships in all mammalian societies . . . are organized to take account of age and sex differences" (Lenski and Lenski 1982:47).

Is the above example an illustration of change or stability? The answer depends on whether the focus of study is on individuals, explaining individuals' reactions to life cycle changes, or on society, identifying the mechanisms by which orderly continuity is maintained. Consequently, in any research it is crucial to identify both the level and the units of analysis.

## Levels of Analysis

Traditionally, sociology is comprised of two major orientations: macrosociology, the study of large-scale social structures and processes such as societies and social institutions; and microsociology, the study of individuals and small groups such as families, friends, and work groups. Actually this dichotomy is a simplification; in fact, sociological variables range over *many* levels of analysis. For example, sociologists may study the structure and processes of the world-system, observe relations among coalitions of nations, compare and contrast individual countries, examine relationships among transnational corporations, analyze social institutions, make inter- and intra-organizational comparisons, study group interaction patterns, or research individual attitudes and behavior. Different levels of analysis often focus on different aspects of behavior, and can call on different types of data. Consequently, as the example of individual change and societal stability demonstrates, it is important to realize that what may apply at one level of analysis may not apply directly to another level.

As an illustration of how a particular phenomenon may be studied at different levels of analysis, suppose a researcher is interested in how modern information and communications technology are diffused throughout society. ICT diffusion could be measured by Internet use. At the most general or global level of analysis, a researcher might focus on the overall proportion of Internet use. For example, according to Nua Internet Surveys, as of August 2001, approximately 513 million people, or 8 percent of the world's population, had accessed the Internet at least once during the previous three months. In this case, a researcher might rightly conclude that the information revolution, as measured by Internet use, is only in its beginning stage. This result could prompt a more detailed analysis, and indeed the researcher would discover that the *global* figure greatly masks what is apparent at the *regional* level. The highest Internet use during this three-month period occurred in North America (57 percent), while Africa's Internet use was the lowest (less than 1 percent).

At the regional level of analysis, a researcher might be interested in finding out whether modern ICT diffusion follows a pattern similar to other differences found between core and peripheral regions. Different levels of analysis often generate different research questions; however, researchers frequently organize their investigations to include several levels of analysis. In this case, the researcher would discover that 32 percent of Europeans and North Americans had accessed the Internet recently, compared to only 3 percent of people in the rest of the world, thus confirming that the digital divide parallels other previously documented development divides.

Should a researcher analyze ICT diffusion at the *individual* level of analysis, the questions driving the research would change. Here interest might focus on why people, as opposed to larger social units, are more or less receptive to technological change. This question would probably lead an investigator to study Internet use in relation to age, education, and income. By now, it should be apparent that the level of analysis is important, both in the initial framing of research questions and in the selection of particular units of analysis.

## Units of Analysis

Units of analysis are the empirical indicators used to measure theoretical concepts or variables. In the example above, "Internet access within the three months prior to August 2001" is the empirical indicator of "modern ICT diffusion." Researchers attempt to construct indicators that best reflect their theoretical concepts, knowing full well that there is no foolproof way to ensure a perfect match.

Indicators are measures of theoretical variables in the same way that a thermometer is a measure of temperature. For any one variable, there are potentially a variety of indicators to measure it. The construction or selection of appropriate indicators of variables is crucial to the research process. The indicators you choose can influence your results dramatically and cause you to draw wrong conclusions (Hagedorn and Hedley 1994:25).

Reconsider Internet use as a measure of modern ICT diffusion. Does it reflect adequately what it is supposed to measure? Some might argue that Internet access is just one of several modern information and communication technologies available, and so selection of this one could possibly bias the results. What about access to a personal computer? A fax machine? A mobile phone? Would these measures reflect more or less diffusion? In determining which empirical indicators to use, researchers are guided by their research questions. For example, why are they interested in modern ICT diffusion? Why do they want to know? Answers to these questions help in the selection of appropriate indicators. For instance, if a researcher is interested in the general rate of growth and diffusion of modern information and communication technologies at both global and regional levels, it might be appropriate to use a variety of indicators, or, alternatively, construct a cumulative index of these technologies that would represent average ICT diffusion. When researchers are attempting to measure complex phenomena such as modern ICT diffusion, they should always use more than one indicator. Multiple measures provide greater assurance to researchers that they are measuring what they intend to measure.

Finally, it is important to keep in mind that measurement always involves error—from a variety of sources. For example, are the results of the Nua Internet Surveys accurate? Could there be more or fewer people on-line than what they report? As the Nua surveyors themselves say, "The art of estimating how many are online throughout the world is an inexact one at best. Surveys abound, using all sorts of measurement parameters. However, from observing many of the published surveys over the last two years, here is an 'educated guess' . . . ." Consequently, the reader of research results must be constantly vigilant about the accuracy of empirical indicators. However, in this particular example, the sheer magnitude of differences between regions of the proportions on-line suggests that, although the results may not be completely accurate, they are most likely reflecting true differences.

An even more complex problem in social research is measuring change. Assuming that researchers have determined the appropriate level(s) of analysis for their research question, and have selected suitable units of analysis, how do they ascertain whether in fact change has occurred?

## Measuring Change

As a concept, change implies an altered state from one time to another, and so it is possible, assuming we are measuring the same thing in the same way at Time 1 and Time 2, to measure the *direction* of change. That is, at Time 2 we may record a value (for example, percent of Internet users) as higher or lower or unchanged from Time 1. Also, provided we have calibrated our measuring instrument, we may record the *magnitude* of this change.

We demand two things from measurement as a process: that it is valid and reliable, and that we can make sense of what we are recording. For example, can we be sure that our two measurements (Time 1 and Time 2) are accurate? Are the direction and magnitude of change from Time 1 to Time 2 indicative of what is to come? Is the difference between Time 2 and Time 1 normal? Given only two measurements, it is impossible to answer any of these questions, but with a number of measurements taken

**Figure 2.2  Annual Global Temperature Differences from Overall Average and Carbon Dioxide Concentrations, 1856–1996**

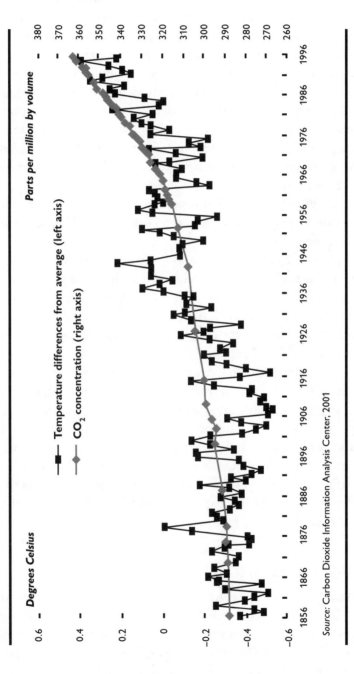

*Source: Carbon Dioxide Information Analysis Center, 2001*

over a sufficiently long period of time, one can be more confident as to both the reliability of measurement and its interpretation.

With many measurements over time, it is possible to compare magnitudes and thus establish *rates* of change. Also, serial measurement permits one to discern the *form* of change (for example, linear or cyclical). However, caution must be taken to ensure that the interval of time is of sufficient duration such that one can correctly identify the pattern being manifested. Figure 2.2 provides two examples of relatively long-term change. The first, showing annual global temperature changes from the overall average, reveals *a definite warming trend* from 1856 to 1996, although within this general trend there are *cycles of cooler and warmer temperatures*. The second example of change ($CO_2$ concentrations) shows a slow and steady growth from 1856 to about 1960 when the rate increased dramatically. Measurement over shorter intervals could produce different interpretations.

Finally, one can conceive of and sometimes measure the *duration* of change, particularly if it is cyclical, and it is therefore possible to record the length of time or duration of the completed cycle before it repeats itself. One can also think of deviations from the normal state of affairs in this regard (for example, the duration of a computer virus before an anti-virus program is developed).

An important point to keep in mind regarding the measurement of social change is that it is severely hampered by the absence of a sufficiently long and detailed historical record. Recorded history reflects only a tiny fraction of the total history of humankind, and even now relatively sophisticated and refined data are primarily limited to the more developed nations. Consequently, if we are concerned with the measurement of long-term global changes, we must be extremely cautious both in our interpretation of what has happened and in our projections of what is likely to occur.[7]

## Validation Strategies

The key to valid measurement is repetition and variation (Hedley 1978). To the extent that varied, or multiple, empirical indicators produce consistent results over repeated occasions, a researcher can be more confident that these indicators are measuring what they are supposed to be measuring. For example, returning to the study of ICT diffusion, if a researcher obtains similar results using several different indicators of ICT, and if these results are repeated in subsequent investigations, then the chances are good that these results represent a true stable finding. The same assurance is not possible with results produced by just one empirical indicator at only one point in time. Extending the principles of repetition and variation to other parts of the research process, it also follows that if different data collection methods, different samples (of countries or people), and different investigators all yield similar results, these too increase confidence in their validity.

These two principles of valid measurement—repetition and variation—are important to keep in mind when evaluating conflicting evidence and interpretations. A time-honored way to distinguish between fact and fiction is to examine the empirical foundations of competing claims. If one claim is supported by just a single study, while another is documented in several different ways by several researchers on more than one occasion, go with the more heavily documented claim. This is certainly the approach I take.

Through the complementary and continuously evolving processes of theory and research, social scientists are guided in their search to understand and explain social change. As Robert Merton (1949) observed more than fifty years ago, the interplay between theory and research is fundamental to the systematic cumulation of knowledge. On the one hand, theory provides an orientation for what to research, a conceptual framework for how to conduct research, and a sound basis for drawing generalizations from research results. In addition, theory can often predict empirical outcomes and point to gaps in our existing knowledge. On the other hand, research leads to the refinement, reformulation, and even rejection of theory. It can also change the focus or orientation of theory, including the initiation of new theory. Theory and research are inextricable elements of the same process. They allow us to construct models of the social world consistent with the reality we seek to understand. Moreover, theoretically informed research can help to guide social policy. And given the magnitude of some of the changes I am describing, in terms of the continuing evolution of humankind on Earth, it is absolutely critical that these changes be assessed and evaluated against the very best theory and research available.

## CHAPTER SUMMARY

2.1 Change is a difficult concept to understand and to measure. In one sense, our needs and circumstances have not changed significantly from our earliest beginnings as a species. Yet in another sense, we are bombarded daily with novel ideas and experiences. Theory and research provide parameters for the study of change. Depending upon the initial questions posed, we try to make sense of the world, both in terms of stability *and* change.

2.2 Modernization and convergence theory propose an evolutionary, unilinear, technologically deterministic perspective on development. Proponents of this perspective state that modernization may be achieved through the adoption of the technologically superior techniques, social institutions, and values of the West. Ultimately, all societies, no matter how dissimilar initially, will converge in patterns of social organization and behavior.

2.3 Dependency and world-systems theory postulate that the global economic and political structure comprises a small core of rich nations and a much larger dependent periphery. Predicated on the basis of a capitalist mode of production originating several hundred years earlier, core nations have institutionalized their initial advantage through the establishment of global trade and investment practices designed to perpetuate a system of unequal exchange: "the on-going process of a world-economy tends to expand the economic and social gaps among its varying areas in the very process of its development" (Wallerstein 1974:350).

2.4 Although development and underdevelopment theories predict very different patterns of global development, they are similar in their description of how world structure has evolved over time. Central to this evolution is the transformation of the world from many diverse nations, each developing more or less independently, to one overall structure of integrated and interdependent global development. With regard to the contemporary human global system, because there is just one common electronic network (the Internet) that provides links to all the computers in the world, the entire system is put at risk, as the love bug virus demonstrated so well.

2.5 The theory of cultural lag contends that changes in the material culture (applications of science and technology) precede changes in the nonmaterial culture (values, norms, and social institutions), thus producing cultural lag. Both cultural lag and technological system theory state that adaptation to the technological environment (technique) represents the most serious challenge to humankind. "The human being who acts and thinks today is not situated as an independent subject with respect to a technological object" (Ellul 1980:325).

2.6 The theories of underdevelopment (dependency and world-systems analysis) provide a better understanding and explanation of contemporary globalism than do the theories of development (modernization and convergence). The bulk of evidence with regard to technological innovation, transnational corporate enterprise, foreign direct investment, strategic global alliances, use of natural resources, and per capita gross domestic products supports the pattern of a core-controlled global system. Support for theories of development is limited to the diffusion of Western institutions, products, and values throughout the world, and the convergent structure of the world system.

2.7 The technological theories of development also offer a realistic assessment of globalism. The theory of cultural lag explains how globalization is occurring through initial changes in the material culture, while technological system theory offers an insightful analysis of how technology itself represents a threat to our existence. Casual observation of problems such as the love bug virus, regulatory control of TNCs, and $CO_2$ concentrations bears testimony at least to the threat.

2.8 Traditionally, sociology is comprised of two major orientations: macrosociology (the study of large-scale social structures and processes) and microsociology (the study of individuals and small groups). In point of fact, however, there are many levels of analysis. In researching social change, sociologists must decide upon which level(s) of analysis they wish to concentrate, because what is revealed on one level may not apply to another. The initial framing of research questions often alerts researchers to the appropriate levels and units of analysis. Units of analysis are the empirical indicators used to measure theoretical concepts or variables. For any one variable, there are potentially many indicators that could be used. Using more than one indicator per variable provides greater assurance to researchers that they are measuring what they intend to measure.

2.9   Provided that researchers measure the same thing in the same way at a minimum of two points in time, they can measure change. Change may be recorded in terms of direction, magnitude, rate, form, and duration. When studying change, researchers should make a reasonable number of observations over a sufficiently long period of time in order to identify correctly the pattern of change being manifested.

2.10  The key to valid measurement is repetition and variation. To the extent that varied (multiple) empirical indicators produce consistent results over repeated occasions, a researcher can be more confident that these indicators are measuring what they are supposed to be measuring.

# 3

# HUMAN CONTROL OF THE GLOBAL SYSTEM

*My concern is with the fact that we are moving ahead very rapidly and are unable to say exactly what the goal is or through what stages we shall pass. Uncertainty is the lot of all technicians and scientists, who are occasionally aware of it. But it is also the situation into which the general populace is thrust without being in the least aware of it.*

*The grasp of things is increasingly behind the times even in supposed looks at the future. The problems that arise are thus increasingly difficult because there is public awareness of them only when they have become vast and inextricable.*

— Jacques Ellul, *The Technological Bluff*

**CONTROL REPRESENTS OUR ABILITY** to reduce uncertainties in our environment such as nature and other people, both in the present and the future. To the extent we achieve control, we can insulate ourselves from the vagaries of this environment. As I have mentioned, one of our strongest drives throughout human history has been to gain relative control over the natural environment to ensure our survival as individuals and as a species. However, during our first 90,000 years of hunting and gathering existence, we achieved relatively little in accomplishing this goal. In fact, it is only within the past 250 years—about ten generations—that we have fundamentally altered our relationship to the natural environment, such that we now live in the science fiction world of earlier visionaries.

Qualitative changes in human control have come about mainly through technological revolutions. One major improvement in human control was the agricultural revolution, a worldwide, but not global phenomenon that took place independently in various parts of the world approximately

10,000 years ago. With the domestication of plants and the invention of the plow, humans gained at least partial control over their basic needs (the acquiring of food, water, shelter, and clothing on a relatively predictable basis), thus moving beyond hand-to-mouth existence. During this period, our ancestors also managed to exceed the capacity of isolated individuals by instituting a division of labor, creating tools, domesticating animals, and harnessing wind, water, and fire. These discoveries allowed early humans to begin planning their *future*, a concept only vaguely realized up to this point. The social communities established during this period mediated in several respects the effects of the natural environment, thus providing other measures of control, such as the generation of surpluses beyond what was required for immediate consumption.

With the cumulative experience of succeeding generations, human beings developed increasingly comprehensive and sophisticated systems of control. The industrial revolution represents a watershed in this regard. Two types of impersonal control mechanisms—bureaucratic organization and mechanical power (the steam engine)—came to epitomize this revolution (Hedley 1992:121–22). First, the systematic application of organizational principles to all sectors of society resulted in the development of a more or less integrated infrastructure capable of sustaining and promoting the additional vast changes that were to follow. Exemplifying these principles of bureaucratic organization were the establishment of a money economy, expansion of maritime navigation and commercial trade, institutionalization of political and legal structures, agricultural reform and enclosure, rationalization of science and education, continued economic differentiation of society, and development of the factory system of production.

Emphasis on the rational organization of social structures and processes resulted in a more centralized, interdependent, and formalized society. Various courses of action were objectively evaluated against the norms of utility, efficiency, and control. Predictability of outcome expanded beyond tomorrow and next season to the more distant "foreseeable future," as planning and a future orientation became major preoccupations. In short, the industrial revolution saw the coordination of human activity within specified space and time parameters on a scale never before even imagined.

Closely interwoven with the theme of rational organization is the equally important element of technological control. The industrial revolution reached a frontier where the outcome of the struggle of humans against an uncertain natural environment became more predictable. Self-determination and expanding horizons replaced fatalistic acceptance as artisans, entrepreneurs, and practitioners alike achieved technical feats previously deemed impossible. Reduced mortality rates, improved standards of living, higher agricultural yields, mechanically driven, machine-based systems of manufacture, and even the shrinking of the earth's surface through increasingly efficient and novel networks of transportation and communication—here was the evidence that verified the techno-scientific might of modern humanity. And when this newly won technical power was channeled into the equally powerful conduit of rational administrative organization, the impact on individuals and society was truly revolutionary. For the first time, people began to live in a technically mediated environment (that is, urban industrial centers) in which innovative infrastructures were set up to cope with the practical exigencies of daily life. Together, bureaucratic organization and mechanical power ushered in an "age of progress" in which many believed it was possible to achieve total control—to reduce to zero the distance between "actual" and "ideal."

As we experience yet another momentous technological revolution, one in which we have crisscrossed the globe with an intricate web of information and communication, some expect we will achieve even greater control over the natural environment and predict future events with greater certainty. In this chapter, I examine the development of human control within the context of globalization. Specifically, I argue that although the evolution of administrative and technical control systems has expanded tremendously the physical and mental capacities of the human race, the substitution of *one complex interdependent set of systems* in place of *many independent systems* is introducing hitherto unanticipated and unintended uncertainties for human existence. I analyze control in relation to each of the four dimensions of globalization I pointed out in Chapter 1—technological, economic, political, and sociocultural. First, however, because of conceptual confusion surrounding the terms "control" and "power," I distinguish between their separate, but related meanings.

## DISTINGUISHING BETWEEN CONTROL AND POWER

According to Gibbs (1994), most social scientists define power in terms of control. Indeed, this is the strategy Gibbs himself employs: "power can be taken as the *capacity* or *ability* for control" (1994:58, italics in original). For Gibbs, the terms "capacity" and "ability" are crucial to the definition, as they "underscore the perceptual character of power." By contrast, Gibbs' definition of control contains explicit reference to overt action: attempted control involves some form of manifest behavior in the belief that "(1) the behavior increases or decreases the probability of some subsequent condition and (2) the increase or decrease is desirable" (1994:27). Thus, an important and generally agreed upon distinction between power and control is that while power involves ability (as perceived by power holders as well as potential objects of power), control refers to actual measurable activity.

Hofstede (1980) provides another useful distinction between power and control. Whereas power involves issues of dominance, inequality, stratification, hierarchy, and authority (or how we vertically array ourselves within society), control invokes notions of rationality, planning, structure, formalization, and standardization (or how we cope with uncertainties produced by nature, other people, and the future). Thus, groups that possess in relative abundance attributes and resources deemed crucial and valuable to social systems, and who consequently have the capacity or ability for control, may overtly institutionalize their power by deploying control mechanisms, strategies, procedures, and systems that regulate activity and behavior within predictable, desirable limits. Examples of such control mechanisms include military and police forces, strategic plans, ritualized customs, bureaucratic rules, formal contracts and agreements, laws, doctrines, assembly lines, computer-aided design and manufacture, hydroelectric dams, and genetic engineering.

These examples highlight yet another distinction between power and control. Generally, power is a function of personal intervention, while control very often involves the introduction of impersonal bureaucratic or technical systems designed to achieve specific outcomes (Scott 1998:310–11). Indeed, establishing structural control is a critical feature of the process by which power becomes institutionalized, and thus normalized.

As an illustration of the distinctions I have made between power and control, let us briefly examine the origins of the capitalist world-system discussed in Chapter 2. Various European nations initially established themselves as the core of this world-system in the sixteenth century because of their immense power which they had gained as a result of their valuable resources—vast accumulations of capital, heavily armed sailing fleets, battle-ready armies, and an overriding desire for conquest to acquire even more capital. Once these European nations expanded into the Americas, Africa, Asia, and Oceania, they consolidated their power after their initial

# BOX 3.1
# CREATING SPACE AND TIME FOR THE WORLD-SYSTEM

How did early explorers know where they were? (In point of fact, many didn't. For example, Christopher Columbus thought he was in India when he reached the Caribbean.) How could Europe establish itself as the core of a world-system if it couldn't accurately define what it controlled? A world-system requires reference points so that it may be established, maintained, and controlled. Reference points were absolutely essential for sailing ships to establish their bearings while exploring and mapping this system.

The stars were the earliest reference points, but because the Earth rotates in relation to the stars, it was necessary for sailors to know exactly when they took their bearings to determine their location. However, early mechanical clocks did not keep time at sea because of the motion of ships.

It was not until 1675, when King Charles II of England appointed the first Astronomer Royal at Greenwich Observatory, and later in 1761 when a clock was made accurate to one-fifth of a second a day, even at sea, that the world-system could be charted accurately.

In 1884, twenty-five core nations formally agreed to make Greenwich (just outside of London) the center of space and time. Because the most comprehensive navigational tables that existed were produced in relation to Greenwich, and because it was becoming increasingly necessary to adopt standard navigational charts and universal time (due to increasing world trade and travel), Greenwich was formally declared as the "prime meridian." This meant that both space and time "began" at Greenwich. The longitude of the Earth was calculated, East and West, from Greenwich at 0° up to 180°, which became the International Date Line.

Thus was created our modern conception of space and time.

*Source:* Factual information taken from www.rogerh.cwc.net/rhwhygmt.htm.

victories by establishing two types of structural control in the form of colonization (Davis 1974). First, in the temperate regions of the world, Europeans settled and attempted to fashion approximations of their homelands in these foreign climes. These areas formed the *semiperiphery* of the world-system. But in the tropics and semitropics, colonial administrations were established for the sole purpose of acquiring raw materials (gold, silver, diamonds, and other goods not indigenous to Europe) that helped to finance the approaching industrial revolution, itself another manifestation of control. These lands became the *periphery* of the world-system.

To make legitimate what they had gained through military conquest, these European countries enacted legislation that designated these new lands as theirs, thus furthering their control over them. Other control structures included the creation of limited product economies in the new colonies, set up explicitly to furnish Europe with the resources it required (see Figure 2.1). In the process, the European core also drew up favorable terms and conditions of international trade and engaged in limited foreign direct investment in the peripheral regions to take advantage of cheap labor costs.

Had the European countries not consolidated and legitimated their power by setting up these control structures, the capitalist world-system would have been extremely unstable, perhaps lasting only until the next uprising. However, by institutionalizing power through these means, Europe solidified its position at the core of a world-system without rival (see Box 3.1).

This examination of the origins of the capitalist world-system highlights the dynamic relationship between power and control. Although the unequal possession of socially valued attributes and resources by individuals and groups results in a graded power hierarchy, possession by itself is insufficient for those at the apex to assume control. They have only the probability or capacity for control. To assert control, they must institute procedures and/or apply mechanisms such that they *"will be in a position to carry out . . . [their] own will despite resistance"* (Weber 1947:152, italics added). Thus, control is the behavioral component of power, which in turn reinforces power.

## DIMENSIONS OF THE GLOBAL SYSTEM

From the introduction to this chapter, we may conclude that human beings have gained increasing control over their fate, largely as a function of epochal technological revolutions. And as we are on the verge of yet another of these portentous revolutions, it is reasonable to assume we will achieve even more control over our earthly existence. However, this revolution is different from those preceding because attempts are now being made *to control the entire world as one interrelated global system*. By definition, globalization involves the *integration* of its various system elements—technological, economic, political, and sociocultural—which means that these same elements are *interconnected* and *interdependent* on a global basis. In turn, these features of the global system introduce a level of *complexity* almost unfathomable to contemplate.

The modern global system has been in the making for the past thirty to fifty years. Motivations for creating it include achieving greater scale, access, speed, and efficiency—or in a word, control. However, as I argue in this chapter, a single system of interrelated (human) elements is more vulnerable to unforeseen risks (natural or human, intended or not) than many (human) systems independently organized. Moreover, given the integrated and expanding global systems already in place, plus increasing human population (projected to level off at nearly 11 billion by 2200 [UN 1998]), plus growing global instability produced by increasing inequality between and within nations, plus rising human aspirations fueled by the Western media and TNCs—all taking place within a finite and increasingly less diverse global eco-environment that is already documented as being under severe strain—the probability of increased human control occurring as a result of further technological innovation becomes less and less likely. In other words, what might be called the "technological fix" is not as viable an option as it once was. Rather, I maintain that the trajectory of human control is now on a downward course. Below I detail the bases for this conclusion.

## Technological Dimension

As I discussed in Chapter 1, the global system in which we are currently living came about largely as a result of the ICT revolution which permitted greater and more comprehensive technical control over virtually all aspects of human activity. To make sense of the massive changes in control that have taken place over the past few decades, I adopt the procedure for identifying and documenting change outlined in Chapter 2; that is, I analyze changes in the direction, form, and duration of human control systems. Figure 3.1 provides an illustrative outline of this analysis.

**Figure 3.1    Changes in Control Introduced by the ICT Revolution**

| Characteristics of Change | Control Features | Illustrations |
|---|---|---|
| Direction of control | Scope: Space Time | TNCs: global control systems Electronically integrated, real time control |
| | Number Range | Microchips offer increased number and range of control applications (e.g., smart homes) |
| | Complexity | WINS global digital nervous system |
| Form of control | Locus | Administrative/Electronic (e.g., computer software & hardware) |
| | Intelligent | Adaptive, self-regulating mechanisms (e.g., smart agents) |
| | Interdependent | Internet: an interlinked network |
| | Standardized | Compatible hardware & software standards to permit machine interfacing |
| | Unobtrusive | Echelon: covert global surveillance |
| Duration of control | Frequency | Continuous electronic monitoring (e.g., security surveillance) |
| | Future orientation | Autonomous, reactive, proactive, forward-looking control systems |

One of the most important changes in *direction* of control, one which facilitated the whole process of globalization, has been expansion in the *scope* of control systems. The microelectronic revolution in the early 1970s was primarily responsible for the creation and deployment of both instantaneous and global control systems that defied the traditional parameters of time and space. As I noted in Chapter 1, prior to this period, both the private and public sectors had to do without the benefits of modern transportation, communication, and information processing, which meant that life—and business—was conducted at a much more leisurely pace over usually much shorter distances. But with the emergence of globally integrated, real-time control, transnational corporate enterprise mushroomed (see Table 1.2) and global capitalism conglomerated (see Table 1.3). Although these developments are not direct measures of the magnitude and rate of increases in the scope of control systems, they are significant manifestations of how control has changed in terms of time and space.

As Figure 3.1 indicates, the microelectronic revolution also permitted increases in the *number* and *range* of activities being monitored and controlled. An important illustration of this empirical observation is the development of computers over the last half century. The first generation of modern (analog) computers, developed approximately fifty years ago, were single-purpose machines, in which specific operating instructions were written for the particular task for which a computer was to be used. Because these early computers were also exorbitantly expensive, only governments, universities, and large corporations could afford them. Consequently, these computers were limited not only in the number and range of possible applications, their prohibitive cost also meant they were restricted to an elite few. By contrast, the current fourth generation personal (digital) computers, first developed in 1971, offer a broad array of applications at reasonable prices, which has led to their widespread and varied use by governments, business, and ordinary citizens.

Today, due to the omnipresence of microchips, the range of applications for computer control is seemingly limitless. Examples include so-called smart homes in which owners can remotely control all their operating systems such as appliances, heating, lighting, audiovisual, and security, and smart cities in which virtually all aspects of modern urban infrastructures are monitored and controlled such as automobile and air traffic control, surveillance, telecommunications routing, power grids, and water quality and supply. In addition, computer control of a wide variety of activities is now employed extensively in business, finance, industry, agriculture, public health, the military, and the sciences and professions.

Finally, concerning changes in the direction of control, control systems have also become increasingly *complex* or sophisticated, due in large part to the cumulation of knowledge and design features. As an illustration of increasing complexity, consider sensor systems—control mechanisms that monitor various aspects of their environment in relation to some preset ideal (see Figure 1.1). When the part of the environment being measured deviates from the ideal, sensors trigger devices to restore the environment to its desired state. The simplest sensor systems are single-purpose, with no feedback. For example, if your car overheats, a sensor activates a light on your dashboard indicating the problem. The problem, whatever it is, then becomes yours to handle. More complex are sensor systems with feedback. A familiar example is a thermostat. Thermostats maintain a prescribed desirable temperature range by measuring the temperature in their environment. When the temperature exceeds or falls below the prescribed range, sensors respond by disengaging or completing electrical circuits, thus turning heating units off or on. In other words, thermostats are self-regulating sensor control mechanisms.

Moving beyond feedback, recent developments in sensor control systems incorporate intelligence (microprocessors and microcontrollers), multifunctionality, and distributed networking capability. One such application of these features is UCLA's Wireless Integrated Network Sensors project (WINS 1998) which provides "distributed network and Internet access to sensors, controls, and processors that are deeply embedded in equipment, facilities, and the environment." Currently, researchers on the WINS project are working to achieve what they call a "global digital nervous system":

On a global scale, WINS will permit monitoring of land, water, and air resources for environmental monitoring. On a national scale, transportation systems and borders will be monitored for efficiency, safety, and security. On a local wide-area scale, battlefield situational awareness will revolutionize operations from armored assault on open terrain to urban warfare. Also, on a metropolitan scale, new traffic, security, emergency, and disaster recovery services will be enabled by WINS. On a local enterprise scale, WINS will create a manufacturing information service for cost and quality control. WINS for biomedicine will connect patients in the clinic, ambulatory outpatient services, and medical professionals to sensing, monitoring, and control. On a local machine scale, WINS condition-based maintenance devices will equip power plants, appliances, vehicles, and energy systems for enhancements in reliability, reductions in energy usage, and improvements in quality of service (WINS 1998).

Developments such as these have prompted futurist Paul Saffo to proclaim that "this decade is being shaped by sensors" (cited in Goode 2000), in that broadband, processing, and wireless networking technologies are all converging around sensors and effectors, which are intelligent agents possessing the characteristics of autonomy, human and machine interactive capability, reactivity, and proactiveness. According to Saffo, sensors will dissolve the human-machine interface. By equipping everyday objects, tools, appliances, and machines with smart agents, Saffo maintains that humans will be able to invite "computers to look into our world and observe the world on our behalf." And he adds, "we are not going to stop there, because the moment we ask them to observe the world on our behalf, we are going to ask them to manipulate it on our behalf." Thus, in terms of control, the ICT revolution will eclipse the industrial revolution through the construction of machines that not only augment human physical and intellectual capacity, but in addition interpret and act upon their environment employing a human perspective.

As control systems have changed in direction in terms of scope, number and range of activities controlled, and complexity, so too have they changed in *form*. The examples above illustrate that the *locus* of control has also shifted—primarily from administrative and mechanical (analog) to administrative and electronic (digital). Whereas the earliest forms of control exercised by humans were almost exclusively personal (using brute force), over time control has become more impersonal and technical. As I mentioned at the beginning of this chapter, the primary control mechanisms employed during the industrial revolution were administrative and technical. This trend has continued as the distinctions between administrative and technical have become progressively blurred with the transformation from mechanical to electronic control. Consider, for example, the major components of a computer—hardware and software. Hardware comprises the technical equipment and devices that make up a computer—objects you can actually touch. On the other hand, software consists of computer operating instructions or programs—ideas, concepts, and symbols. Hardware is technical; software is administrative—but neither can function without the other. A computer embodies what Ellul refers to as technique or "any complex of standardized means for attaining a predetermined result" (Merton 1973:vi). Computers (and technique) represent a genuine fusion of rational organization and technical apparatus—a fusion that increasingly characterizes control systems in the global age.

Control systems have also been made more *intelligent* over time. Given the ubiquity of microchips, virtually all control mechanisms now contain a self-regulating, feedback function in which they are able to monitor and adapt to changes in their environment in order to accomplish pre-established objectives. The study and application of feedback dates back to the 1950s and '60s when scientists first became interested in cybernetics and systems theory. It is important to note, however, that smart machines are only as smart as their software or operating instructions render them; they are not fail-safe. It is certainly conceivable that unanticipated elements in either the system or the environment could cause system malfunction. Consider, for example, a very complex system such as a modern aircraft with all of its automated navigational equipment flying in an even more complex environment. Occasionally, system malfunctions occur, due either to software anomalies or unforeseen environmental contingencies such as an electrical storm.

Another feature of modern control systems in the global age is increasing *interdependence*. The notion of interdependence or a networked system means that previously independent systems such as computers are reconfigured into one overarching interlinked system such as the Internet. A necessary condition for achieving interdependence is the establishment of a common protocol by which individual computers and computerized systems can communicate with each other (Libicki 1995). Consequently, *standardized* or compatible hardware and software is another growing aspect of modern control systems. Standardized networked systems offer great advantage not only in relation to control, but also in terms of access, speed, cost, efficiency, and effectiveness. Indeed, interdependence among standardized units has become a hallmark of globalization. However, serious threats, both internal and external, also pose risk for these interdependent systems. Either deliberate or unintentional forces can cause massive disrupting chain reactions or cascading effects throughout the entire interconnected network. This very scenario is what allowed the love bug virus to infect so many of the world's computers in May 2000, owing to their common link to the Internet and the popularity of Microsoft standard operating systems.

A slightly different example of a potentially massive global crisis stemming from the interdependence and standardization of computerized control systems was the so-called "millennium bug," or the Y2K problem. Prior to 1996, in order to save space and increase operating speed, all computers recorded the year in two rather than four digits (World Bank 1998). Until the turn of this century, this standard convention worked well. For example, suppose we were in 1966, and a computer was programmed to evaluate a person's age who was born in 1940. The computer would calculate "$66 - 40 = 26$," which is correct. However, the same operation done in 2000 would yield "$00 - 40 = -40$." Even if the computer ignored the minus sign, the answer is still wrong. Some years prior to 2000, experts began worrying about what would happen on January 1, 2000, when millions of computers around the world began to process date-specific information in medical life-support systems, aircraft navigational equipment, and other systems. Given the pervasiveness of computerized systems throughout the world—such as power generation, telecommunications, water treatment and distribution, transportation, health care, and financial services—and the fact that in many cases these systems are either directly or indirectly linked, the potential for global catastrophe was real. "The failure of just one link in the chain of this . . . [global]

network could conceivably cause substantial damage to other sectors, even if not directly linked" (World Bank 1998).

Although Y2K did not result in the calamitous outcome that some predicted, this was mainly due to precautions taken *before* 2000. Globally, the costs estimated to fix the Y2K problem range from $600 billion to $1.6 trillion (World Bank 1998). For example, a major industrial food conglomerate spent $20 million—$150,000 on each of its 130 factories— while the average cost for a major bank was more than $250 million. Had these precautions not been taken, some of the grim scenarios resulting from these millions of commonly programmed, interlinked computer systems might well have played their course.

Another change in the form of control systems, stemming from the continuing development of the microelectronics industry, is its increasingly *unobtrusive* nature. One reason why control has become less perceivable is that now it is often integrated into equipment and machinery such that users are not immediately aware of the control functions. A classic example is an assembly line which by its mere operation not only moves product components through a factory, but also controls the rate of work accomplished. More recently devised computer-aided design and manufacture (CAD/CAM) also incorporate control functions in their operating programs. For instance, although the manifest role of computers in CAD/CAM is to produce designs and manufacture end products according to user specifications, system software, particularly at the design stage, also contains control parameters that dictate outside limits in terms of geometric, design, and engineering principles, thus increasing the probability of producing optimal designs and products that actually work (Machover 1996).

Control systems have also become more covert not only because the technology for concealed electronic observation has vastly improved, but because systems are designed deliberately to acquire information surreptitiously. Examples include electronic surveillance, remote sensors, vehicle recognition tracking systems, computer, telephone, and other electronic monitoring, computer data banks, and national and international communications intercept satellite networks (European Parliament 1998). Such control systems are put in place ostensibly to monitor the activities of people who pose threats to society; however, they are also used to track employees, consumers, citizens, and even family members. Box 3.2 provides a description of Echelon, a covert global surveillance system.

Finally, let us examine changes in the *duration* of control, or the

## BOX 3.2
## ECHELON: A GLOBAL SURVEILLANCE SYSTEM

In August, 1988, the *New Statesman* published an article by investigative journalist Duncan Campbell, in which he revealed the existence of a global electronic surveillance system called Echelon. Originating decades earlier, shortly after World War II when the United States and other English-speaking countries entered into a secret agreement to gather "signals intelligence," Echelon now has the capability to monitor as many as three billion electronic communications every day.

The purpose of the network is to collect signals intelligence (Sigint) by covertly intercepting foreign and international communications. Other parts of the Sigint system intercept messages from the Internet, from undersea cables, from radio transmissions, from secret equipment installed inside embassies, or use orbiting satellites to monitor signals anywhere on the earth's surface. The system includes stations run by the United States, Britain, Canada, Australia, and New Zealand (Campbell 2000).

Echelon intercepts electronic messages indiscriminately, and then encrypts and relays them to regional monitoring stations where they are analyzed by "dictionary" computer programs that scan each message for preselected key words or phrases such as "bomb," "revolution," or significant names and places.

Although the original purpose of Echelon was and continues to be the gathering of military and political intelligence to protect national security, both the European Parliament (1998) and the American Civil Liberties Union (n.d.) provide evidence which indicates that this intelligence has also been used to gain national economic advantage and to stifle political dissent. Because Echelon is a top secret operation, not subject to public scrutiny, it is impossible to know exactly the extent to which it may have abused its mandate. However, there is no doubt that its entire operation involves a monumental invasion of the privacy of individuals, groups, and organizations worldwide.

period during which controls are in actual operation. The shift to electronic monitoring of the environment has resulted in greater *frequency* of control, or the rate at which control mechanisms are applied to compare what is occurring with what should be occurring. During human history, control systems have moved from being mainly sporadic to intermittent to continuous. Prior to the industrial revolution, when humans were the principal agents of control, they most often assessed situations on an ad hoc basis, attempting to ensure that reality conformed to expectation. However, with the industrial revolution, impersonal control mechanisms—bureaucratic rules and mechanical means—became built-in features of continuing operations, occurring at regularly defined intervals. And with the further advent of the microelectronic revolution, continuous monitoring and adaptive control of system performance became possible. Whether the system in question was a single machine, a network of machines, an entire factory, or even a large transnational corporation, continual self-regulating control became an integral element of system operation.

Another aspect of the duration of control in the global age is its *future orientation*. Because microelectronic control systems are also "smart"— they are autonomous, have human and machine interactive capability, can react to their environment, and make adaptive responses consistent with defined objectives—they can be programmed to operate into the indefinite future, thus increasing the predictability of ongoing operations. However, sometimes the future does not behave like the present, as Y2K demonstrated.

As I mentioned, Figure 3.1 summarizes all the changes in control systems I have discussed. Although I focused on each control feature separately, it may be seen that they form an interrelated constellation of control made possible largely by the microelectronic revolution originating in the 1970s. Intelligent, complex, interdependent electronic control systems, responsible for monitoring a vast range and number of activities, now span the globe, constantly assessing their environment and making corrective adjustments to maintain equilibrium into the open-ended future. Although the particular illustrations listed in Figure 3.1 are extremely impressive from a scientific and engineering perspective, nevertheless there remain serious technical concerns that need to be addressed. If any one of the many thousands of highly complex, networked control systems now in place should malfunction, due either to anomalies within the system or incursions from the environment outside, the consequences to systems such as air traffic control could be devastating. Thus, the technological structure that supports globalization is itself vulnerable.

## Economic Dimension

Nowhere have these electronic control systems been adopted as enthusiastically as by corporations. Modern business corporations may be characterized as goal-oriented control systems. Their purpose is to negotiate the many elements such as suppliers, markets, and laws that comprise their environment in order to expand market share. Since their origin in the mid-nineteenth century, they have employed several distinct control strategies in the pursuit of this goal:

1. expansion in the size of operations to achieve economies of scale;

2. horizontal integration or the merging of similar firms to control markets;

3. vertical integration or the acquiring of firms that either supply raw materials (backward integration) or handle output (forward integration) to attain greater control over production and distribution;

4. spatial dispersion or regional relocation to expand markets (including the labor market);

5. product diversification to develop new markets; and

6. conglomeration or mergers with companies on the basis of their financial performance rather than on what they produce (Chandler 1962; Fligstein 1990).

Establishing an electronically integrated transnational corporation simply represents a new control strategy in this evolutionary chain.

The move toward transnational investment may be seen as a logical and rational extension on the part of business enterprises to adapt to and control their environment. Because of technological advances in transportation, communication, and information processing during the past four decades, spatial dispersion on a global basis is an asset that carries few if any of the liabilities previously associated with it. Not only are transnational corporations flexible and adaptable, they are technologically enhanced such that they can deal effectively—in real time—with their total global environment. In so doing, they achieve advantages not available to non-transnational organizations bound by the physical, economic, legal, and social constraints of just one country. Because resources and markets are

Table 3.1  National Regulatory Changes to Foreign Direct Investment Policy

| DESCRIPTION | 1991 | 1992 | 1993 | 1994 | 1995 | 1996 | 1997 | 1998 | 1999 | Total |
|---|---|---|---|---|---|---|---|---|---|---|
| Number of countries introducing regulatory changes to FDI policy | 35 | 43 | 57 | 49 | 64 | 65 | 76 | 60 | 63 | n.a. |
| No. of regulatory changes | 82 | 79 | 102 | 110 | 112 | 114 | 151 | 145 | 140 | 1035 |
| Percent more favorable to FDI | 98 | 100 | 99 | 98 | 95 | 86 | 89 | 94 | 94 | 94 |

*Source*: Adapted from UNCTAD 2000:6.

geographically dispersed, and because all countries have different laws and customs, TNCs can systematically select where in the world it is most profitable to conduct particular kinds of business. In many ways, the electronically integrated transnational corporation is the ultimate empirical manifestation of the fusion between rational organization and technological mastery.

Variability in the global environment is a major key to transnational corporate control. Consider, for example, what has been termed "the policy environment," encompassing national laws on tariffs, financing, competition, labor, environmental protection, consumer rights, taxation, transfer of profits, and so forth. These laws vary, sometimes remarkably, among nations. TNCs carefully consider all these laws, together with many other factors, in making their decisions on which countries represent optimal choices for certain kinds of activities (Hedley 1999).

In the mid-1980s, the global policy environment began to change. Prompted largely by the conservative regimes of Ronald Reagan in the United States and Margaret Thatcher in the United Kingdom, and later reinforced by the collapse of the Soviet bloc, most countries in the world started deregulating and liberalizing their foreign investment policies. Table 3.1 presents data on changes to these policies introduced by countries during the 1990s. Of the 1035 regulatory changes made during this period, 94 percent of them were more favorable to foreign direct investment by transnational corporations. Inducements offered included more liberal entry and operational conditions, more fiscal and non-fiscal incentives, more sectoral liberalization (that is, permitting FDI in industries previously excluded), and more guarantees and protection (UNCTAD 1999:115–20; 1998:55–74). However, although the general changes made were in the direction of liberalizing national foreign investment policy, considerable variation in specific national regulations remained. Hence, both the general move to liberalization as well as the continuing regulatory differences among nations benefitted TNCs. Not only is the general policy environment now more receptive to foreign investment, TNCs can also still selectively choose among different national policies.

Consequently, in the inter-nation competition to attract foreign investment during the 1980s and '90s, between-nation variability resulted in an erosion of state sovereignty and a corresponding increase in the control of transnational enterprise. Indeed, the global-spanning capabilities of TNCs, together with the variable national environment in which they operate, have prompted some analysts to declare that the balance of power between corporation and state has tipped very much in favor of corporations (Korten 2001). Table 3.1 and the fact that an increasing number of countries have offered "preferential tax regimes" to TNCs over the past four decades (UNCTAD 1998:74–87) provide evidence for this declaration. For example, consider the United States: in 1957, the corporate share of local property tax revenues was 45 percent; however, thirty years later, its share had dropped to just 16 percent (Reich 1992:281). Quite clearly, big business is profiting immensely in a globalized world.

To understand just how large TNCs actually control their far flung operations, consider General Motors as an illustrative case. As I indicated in Chapter 1, it was the largest TNC in terms of annual revenues ($176.6 billion) in 1999, making it the twenty-third largest economy in the world. It employs nearly 400,000 people, has manufacturing operations in fifty countries, and conducts business in 150 more (GM 2001). In 1999, it recorded profits of $6 billion, up 103 percent from the year before (*Fortune* 2000:F–1). How does GM manage to control everything it does?

Toward the end of the 1980s, senior executives at General Motors were asking themselves pretty much the same question (Bliss 1996). During the two decades previous, GM had been moving from manual to automated design and production control, but not in a coordinated fashion, with the consequence that it had many incompatible computer-aided design, engineering, and manufacturing systems (CAD/CAE/CAM). "As a result, GM lacked the capability to communicate technical data across vehicle groups, component groups, and supplier base to synchronize product development. . . . The inability to transfer CAD/CAM data between dissimilar systems was one of the biggest obstacles to integrating the vehicle design and build process" (Bliss 1996:312). Moreover, in order to remain competitive, GM had to reduce the time and cost of bringing new products to market, while maintaining and improving quality control. GM's goal was to achieve a twenty-four-month "fast-to-market" product cycle. To attain this objective, it required total and compatible electronic design, engineering, and manufacturing capability, or computer-integrated manufacturing (CIM).

The key to CIM was to develop *standard* workstation configurations and *single* software architecture. "In general, the more standard the environment, the easier it is to support" (Bliss 1996:315). Consequently, GM developed strategic alliances with certain key hardware and software suppliers. Because GM is also one of the world's largest buyers of this kind of technology, its efforts to standardize its global operations had tremendous impact on the entire computer and software industry, resulting in *many other companies adopting the same standards as GM.* In addition, GM's many parts and components suppliers were also prodded to adopt compatible systems.

Today, operating through a *central* Technical Data Management Facility, GM "has created a global infrastructure for all GM business entities, such as worldwide purchasing, financial, manufacturing, personnel, sales, service, and marketing departments. This *integrated worldwide infrastructure* includes computing, communications, networking, and data management, and will also be used by GM suppliers and dealers worldwide" (Bliss 1996:316, italics added). By moving to *common processes and systems*, GM has achieved its fast-to-market objective, reduced costs, improved its competitive position in the industry, and gained greater control over its entire global operations.

Is GM's case unique? Industry analyst Charles Clarke (2001, italics added) reports that "in recent years *all* automobile manufacturers have attempted to reduce the number of disparate computer applications and systems they use in order to streamline their processes."

The ultimate goal for automobile manufacturers is to engineer a car around the clock, around the globe. Twenty-four-hour engineering with worldwide partners will lower the cost and development time. . . . The objective is to allow designers to collaborate globally, across time zones, so that when one person goes home another takes over in another part of the world. The globalisation of the industry and the sharing of vehicle platforms across international markets aids this process (Clarke 2001).

The automotive industry appears to be a global success story, but let's examine the implications of what is involved when a transnational corporation sets up an electronically integrated worldwide infrastructure. First, let me provide some background facts:

- In April 2002, the Computer Security Institute released its seventh annual *Computer Crime and Security Survey* of computer security practitioners working in large American corporations and government agencies. The results were by now predictable: cyber-crime is a growth industry. Of the 503 organizations questioned, 90 percent had detected computer security breaches within the past year, and 80 percent incurred financial losses in the hundreds of millions. However, only 34 percent reported these incursions to law enforcement authorities.

- The CERT Coordination Center (2001), a major U.S. reporting agency for Internet security problems, has maintained records of the number of "incidents reported" regarding "security compromises" from 1988 to 2000. Of the total 47,711 incidents reported during this twelve-year period, nearly half (46 percent) were in 2000; two-thirds occurred between 1999 and 2000. Not only do these statistics reveal a huge increase in breaches of security, but given the figures reported in the item above, they are more than likely gross underestimates of the actual incursions that took place.

- The *Virus Bulletin* (2001) compiles a monthly list of computer viruses "in the wild" (as confirmed by a minimum of two "virus information professionals"), as well as the number of reported attacks associated with each virus. The number of invasions reported worldwide in January 2001 (6,177) exceeded by far the total number of incidents reported for each January in the preceding six years (4,486). In April 2001, 222 viruses were confirmed as being "in the wild."

- In October 2000, hackers broke into Microsoft's computer network (CNN 2000c). According to the *Wall Street Journal* (cited in CNN 2000c), "passwords used to transfer the source code behind Micosoft's software were being sent from the company's computer network in Washington to an email account in St. Petersburg, Russia." It further reported that "the unknown hackers were believed to have stolen blueprints to [Microsoft's] most valuable software, including latest versions of Windows and Office."

- In May 2001, Microsoft issued a "Security Bulletin" announcing a "buffer overflow vulnerability in its Internet Information Services (IIS) 5.0" (Microsoft 2001). Hackers could exploit this vulnerability and gain system-level access to any of the many thousands of Windows 2000 servers running IIS 5.0. System-level access would allow hackers "to take any action desired, such as installing malicious code, running programs, reconfiguring, adding, changing, or deleting files" (NIPC 2001).

- Vladimir Levin, the Russian convicted of masterminding the largest computer bank robbery in cyber-history ($10 million from Citibank in 1994), is currently serving a three-year sentence in the United States (PBS 2001). Levin funneled "millions in cash from Citibank branches worldwide to his accomplices' accounts in California, Israel, Finland, Germany, the Netherlands and Switzerland, all without ever leaving his computer keyboard in St. Petersburg, Russia" (*USA Today* 1999). According to Myron Cramer, principal research scientist at Georgia Tech Research Institute, "It's my belief that this is not an isolated incident." "Cramer bases his belief 'on my experiences working with the commercial (sector). When they see problems, they deny that it happened and cover up all evidence that it happened . . . to avoid loss of public confidence in their industry or to avoid getting in trouble with their bosses'" (cited in *USA Today* 1999).

- In 1998, nearly two thousand Web sites were providing advice, expertise, and techniques to would-be hackers (CNN 1998).

- "According to the Frost & Sullivan consulting company, the [American] information security industry will grow from $1.13 billion in 1998 to $24.75 billion in 2005" (Hudack 1999), an increase of over 2000 percent in seven years.

All these facts, plus the italicized portions of the GM story above, highlight the increasing likelihood of massive system failures in the future. Principally because most modern computerized control systems use standardized or compatible hardware and software and operate within vast interlinked networks, the chances are high that interventions—

intentional or unintentional, human or natural—will occur with possibly devastating consequences. Y2K is a recent example of disaster averted, but not without substantial cost and emotional turmoil. Certainly, as I mentioned in Chapter 1, these events raise a profound paradox: the very systems that are put in place to increase predictability and control are themselves producing acute uncertainty, not only for those responsible for these systems, but for humanity at large.

Recent work in electronic system architecture (that is, software design) has attempted to deal with the security and dependability problems inherent in hierarchical, standardized, networked control systems in which all subsystems are linked to and controlled by a single central system, as is the case with GM's Technical Data Management Facility. This type of architecture, originally designed for high-volume, routine tasks in a stable environment, is not well suited to processing variable tasks in a relatively unstable environment. Centralized architecture generally is not sufficiently flexible to deal with atypical cases, and in addition, if one subsystem is put at risk due to environmental contingencies, the entire system is rendered vulnerable. In such variable, unstable situations, "distributed" or decentralized control architecture is more appropriate (Class Technology 2001; Prabhu n.d.). Distributed control systems allocate autonomy and responsibility to individual subsystems to make their own decisions, which at the same time must be consistent with overall system objectives. In order for subsystems to make optimal system decisions, each subsystem is provided with adequate but limited information about the total operating system. Consequently, should an individual subsystem become vulnerable, the entire system is not compromised. Moreover, any subsystem failure is limited only to that subsystem; it does not reverberate through the entire system.

Although distributed control systems are superior to hierarchical systems in terms of security and dependability problems arising in their environment, there are two essential reasons why they are not impervious: first, any networked system must have at least some lines of communication among and between units; and second, individual units must use a common protocol in order to comprehend one another. In other words, although the problems of interdependence and standardization are reduced in distributed control systems, they are not eliminated. Therefore, the price for the greater access, speed, and efficiency of networked versus independent systems must be higher risk tolerance. As I note in the next section, this issue is not limited to business corporations; it also applies to political structures.

## Political Dimension

Because of two demographic variables—population growth and migration—human populations are increasingly concentrated in urban agglomerations. In 1900, only one-tenth of the world's population lived in cities, but by 2006, it is estimated that half will live in urban areas, and by 2025, nearly two-thirds will be urbanized (Sweet 2000; World Bank 2000:46–49). Currently, 20 percent of the world's population (1.2 billion) live in the 386 cities numbering one million and more, including Tokyo-Yokohama, the world's largest city (34.5 million) (Brinkhoff 2001). The most densely populated countries, the city-states of Hong Kong and Singapore, have approximately 7,000 and 5,300 people per square kilometer respectively (World Bank 2001:274–75). However, even in Australia, one of the least densely populated countries (2 people per square kilometer), 63 percent of its population lives in the five cities that number at least one million (Brinkhoff 2001). Overall, in the high-income developed countries, 77 percent of the citizens are urbanized (World Bank 2001:277).

These statistics reveal the fact that not only are more and more people living in technically mediated environments (in other words, cities), but that it is the growing responsibility of national and local governments to provide complex, interdependent, critical infrastructures—including national transportation and communication networks—to serve the needs of citizens and to protect their safety and security. This is an overwhelming mandate of governments today. Quite literally, in today's highly complex urbanized environments, ordinary people cannot fend for themselves as they once could. They are dependent for their very survival on the uninterrupted, adequate functioning of these infrastructures. And given that these infrastructures are computerized and interdependent, and given also the widespread availability of inexpensive computers, the potential threats to infrastructures now are greater than they ever have been.

The problems of coordinating and managing highly urbanized populations within an integrated national context in a globalizing world are immense. Although the incorporation of new information and communications technologies into local and national infrastructures permits governments to provide better, more comprehensive services to citizens, it also increases risk. In this regard, note what the director of the newly established American National Infrastructure Protection Center (NIPC) has to say:

Our society is increasingly relying on new information technologies and the

Internet to conduct business, manage industrial activities, engage in personal communications, and perform scientific research. While these technologies allow for enormous gains in efficiency, productivity, and communications, they also create new vulnerabilities to those who would do us harm. The same interconnectivity that allows us to transmit information around the globe at the click of a mouse or push of a button also creates unprecedented opportunities for criminals, terrorists, and hostile foreign nation-states who might seek to steal money or proprietary data, invade private records, conduct industrial espionage, cause a vital infrastructure to cease operations, or engage in Information Warfare (NIPC n.d.).

Because of these concerns, NIPC was established in 1998 "to serve as the U.S. government's focal point for threat assessment, warning, investigation, and response for threats or attacks against . . . critical infrastructures" (NIPC n.d.), and since the terrorist attacks on the World Trade Center in New York City and the Pentagon in Washington, D.C., on September 11, 2001, NIPC views its mandate as crucial for the security of Americans everywhere. Included within its mandate are natural and inadvertent interruptions of infrastructure operations such as earthquakes and human error, as well as those occurring intentionally. The critical infrastructures identified by NIPC are telecommunications, banking and finance, water supply systems, transportation, emergency services, government operations, electrical power, and gas and oil storage and delivery.

Paralleling and predating NIPC is the Information Survivability Program of the Defense Advanced Research Projects Agency (DARPA), the central research and development organization for the U.S. Department of Defense. In the mid-1990s, rather than attempting to design totally secure systems, which is judged to be impossible, DARPA concentrated its efforts on developing systems and networks with "high fault tolerance,"— in other words, systems that could successfully withstand deliberate attacks and natural environmental contingencies. According to the then-director of the program, "survivability is the ability of a system to continue the adequate performance of its critical services and functions even after (unforeseen) successful attacks have taken place" (Shrobe cited in Wilikens and Jackson 1997). To achieve its objective, DARPA has established a multifaceted research agenda:

DARPA is developing technologies for use in building hardened information systems and networks that have strong barriers to attack, can detect malicious and suspicious activity, can isolate and repel such activity where possible, and can guarantee minimum essential continued operation of critical systems functions in the face of concerted information attacks (DARPA 1998).

In a similar vein, the European Commission (2000) launched a "Dependability Initiative" in 1999. Dependability is defined as "the trustworthiness of a computer system such that reliance can justifiably be placed on the service it delivers." Dependability incorporates the features of reliability, availability, safety, and security. To date, the Commission has funded sixty projects divided into five dependability sub-themes pertaining to large-scale information infrastructures and embedded systems. In an overview of the problems associated with dependability, Wilikens and Jackson (1997) highlight the same dilemma identified by NIPC: the huge and growing reliance and dependence on digital information systems by all sectors of society in the face of increasing dependability concerns about these same systems. Put another way, these systems are large-scale, networked and integrated, and use homogeneous open hardware, software, and communications architecture. Wilikens and Jackson conclude by stating that "threats and risks to the dependability of networked information systems are probably growing at a rate comparable to the growth of the Internet itself."

Japan has been slower than either the United States or European Union to acknowledge the risks inherent in complex networked systems. Although it has long been concerned with natural disasters and the infrastructural disruptions they cause, given its location in the typhoon belt and the so-called Pacific "Ring of Fire" that is noted for its many active volcanoes and geological faults (Furukawa 2000), Japan has only recently begun "to grasp the staggering complexity—and the implications—of the world-spanning interconnections between easily-accessed computer networks and crucial elements of national infrastructure, such as transportation, power, water, defense, and banking systems" (Miyawaki 1999). It was not until some recent calamities—the devastating Kobe earthquake and the nerve gas attack in Tokyo's subways, both occurring in 1995—that the Japanese government finally came to terms with "its critical shortage of contingency management" (Nakamura 2000:1) by creating an Office for National Security Affairs and Crisis Management. Also established in 1998, largely by corporations to deal with the Y2K problem, was Japan's Commission on Critical Infrastructure Protection (Miyawaki 1999).

In the developing countries of the world, urban infrastructure problems are far more basic. Just being able to provide essential services constitutes a major challenge for many governments. Table 3.2 presents data on various infrastructural features for 164 of the most populous cities in the world. Collected under the auspices of the UN Commission on Human Settlements (2001), these data reveal that while virtually all major metropolitan urban households in developed countries have water, sewer, electricity, and telephone service, this is often far from the case in large cities located elsewhere. For example, in Africa, with the exception of electricity, fewer than half the households in major cities have such basic amenities. One reason for this is that the shantytowns surrounding large cities are growing at faster rates than the cities themselves. These data reinforce the conclusion I drew in Chapter 1 that there are two global realities. Obviously, governments in the North and South have very different sets of problems.

Returning to the problems of developed countries, not only must governments cope with the relatively new threats to interdependent societal infrastructures, they must also contend with more traditional contingencies. One such problem is organized crime, which has revamped itself by adopting strategies similar to legitimate business, such as taking advantage of information and communication technologies and becoming more transnational in its operations. According to the Center for Strategic and International Studies (CSIS n.d.) based in Washington, D.C.:

The rise of transnational organized crime is an unfortunate by-product of globalization, through which technological advances and lower barriers to trade have created a seamless electronic environment and empowered new classes of actors which bypass nation-states. Like legitimate business, transnational criminal enterprises are embracing globalization by adopting new communications and transportation technologies which allow them to pursue global markets. The criminal organizations are not monolithic, but act as networks, pursuing the same types of joint ventures and strategic alliances as legitimate global businesses.

The *International Crime Threat Assessment* (ICTA 2000), an evaluation produced by the U.S. Government, reports "a significant increase in the range and scope of international criminal activity since the early 1990s" due to several related factors:

1. Advances in modern ICT
2. Globalization of legitimate business
3. End of the Cold War
4. Economic and trade liberalization
5. Proliferation of international travel

Table 3.2   Metropolitan Infrastructure Indicators, 1998

| World Region | # of Cities | Percent of Households Connected to | | | | % Households Access to Potable Water[a] |
| | | Water | Sewer | Electricity | Telephone | |
|---|---|---|---|---|---|---|
| Industrialized countries | 9 | 100 | 100 | 100 | 99 | 100 |
| Transitional countries[b] | 36 | 91 | 90 | 99 | 74 | 97 |
| All developing countries | 119 | 76 | 64 | 86 | 52 | 89 |
| Latin America[c] | 48 | 84 | 64 | 91 | 52 | 89 |
| Arab States | 14 | 79 | 66 | 92 | 42 | 88 |
| Asia Pacific | 28 | 66 | 58 | 94 | 57 | 95 |
| Africa | 29 | 48 | 31 | 54 | 16 | 74 |

*Source*: Adapted from the UN Commission on Human Settlements (2001).
a. Access is defined as having safe or potable water located within 200 meters of the dwelling.
b. Former Soviet bloc countries located in eastern and central Europe.
c. Includes Caribbean countries.

This global environment provides organized crime the opportunity to move goods and services worldwide with virtual impunity and to transfer funds at the speed of light. As evidence of this assertion, consider that U.S. Customs, due to increasing volumes, now inspects only about 3 percent of the goods entering its borders, a number destined to be lower in the future.[1] Moreover, the previously risky business of money laundering (estimated at $1 trillion annually) is now made significantly easier due to the capacity to move huge sums across borders electronically, and because banks are also globalized. Similar to their problems with TNCs, nation-states are severely limited in their ability to control transnational crime because while they must respect the sovereign rights of other states, organized crime prospers in a world without borders (ICTA 2000).

More sophisticated and professional than in previous times, and employing a diversified range of highly skilled experts, including those it bribes, organized crime has launched new initiatives in addition to its traditional pursuits. For example, it is taking advantage of the global digital age by distributing child pornography on the Internet, engaging in industrial espionage by downloading corporate computer files, committing electronic fraud and embezzlement by accessing credit card numbers and commercial accounts, and violating intellectual property rights by counterfeiting trademarked products (ICTA 2000).

Another new profitable enterprise is environmental crime. "The US Government estimates that local and international crime syndicates worldwide earn $22–31 billion annually from hazardous waste dumping, smuggling proscribed hazardous materials, and exploiting and trafficking protected natural resources" (ICTA 2000). In addition, organized crime has established connections with various terrorist groups and rogue states through which it provides a whole range of contractual services, including sanctions violations, illicit technology transfers, and the smuggling of chemical and biological materials for weapons of mass destruction.

According to the authors of the *International Crime Threat Assessment*, in the next decade international criminal organizations will become increasingly adept at "exploiting computer networks upon which all modern government, public, private, and financial services will depend." Given this capability, it is certainly conceivable that organized crime could eventually hold individual nation-states (and corporations) for ransom in that "many countries are likely to be at risk of organized crime groups gaining significant leverage or even control over political and economic systems."

Consequently, similar to the private sector, and for the same reasons, governments in all developed countries are increasingly vulnerable in their attempts to provide basic essential services to their citizenry. This vulnerability extends to all individuals and organizations, linked in any way to interdependent, networked, computerized control systems. In addition, as I noted in my discussion of the "Economic Dimension" of the global system, governments face another substantial challenge to their control due to their inability to regulate adequately the activities of border-straddling transnational corporations.

## Sociocultural Dimension

Of all the dimensions of the human global system I have discussed, the sociocultural appears to be the most resilient in terms of maintaining diversity, thereby representing an alternative to the monolithic force of globalization. Although it is certainly true that highly organized interests in the developed core nations have strategically employed electronically integrated control systems to gain further domination over the total world-

**Table 3.3  Characteristics of Forces for Cultural Convergence and Diversity**

| | FORCES FOR | |
| --- | --- | --- |
| **CHARACTERISTICS** | **CULTURAL CONVERGENCE** | **CULTURAL DIVERSITY** |
| Constituency | Elite core corporations & nation-states | Core & periphery multicultural people |
| Motivation | Economic and political | Broad-based social welfare & ecological viability |
| Objectives | Power and control | Sustainable development in a variety of forms |
| Area of activity | Global, but concentrated in core nations | Local, but can mount global campaigns |
| Type of activity | High-end goods & services | Diversified |
| Resource mobilization | State and financial institutions | Formation of social movements |
| Type of organization | Corporations & nation-states | NGOs (grassroots orgs. & grassroots support orgs.) |
| Organization structure | Centralized hierarchies | Participative democracies |
| Formalization | Highly formalized | Non-institutionalized (more committed than organized) |
| Direction of communication | Top-down | Bottom-up |
| Means of outside communication | Mass media | Petitioning, lobbying, demonstration & protest (face-to-face & electronic) |

system through the superimposition of a Western world culture, at the same time there has been an amazing, as well as increasing, resistance to these efforts in both the core and the periphery. In this section, I first present evidence for global cultural convergence, and then provide data that support cultural diversity. As is usual in these kinds of debates, the actual empirical outcome most likely will fall somewhere between these two extremes.

Table 3.3 outlines defining characteristics of the forces for cultural convergence and cultural diversity. However, because I am attempting to classify very complex phenomena, you should interpret these characteristics cautiously. Although they apply broadly to these two sets of forces, they do not fit perfectly into each and every case. But considered together, they provide a useful snapshot of these opposing ideologies.

Concerning these contradictory views, it is much easier to identify the

forces for convergence because they are extremely concentrated and dominate the global scene. They comprise major transnational corporations
such as the *Fortune* "Global 500" and countries (especially the Triad—
the United States, European Union, and Japan) in the core of the world-
system. These are the major players promoting globalization. On the other
hand, it is difficult to catalog the forces for diversity, precisely because
they are so diverse. As I noted in Chapter 1, while there may be more than
30,000 international NGOs worldwide, this number is nowhere close to
the millions of grassroots organizations and groups all over the world—
including the core—engaged in achieving *their* visions of development.
They represent the peoples of the world in all aspects of their multifaceted
lives. To the list of human rights and civil liberties, empowerment and
government accountability, financial cooperatives and technical assistance,
poverty alleviation and community development, community health and
disease prevention, agricultural and environmental sustainability, and education and technical training that I outlined in Chapter 2, we must also
add issues of ethnicity, language, religion, and cultural heritage. And this
list is by no means exhaustive of the many concerns being addressed.
However, together they provide an indication of who the forces for diversity are. In addition, many of these organizations are supported by a wide
variety of UN agencies, development-assistance organizations, and chari-
table foundations. Although the forces for convergence may be far more
organized in both their objectives and how to achieve them, nevertheless
the forces for diversity, because they are so numerous and diverse, represent a significant counterforce to globalization as it is presently conceived.

Examining now the forces for convergence, as Table 3.3 (and Box
1.2) indicate, they are assisted hugely by the Western mass media, which
are dominated by just a few transnational American and American-based
corporations. Spanning newspapers, magazines, books, music publishing,
radio, TV and cable networks, film production, motion picture theaters,
the Internet and much more, they provide a seamless global distribution
and transmission network.

The media companies have two major avenues or methods with which
to get their message across, and in the process provide a relatively uniform global overlay of Western values, customs, and modes of living. First,
the *content* they distribute and transmit is highly cultural-laden. Not only
do most movies, TV series, and music display Western points of view,
even the news—including what is and is not presented—contains core
perspectives. For example, in reporting an increase in oil prices by OPEC,

## BOX 3.3
## LOST IN TRANSLATION

- In China, Kentucky Fried Chicken's slogan "finger-lickin' good" was translated as "eat your fingers off."
- Coors put its slogan, "Turn it loose," into Spanish, where it was read as "Suffer from diarrhea."
- Clairol introduced its "Mist Stick," a curling iron, into Germany only to find that "mist" is slang for manure. Not too many people had use for the "manure stick."
- General Motors introduced its Nova into Spain and wondered why its sales were so low. "No va" in Spanish means "It doesn't go."
- When Gerber began selling baby food in Africa, it used the same label as in the United States—a photo of a beautiful baby. Later it learned that in Africa most companies routinely put pictures on the label of what's inside, since most people can't read English.
- In Taiwan, Pepsi's "Come alive with Pepsi" came out as "Pepsi will bring your ancestors back from the dead."
- Electrolux, a Swedish vacuum cleaner company, tried to market its products in the United States using the slogan "Nothing sucks like an Electrolux."
- In Brazil, Ford changed the name of Pinto to Corcel because Pinto is slang for "small male genitals."
- Colgate introduced a toothpaste in France called Cue, the name of a notorious porno magazine.
- In Italy, a campaign for Schweppes Tonic Water was translated into "Schweppes Toilet Water."
- In China, a phonetic adaptation of Coca-Cola came out as "Bite the wax tadpole."

*Source:* Picked up from various Internet sites. Regardless of their authenticity, these ads do make a point.

one editor at the reputable *Washington Post* explained that "the world's supplies of oil and price levels are *manipulated* and controlled by *greedy*

Arabs" intent on *"blackmailing* the United States" (cited in El-Farra 1996, italics added), even though at the time only seven of the thirteen member states of OPEC were Arab, and only one Arab country was among the top five producers. Clearly, this news story and others less blatant contain more than an objective reporting of the facts. In fact, most sociologists are of the view that it is impossible to interpret events objectively (Hedley 1994). No matter how careful we might be, our personal and cultural circumstances influence or color how we see the world. If this is the case, *and* the media are overwhelmingly dominated by American interests (as they are), then most of what is reported in the world news necessarily contains a biased American perspective. A more subtle, but nevertheless systematic form of cultural bias takes place in translating media content from one language to another, most often from English to some other language. For some humorous, yet telling illustrations of the difficulty of translating not just words, but also cultural frames, see Box 3.3.

Box 3.3 also reveals the other main avenue by which the global media get the message out: *advertising.* Thousands of brands, slogans, jingles, products, services, and companies have become household names around the world, thanks to the effectiveness of advertising by these media giants. And virtually all those advertising are major core corporations. For example, in the United States, "the 100 largest corporations . . . pay for roughly 75 percent of commercial television time and 50 percent of public television time" (Korten 2001:154). The media in all their forms continuously keep these corporations and their products in our consciousness. In turn, this creates a repeating and reinforcing cycle: increasing brand recognition leads to increasing brand loyalty, which translates into greater profit margins for the recognized firms, which results in greater industry consolidation (by squeezing out the "bottom players"), which produces greater convergence in the message being transmitted, which leads to increasing brand recognition and loyalty, . . . and so on. In other words, advertising is an equal partner to content in the ability of the global mass media to provide a universal and uniform view of global reality. David Korten (2001:155), author of the influential book *When Corporations Rule the World*, describes the symbiotic relationship between media content and advertising, and how together they produce a socialization effect that challenges the impact of public education:

The Economist reported that in 1989, global corporate spending for advertising totaled more than $240 billion. Another $380 billion was spent on packaging, design, and other point-of-sale promotions. Together, these expenditures amounted to $120 for every single person in the world. Although the bulk of this corporate expenditure is directed toward creating demand for specific products, it also contributes to creating a generalized global consumer culture and to making a connection in the public mind between corporate interests—in particular the interests of large corporations—and the public interest.

Overall, corporations are spending well over half as much per capita to create corporation-friendly consumers as the $207 per capita ($33 for Southern countries) the world spends on education. Furthermore, growth in advertising expenditures far outpace increases in education spending. Advertising expenditures have multiplied nearly sevenfold since 1950—one-third faster than the world economy.

And considering that the average American youth spends 1,500 hours per year in front of a television set—exposed to approximately 30,000 TV commercials—compared to the 900 hours spent annually in the classroom (TV Free America 1998), the impact of media content and advertising may well be greater than what is learned in school.

Similar to my examination of General Motors, let us now focus on AOL Time Warner, the largest of the media corporations, to get a fuller understanding of how it represents a major force for global cultural convergence. The history of AOL Time Warner is a history of corporate mega-conglomeration. Time and Warner Bros. began independently in the 1920s, Time primarily in magazines (for example, *Time, Life, Fortune, Sports Illustrated, People*), Warner Bros. in movie production and music publishing (AOL Time Warner 2001). In 1989, these two by then huge corporations merged to become the largest media and entertainment company in the world. And the further acquisition of the Turner Broadcasting System (TV, movie, and cable networks, CNN, Home Box Office, the Atlanta Braves, and the Atlanta Hawks) in 1996 served to reinforce its dominance. Then in 2001, Time Warner and America Online, the Internet leader in advertising, marketing, and commerce, joined in "the largest business merger of any kind in history" (FAIR 2000). As a result, AOL Time Warner now claims that its brands "touch consumers [worldwide] more than 2.5 billion times each month." In terms of revenues, which were more than $35 billion in 2000, it is among the 100 largest corporations in the world (*Fortune* 2001:152).

Given its preeminence as the most powerful global voice in information and communication, AOL Time Warner is not without its critics. Various consumer and public interest groups (that is, NGOs) have identified a number of related concerns, all relevant to the case for cultural convergence (Multichannel Video Compliance Guide 2000; FAIR 2000):

- reduced competition due to increasing conglomeration among all leading media corporations;

- cross-ownership (for example, AT&T, also a major communications corporation, owns substantial shares of AOL);

- reduced access for competing firms;

- less choice of on- and off-line content for consumers;

- reduced privacy for consumers (for example, AOL regularly tracks visitors to its sites in its effort to build consumer profiles); and

- lack of public accountability and social responsibility of these media giants.

In short, critics claim that the size and the power of these super media corporations lead not only to convergence in the messages being transmitted, they could also result in substantial abuses of power.

Now let us look at the forces for cultural diversity. Paradoxically, many of the recent initiatives of global capitalism (including the merger of AOL and Time Warner) have served as rallying calls for NGOs and concerned citizens worldwide to proclaim their visions of global development. Although the hundreds of thousands of groups advancing these alternative visions may not agree with each other on either priorities or procedures, they are united in their unshakable conviction that the present Western-dominated, corporate perspective on globalization is flawed. Whether it was the electronically mediated campaign against the Multilateral Agreement on Investment in 1997 (see Box 1.3), or the demonstrations against the World Trade Organization in Seattle in 1999, or the protests against the Summit of the Americas in Quebec City (2001), or the mass support for implementation of the Kyoto Protocol in Bonn (2001), or the criticisms of the "neoliberal agenda" of the G-8 nations in Genoa (2001), the message was the same. Based on the underlying principles of human social welfare and environmental sustainability, the protesters' message comprised four overlapping themes, each representing a criticism of corporate-led globalization: 1) active democratic involvement of all peoples in their own development; 2) greater socioeconomic equity for all humankind; 3) more local autonomy and sense of community; and 4) sustainable development. Together, these themes comprise a substantially more diverse agenda for global development than is presently in place. Moreover, given the momentum of recent events, it is likely that the advocates of this agenda will continue to press for their visions of global development.

The forces for cultural convergence and the forces for cultural diversity represent radically opposed worldviews. As Table 3.3 reveals, currently the forces for convergence are stronger, more institutionalized, and more recognized as being legitimate than the forces for diversity. These are the forces of the status quo. Their roots date back to the sixteenth century, and over the past few decades they have instituted electronically integrated systems of global control to achieve more efficiently their overriding objective: "the endless accumulation of capital" (Wallerstein 1999:35). On the other hand, the forces for diversity, although not as strong nor as organized, are more reflective of the aspirations of the overwhelming majority of the world's population. As the recent protests against corporate-led globalization have demonstrated, theirs is not a cause to be taken lightly. Also, the development objectives of the forces for diversity are more consistent with the concept of sustainable development. We will return to these opposing views of development in Chapter 5.

## OVERVIEW OF THE GLOBAL SYSTEM

I began my discussion of the global system by asserting that although human beings have gained increasing control over their fate during the course of history, the trajectory of human control is now on a downward course. The reasons I advanced for making this assertion include the scale and complexity of integrated global control systems, and the fact that they necessarily involve interdependent subsystems that rely upon a common protocol for communication. In addition, the following features of the context within which globalization is taking place further exacerbate the probability of achieving effective control: increasing human population, rising aspirations, increasing disparity within and between nations, and a finite, already strained, global eco-environment. Given my foregoing analysis, what sense can we make of my hypothesis that we are now running out of control?

First and foremost is the technical information and communications infrastructure that supports modern globalization. If it is not sound—that is, survivable, dependable, reliable, secure—it cannot then sustain a global superstructure, which is to say the economic, political, and sociocultural institutions that rely upon it. Figure 3.1 specifies how particular features of control systems have changed over the past four decades. Considering them as a whole, we may conclude that qualitatively different systems of control have been introduced during the latter half of the twentieth century. These systems, while offering greater scale, access, speed, and efficiency than the systems they replaced, are nevertheless subject to greater risks of being compromised. I have outlined the structural bases of these risks, provided examples of malfunction due to these risks, and indicated how we may expect even more system failure in the future. Particularly in light of the terrorist attacks on September 11, 2001, the following testimony by high-ranking experts deserves our serious attention:

*Linton Wells, Acting U.S. Assistant Secretary of Defense:*
The Department is increasingly dependent on a "global information environment" over which it has little control, said Wells. That dependence increases U.S. vulnerability to threats externally—and internally. . . . "Current intrusion techniques are extremely limited in their ability to identify attacks" (Nando Times 2001).

*U.S. Army Major General David Bryan, Commander of the Military Joint Task Force for Computer Network Operations:*
"We have to continue to improve [network defenses] because the threat continues to improve," he said, referring to the department's more than two million computers, 100,000 local-area networks, and 100 long-distance networks (CNN 2001).

*Howard E. Shrobe, Chief Scientist, U.S. Defense Advanced Research Projects Agency, 1994–97, responsible for the "Evolutionary Design of Complex Software" and the "Information Survivability" programs:*
"An appropriate intellectual community with the critical mass to attack large scale [computer network] survivability does not yet exist" (cited in Wilikens and Jackson 1997).

*Paul Higdon, Head, Digital Crimes Department, Interpol:*
"Critical information infrastructure protection and cybercrimes will be the challenge of the twenty-first century." In a worst-case scenario, Interpol believes cyber-terrorists could paralyze an entire

city. In the United States, as many as seventeen million people are thought to have enough computer knowledge to stop the distribution of electricity, drinking water, as well as other critical items needed in a large city (WITSA 1999).

*Jeffrey Hunker, Senior Director for Critical Infrastructure Protection, U.S. National Security Council:*
The government is dealing with an "enormous educational deficit" when it comes to IT security, he said. . . . "I believe that we are going to get nailed seriously" (CNN 2000d).

As I have mentioned in regard to control in a globalizing world, we face a profound paradox. On the one hand, a primary objective of globalization is to achieve greater control over the environment and human activity into the foreseeable future. On the other hand, however, the very structure of globalization renders it vulnerable to a plethora of foreseen and unforeseen risks. This paradox is consistent with Ellul's observation that "the greater the technical progress, the larger the number of unpredictable effects" (1990:70). I return to this issue in Chapter 5. Suffice it to say here that because the reliability and dependability of the global technical infrastructure are in question, severe repercussions could follow for the economic, political, and sociocultural institutions that rely upon it. And to complicate matters even further, in the following chapter I introduce yet another set of uncertainties for the viability of globally integrated control systems—the global eco-environment within which they operate.

## CHAPTER SUMMARY

3.1    Control represents our ability to deal with uncertainties in our environment such as nature and other people, both in the present and in the future. Attempted control involves some form of overt behavior in the belief that "(1) the behavior increases or decreases the probability of some subsequent condition and (2) the increase or decrease is desirable" (Gibbs 1994:27).

3.2    Power, a concept related to control, is "the *capacity* or *ability* for control" (Gibbs 1994:58, italics in original). Whereas power involves the potential for control, as perceived by power holders as well as potential objects of power, control involves overt action.

Control is the behavioral component of power, which in turn reinforces power.

3.3    Throughout history, human beings have gained increasing control over their fate, largely due to technological revolutions such as the agricultural revolution approximately 10,000 years ago and the industrial revolution in the late eighteenth century.

3.4    As we are now experiencing another technological revolution, one in which human beings are attempting to control the entire world as one integrated human global system, it is reasonable to assume we will gain even more control over what we do and what we want to do. However, because this revolution involves the establishment of just one system of interdependent elements, its inherent structure renders it highly susceptible to chain reactions that could cause massive system failure. Consequently, I put forward the thesis that the trajectory of human control is now on a downward course.

3.5    Figure 3.1 summarizes the changes in technical control introduced by the information and communications technology revolution that began in the 1970s. Intelligent, complex, interdependent electronic control systems, responsible for monitoring a vast range and number of activities, now span the globe, constantly assessing their environment and making corrective adjustments to maintain equilibrium into the open-ended future.

3.6    Regarding the economic dimension of the global system, the balance of power between corporation and state has shifted in favor of corporations as a result of globalization. Operating within a borderless world, transnational corporations can capitalize on the variable policy environment among nation-states to select where in the world it is most profitable for them to conduct business.

3.7    Although transnational corporations have been able to deploy integrated electronic systems of global control to profitable advantage, mounting evidence indicates a high probability of massive system failures in the future. Principally because most modern computerized control systems use standardized, compatible hardware and software and operate within vast interlinked networks, the chances are high that interventions—intentional or unintentional, human or natural—could occur with possibly devastating results.

3.8    Concerning political control of the global system, during the past decade governments at all levels in the developed countries have instituted extraordinary measures to protect their electronically interdependent infrastructures that provide crucial services to largely urban populations. These procedures were introduced because of the realization that while the interconnectivity of essential infrastructures produces enormous gains in efficiency, productivity and communications, it also introduces new vulnerabilities for reliable system functioning. The tragic events of September 11, 2001 provide an ominous foreshadowing of what these new vulnerabilities could mean in terms of lives lost and damage incurred.

3.9    Table 3.3 reveals two major worldviews on the sociocultural dimension of the global system. On the one hand, the thrust of dominant elite core corporations and nation states is to establish a Westernized world culture reflecting the values of global capitalism, while on the other hand, grassroots NGOs and ordinary people everywhere are posing an alternative vision of development based on the value of cultural diversity—in other words, the active involvement of all peoples in their own development, greater socioeconomic equity, local autonomy, and sustainable development. Whereas the capitalist core is aided hugely by the Western-dominated mass media in getting its message out, the forces for diversity communicate their message by mounting both physical and virtual grassroots campaigns and demonstrations.

3.10   Because a globalized system of control relies first and foremost upon the worldwide information and communications infrastructure that supports it, and because there are systemic dependability problems with this infrastructure such as interdependence, the thesis that the trajectory of human control is now on a downward course cannot be rejected. Rather, primary indications reveal that the very structure of globalization renders it vulnerable to a plethora of foreseen and unforeseen risks. In the words of Jacques Ellul (1990:98), "the more technique advances, the more serious the risk and the greater its probability."

# 4
—

# THE GLOBAL ECOLOGICAL ENVIRONMENT

*The planet is fine. Compared to the people, the planet is doing great. Been here four and a half billion years. Did you ever think about the arithmetic? The planet has been here four and a half billion years. We've been here, what, a hundred thousand? Maybe two hundred thousand? And we've only been engaged in heavy industry for a little over two hundred years. Two hundred years versus four and a half billion. And we have the CONCEIT to think that somehow we're a threat? That somehow we're going to put in jeopardy this beautiful little blue-green ball that's just a-floatin' around the sun? The planet has been through a lot worse than us. Been through all kinds of things worse than us. Been through earthquakes, volcanoes, plate tectonics, continental drift, solar flares, sun spots, magnetic storms, the magnetic reversal of the poles . . . hundreds of thousands of years of bombardment by comets and asteroids and meteors, worldwide floods, tidal waves, worldwide fires, erosion, cosmic rays, recurring ice ages . . . And we think some plastic bags, and some aluminum cans are going to make a difference? The planet . . . the planet . . . the planet isn't going anywhere. WE ARE!*

—George Carlin

**DEPENDING UPON THE LEVEL OF ANALYSIS,** the planet is both an environment and a system. Considered as an environment (for the human species), its attributes affect us, as do we affect it. It is in this sense that George Carlin launches his tirade against humankind: we are not putting the planet, as a system, in peril; rather we are placing ourselves, as one miniscule subsystem within a vast multi-level ecosystem, at severe risk due to our lack of understanding of and interference with our natural environment. Were the human species to disappear from the face of the Earth tomorrow, says Harvard zoologist/biologist/ecologist Edward O. Wilson, "the rest of life . . . would benefit enormously." On the other hand, if ants "were to disappear, there would be major extinctions of other species and probably partial collapse of some ecosystems" (cited in Suzuki and Dressel 1999: 13–14).

Just how likely is it for us to "disappear"? The answer upon which most environmental experts agree is "very likely, IF . . . we continue as we have in recent decades." In other words, as a species, we have to do something—and soon! Again citing Wilson (1999):

The world environment is changing so fast that there is a window of opportunity that will close in as little as the next two or three decades. I've always thought that we would lose a lot of biodiversity, but how much is hard to say. It could be something like 10 percent of species. But that is far better than the 50 percent or more we will certainly lose if we let things continue as they are today.

Similar to the human global system I described in Chapter 3, the global ecosystem consists of an extremely complex, multifaceted series of interdependent subsystems. Consequently, it is subject to similar types of risks for us as I pointed out with regard to the human global system. The key to our survival is the biological diversity of the global ecosystem. As I mentioned in Chapter 1, biodiversity is important not only for that part of the natural environment that humans use directly such as air, water, food, and shelter. It is also important precisely because of the interdependence of the entire biosphere—an interdependence we are nowhere close to understanding. For example, the loss of even a single component such as ants could produce unanticipated destructive ripple effects—for humans—throughout the entire system. Biodiversity contributes to ecosystem stability, productivity, and sustainability. "The Earth's biodiversity is a capital resource that provides vital ecosystem services, goods such as food, fuel, fiber and medicines, and the aesthetic, recreational and cultural riches associated with nature" (IBOY 2001).

Although the impact of humans on the environment has been negligible over most of the course of human history, during the last 250 years (since the industrial revolution), but especially during the past few decades, we have exploited the planet in serious ways and greatly diminished its biodiversity. Table 4.1 tells part of the story. During the past fifty

Table 4.1    Some Impacts of Humans on the Global Environment

| World Indicators | 1950 | 1960 | 1970 | 1980 | 1990 | 1999[a] | 1950–99 % increase |
|---|---|---|---|---|---|---|---|
| Population (billions) | 2.56 | 3.04 | 3.71 | 4.45 | 5.28 | 6.00 | 134.4 |
| Grain area harvested (mill. hectares) | 587 | 639 | 663 | 722 | 694 | 674 | 14.8 |
| Fossil fuel consumption (mill. tons of oil equivalent) | 1666 | 2964 | 4846 | 6300 | 7151 | 7647 | 359.0 |
| Automobile fleet (millions) | 53 | 98 | 194 | 320 | 445 | 520 | 881.1 |
| Paper & paperboard production (mill. tons) | n.a. | 77[b] | 126 | 170 | 240 | 294[c] | 281.8[d] |
| Urban population (billions) | 0.75 | 1.02 | 1.36 | 1.75 | 2.28 | 2.80 | 273.3 |
| Gross World Product (trill. 1998 dollars) | 6.3 | 9.9 | 16.1 | 23.3 | 31.4 | 40.5 | 542.9 |

*Source*: Adapted from Brown et al. (2000).
*Notes*:
a. Preliminary figures.
b. 1961 figures.
c. 1998 figures.
d. 1961: 98 percent increase.

years, we have more than doubled the world's population—increasing demand on a finite supply—and multiplied by nearly seventeen the world's automobile fleet, which is one of the major sources of harmful carbon dioxide emissions. Not only do more than half a billion cars require environmentally degrading fossil fuel, they also need roads on which to run. For example, in the United States, with its 214 million motor vehicles—which amounts to three vehicles for every four people—there are 3.9 million miles of paved roads. This is enough to circle the equator 157 times, with additional space required for parking (Brown 2001).

Table 4.1 also reveals that the computer age with its electronic databases has yet to usher in the paperless society as was promised. More than 70 percent of the almost 300 million tons of paper produced in 1998 was consumed in developed countries, almost half for packaging. In fact, 90 percent of all paper is used only once and then thrown away in forms such as packaging, newspaper, sanitary and household paper. "Of [all] the wood harvested for 'industrial' uses (everything but fuel), fully 42 percent becomes paper. This proportion is expected to grow in the coming years since the world's appetite for paper is expanding faster than for other

## Table 4.2    The World's Largest Cities

| CITY | COUNTRY | POPULATION (millions) |
|---|---|---|
| 1. Tokyo-Yokohama | Japan | 34.50 |
| 2. New York | USA | 21.40 |
| 3. Seoul | South Korea | 20.25 |
| 4. Mexico City | Mexico | 19.30 |
| 5. Bombay | India | 18.95 |
| 6. São Paulo | Brazil | 18.45 |
| 7. Osaka | Japan | 17.90 |
| 8. Los Angeles | USA | 16.60 |
| 9. Cairo | Egypt | 14.70 |
| 10. Manila | Philippines | 13.80 |
| 11. Buenos Aires | Argentina | 13.40 |
| 12. Jakarta | Indonesia | 13.40 |
| 13. Calcutta | India | 13.20 |
| 14. Moscow | Russia | 13.20 |
| 15. Delhi | India | 12.25 |
| 16. London | England | 11.80 |
| 17. Shanghai | China | 11.80 |
| 18. Rio de Janeiro | Brazil | 11.20 |
| 19. Karachi | Pakistan | 10.75 |
| 20. Istanbul | Turkey | 10.60 |
| 21. Teheran | Iran | 10.60 |
| 22. Dhaka | Bangladesh | 9.80 |
| 23. Paris | France | 9.75 |
| 24. Chicago | USA | 9.30 |
| 25. Beijing | China | 8.50 |

Source: Brinkhoff, 2001.

Note: Cities are defined as "urban agglomerations," that is, "a central city and neighbouring communities linked to it by continuous built up areas or many commuters. . . . Some agglomerations have more than one central city."

major wood products" (Brown et al. 2000:78).

Also making a major impact on the planet is the growing urban population. Nearly half of us now live in technologically created environments called cities, a quadrupling of our numbers since 1950. "Local environmental problems, such as water and air pollution, are worst in cities where population size or growth exceeds the capability of governments to build and maintain critical water, waste, and transportation infrastructure" (Brown et al. 2000:104). Table 4.2 lists the twenty-five largest cities in the world, twenty-one of them numbering more than ten million. In 1950, there were just ten metropolitan areas with populations of more than five million; today there are fifty-two (Brinkhoff 2001).

Finally, Table 4.1 displays a more than 500 percent increase in the world production of goods and services since 1950. Especially since 1960, this increase is largely attributable to the global activities of transnational

---

## BOX 4.1

## OUR ECOLOGICAL FOOTPRINT

An "ecological footprint" is "a measure of the 'load' imposed by a given [human] population on nature" (Wackernagel and Rees 1996:5). "The Ecological Footprint concept . . . accounts for the flows of energy and matter to and from any defined economy and converts these into the corresponding land/water area required from nature to support these flows" (p. 3). Wackernagel and Rees became interested in developing a specific measure of our ecological footprint when they were confronted with two sets of opposing trends: 1) a more than 70 percent per capita decrease in eco-productive global land area over the past century, due to expanding world population and human land degradation; and 2) a 300 percent per capita increase in land area use appropriated by North Americans, due primarily to rising material expectations, but also to population growth.

Statistics such as these raise a number of obvious but extremely important questions:

1.    What is the total sustainable carrying capacity of the Earth?

2. What is the present aggregate demand by people on the global ecosystem?
3. What is a fair "Earthshare" if all the ecologically productive land were divided equally among the global population?
4. What are the actual Earthshares among the world's people?

To answer these questions, the researchers devised the ecological footprint index. They constructed a "consumption—land-use matrix" that listed people's consumption and waste-assimilation demands on the environment (for example, certain types of food, housing, transportation, and consumer goods and services) against various types of land that would be required to satisfy these demands (for example, fossil energy consumed [expressed in the land area necessary to sequester the corresponding $CO_2$], degraded land or built-up environment, garden, crop, pasture, and forest). With statistics collected by various agencies such as the World Resources Institute, they could thus compute an overall ecological footprint for any given population.

Answers to the preceding questions are:

1. Of the total surface area of Earth (51 billion hectares), roughly 75 percent of it is covered by either water or ice. Of the remaining 13.1 billion hectares, 7.4 billion are ecologically productive—cropland, permanent pastures, forests and woodland—for active human use.
2. The present aggregate demand for ecologically productive land for four major human requirements is 9.5 billion hectares, that is, almost 30 percent more than the productive land available. "Agriculture occupies 1.5 billion hectares of cropland and 3.3 billion hectares of pasture. Sustainable production of the current roundwood harvest (including firewood) would require a productive forest area of 1.7 billion hectares. To sequester the excess $CO_2$ released by fossil fuel combustion, an additional 3.0 billion hectares of carbon sink lands would have to be set aside" (p. 90).

    How is it possible to use 30 percent more land than is available? The answer is, it is not possible *in the long run*. In other words, we are using the essential products and processes of nature more quickly than they can be renewed, and discharging waste more rapidly than it can be absorbed. Rather than reaping "natural interest," we are cutting into "natural capital," thus providing future generations with less ecologically productive land than we have at present.

3. A fair "Earthshare" comprises a circle of land 138 meters in diameter. Approximately one-quarter of this circle is arable land, with the rest consisting of pasture, forest, and wilderness. A tiny fraction of the circle is built up for human habitation. The global average ecological footprint is 7.1 acres per person, which actually represents a 1.8 acre per capita deficit in terms of the Earth's total biocapacity.

4. In a new Ecological Footprint study located at the Web site, "Redefining Progress for People, Nature, and the Economy," Wackernagel and his co-researchers (2001) computed the global acres per capita presently required by the citizens of various countries. Here are some of their results:

| | | | |
|---|---|---|---|
| United States | 30.8 | South Korea | 12.1 |
| Australia | 22.1 | Mexico | 7.6 |
| Canada | 21.5 | Egypt | 4.5 |
| France | 17.9 | China | 4.4 |
| United Kingdom | 15.6 | Indonesia | 3.4 |
| Germany | 14.9 | Ethiopia | 1.9 |
| Japan | 13.8 | India | 1.8 |

What do these figures mean? Consider, for instance, the 30.8 acres per capita, which is the equivalent of "30 football fields without their end zones," used by Americans. This figure is more than four times the 7.1 acre global footprint per capita, which in turn is 1.8 acres more than the Earth can sustain in the long term. In other words, if everyone on Earth lived like an average American, we would need six Earths to satisfy the aggregate material demand. As Wackernagel and Rees (1996:102) conclude, "consumption by the [most] affluent 1.1 billion people [that is, the richest 20 percent, most of whom live in the North] alone claims more than the entire carrying capacity of the planet."

What is *your* ecological footprint? Is it above or below your fair Earthshare? Why don't you visit the "Redefining Progress" Web site at www.rprogress.org to find out your own individual ecological impact on Earth.

corporations. Similar to Table 1.2 which reported the rise of foreign direct investment by TNCs during the twentieth century, increases in gross world product are also most pronounced from 1960 on. Indeed a large part of the rationale for globalization is to stimulate economic growth. Of the top twenty-four TNCs listed in Table 1.3, seven manufacture automobiles and three refine petroleum, thus explaining in substantial part the huge increases in the world automobile fleet and fossil fuel consumption over the past fifty years.

Also contributing to the upward trend of the gross world product has been product diversification (for example, the entire microelectronic industry—again largely stimulated by TNCs) and rising standards of living and aspiration. These developments have expanded global production and consumption, which in turn have exacted a further toll on the environment.

Except for population, most of the tremendous increases reported in Table 4.1 are the result of activities in the developed countries. However, given the huge and growing population base in the South, there is no reason to expect these figures to decline any time soon, unless there is a substantial change of will in both the North and South. After all, many in the South are simply attempting to attain the lifestyle that is seductively presented to them by the Northern media. For a dramatic illustration of the total impact of humans on the environment and how this varies by countries in the North and South, see Box 4.1 on *Our Ecological Footprint*.

The principal driver of all the developments listed in Table 4.1 is cumulative technology. In an intriguing paper, biohistorian Stephen Boyden (1996) traces the impact of humans and their technologies on the natural environment over the course of human history. Boyden develops an energy-based index to measure all human behavior, which he divides into four main activities: extraction, production, consumption, and pollution (that is, waste elimination). He then separately measures human "bioenergy" use, described as "the inputs, throughputs and outputs of organic material, water and oxygen flowing through human bodies," and "technoenergy" use, described as "the inputs, throughputs and outputs of materials and energy as a result of technological processes [in which people engage]". On average, Boyden judges that an active adult expends about ten megajoules (MJ) of bioenergy in one day.[1] So, for any given population, the amount of bioenergy used in a year equals 10 MJ x 365 days x the number of people in the population.

**Figure 4.1    Total Energy Use of Humankind in Three Periods of History**

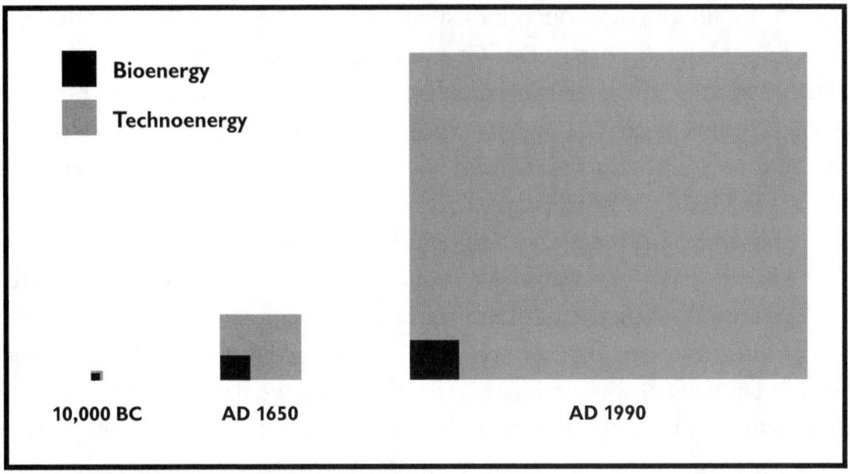

■ Bioenergy

▨ Technoenergy

10,000 BC        AD 1650                    AD 1990

*Source*: Boyden, 1996.

Boyden calculated the total bio- and techno-energy expended by humans at various times in history. For example, because hunters and gatherers used fire and crude rock tools in their struggle for survival, Boyden estimated that early humans used about twice as much total energy than they otherwise would have—half bioenergy and half technoenergy. As humans evolved, they developed further technological means such as plows, tools, and domesticated animals to help them in their daily living. Hence, while bioenergy remained relatively constant, affected only by population fluctuations, technoenergy expanded exponentially.

Figure 4.1 presents the total energy use by humankind for extraction, production, consumption, and pollution at three points in history. The first date, 10,000 BC, reveals an equal proportion of bioenergy and technoenergy use for a very small world population of hunter-gatherers. The second date, 1650, represents the acme of the agricultural era during which people had developed a whole range of tools, implements, and armaments constructed from a variety of materials. At this time, Boyden calculated the ratio of bioenergy to technoenergy use at about 1:2.5. The final date depicted is contemporary (1990). Here, the bio-technoenergy use ratio is approximately 1:50.

Although the impact of bioenergy use on the environment has increased substantially during the past 12,000 years due to an expanding world population, it is insignificant compared to the impacts of technoenergy use. The developing countries are responsible for most bioenergy use, in that they comprised 80 percent of the world population in 1990, while the developed industrialized countries are the major users of technoenergy at 75 percent. Overall, "total energy use by humankind today [which is still increasing rapidly] is about 10,000 times what it was when farming began" (Boyden 1996). These conclusions are consistent with the relative sizes of our ecological footprints in various world regions (see Box 4.1). In addition, they provide reference points on the impact of humans on the global ecology throughout history.

Boyden's analysis reveals a profound paradox: the overwhelming share of the energy devoted to human extraction, production, consumption, and pollution is used by the very technologies we have devised to control our life chances on planet Earth. And the more we have substituted machine- and capital-intensive technology for labor-intensive technology, the more aggravated the impact of technology on the environment has become. Consequently, we have another set of factors to corroborate the hypothesis that for the first time in history, the trajectory of human control is on a downward course.

In Chapter 3, I suggested that we are now beginning to run out of control because we are attempting to devise one overarching, extremely complex, interdependent global system. And given the conceivability, potential, and indeed preliminary indications that any number of eventualities could cause this system to malfunction, the risk for humankind is perhaps more than we can bear. In this chapter, I am describing an even more complex, more interdependent global system that, because of our concerted but unintended actions prompted largely by technologically enhanced global enterprise, is showing many signs of serious stress. From a systems perspective, the solution for system viability is similar for both the human global system and the global ecosystem: increase diversity and reduce interdependence. Through these means, both systems could become more resilient in the face of unknown and unpredictable environmental and system uncertainties. In Chapter 5, I offer some actual approaches and strategies that could incorporate these system features.

In the remainder of Chapter 4, I present four major categories of how humans encroach upon the eco-environment, along with illustrative examples. These are what I term flash points, demanding our attention as we attempt to formulate long-term approaches that will allow our grandchildren's children to enjoy the bounty and the beauty of the earth in the same way we do.

# HUMAN ENCROACHMENT ON THE ECO-ENVIRONMENT

Human beings engage with their environment on three main levels: ecosystems, species, and organisms. In many cases, their activities intervene on all three levels simultaneously. For instance, activity at the ecosystem level necessarily involves the species and organisms that inhabit the system, as involvement with a particular species also includes the organisms that constitute it. However, modification of either species or organisms also produces effects on the ecosystems in which they live. Thus, virtually any activity has consequences beyond its immediate impact.

In the subsections below, I discuss different types of incursions by humans on their environment. In actual fact, although I treat each subsection separately, there is much overlap among them. For example, when people convert the natural habitat for their own purposes, such as building a town, not only does this action result in habitat loss and fragmentation, it also involves pollution of this same habitat, as well as biotic changes to the environment, and exploitation of wild living resources. Just as there is interdependence among ecosystems, species, and organisms, so too are various human activities mutually interrelated.

## Habitat Loss and Fragmentation

Much of all human activity involves habitat loss and fragmentation. Consider, for example, resource extraction (mining, oil and gas, forestry, and fishing), agriculture, factories, construction, cities and towns, transportation, communication and energy networks, and dams and reservoirs. In all these endeavors, humans substantially modify the natural environment. McNeely et al. (1995:751) report that only 27 percent of the world's land surface (other than rock, ice, and barren land) is "undisturbed" by humans. More than one-third (36 percent) is completely "human-dominated," and the remainder is "partially disturbed." However, given the global impact of humankind and the interdependence of the entire biosphere, even the undisturbed land cannot be considered totally free from the effects of humans.

Habitat loss and fragmentation may be either reversible or irreversible, meaning that in some cases, given sufficient time, land used for forestry and agriculture may be returned to its original state, whereas land devoted to mining, oil and gas extraction, and metropolitan areas may not. Generally, the greater the technoenergy involved in the conversion of land for human use, the less likely the modification will be reversible.

When humans do appropriate land, most often the ecosystems involved become less diverse because the land is designed to accommodate particular human purposes. Consider modern intensive agriculture. Initial clearing of wild grassland or forest immediately incurs loss of vegetation, insects, birds, and wildlife. The subsequent planting of a few high-yield varieties of fertilized crop species protected by pesticides further reduces biodiversity not only of ecosystems, but also of species and organisms. For example, the Worldwatch Institute (1999) reports that farmers in China are now growing fewer than 10 percent of the wheat varieties they did in 1949, and in Mexico, only 20 percent of the corn varieties cultivated in the 1930s are now being harvested. Largely due to practices adopted by modern agribusiness, which favors mass-produced, pest-resistant, high-yield, uniform crops and stock, genetically designed species are developed and grown, thus excluding other varieties of the same species.

Contributing to this loss of biodiversity has been, first, the consolidation and then integration of the global agro/food system. In the case of consolidation, between 1935 and 1970 the number of farms in the United States decreased by half, while their size more than doubled due largely to mechanization and expanding economies of scale (Collins 2001). Similar consolidating patterns also took place in other agricultural exporting countries, extending as well to agricultural handling, transportation, processing, and retailing. Coincident with these developments, the agro/food system moved from being mainly a family owned and operated enterprise to a corporate dominated agribusiness.

Integration followed consolidation. During the past two decades, giant corporate retailers have acquired or otherwise control the entire food chain from farm to store, with the result that most food sectors, including grain, meat, poultry, and dairy products, are now organized into global "food chain clusters" (Hendrickson et al. 2001). Similar to automobile manufacturing and retailing, now dominated by just seven TNCs (see Table 1.3), consolidation and integration in the agro/food system have led "some analysts [to] predict there will be only six or so global food retailers in the near future"[2] (Hendrickson et al. 2001). Not only does this concentration reduce choice for consumers, it also creates less diversity in the actual food produced because these few retailers can dictate particular terms and conditions to all their food suppliers.

In addition to land being appropriated for specific human purposes, sometimes there are competing claims for the same land area. For example, space-cramped urban areas are increasingly taking over surrounding farmland for residential use. But, given the expanding global population which is expected to approach ten billion by 2050, can we afford to give up valuable finite farmland for urban use? In an ingenious project, NASA climatologist and remote sensing specialist Marc Imhoff attempted to answers this question (Weier 2000). Using satellite images of city lights at night, Imhoff and his research team constructed a map of all urbanized areas in the United States and several other countries. They then superimposed these maps on other maps representing differing levels of soil quality. For the United States, Imhoff found that only five percent of the total land area with the highest quality soil had been urbanized to date. However, urban sprawl is occurring in just those areas with the best soil, thus presenting a warning for future urban development. China, with more than four times the population of the United States, approximately the same land area, and poorer soil quality, is not faring as well. Imhoff concludes that given continuing population growth and limited good farmland, "city planners need to start building and developing city infrastructure on rocky, non-level, and arid soils" (Weier 2000).

Not only do humans convert the world's land area to suit their purposes, they also have the technological capability to alter ocean habitats. For example, large industrial fishing vessels (those at least seventy-five feet long and one hundred Gross Register Tons in weight) with massive fifteen-foot-wide bottom-dragging dredges, forty-mile-long drift nets, and eighty-mile longlines with up to 50,000 hooks cause major disruption to marine ecosystems (Fitzpatrick and Newton 1998). Equipped with sophisticated navigational, remote sensing, hydraulic, processing, and refrigeration systems, these factory ships represent nearly 60 percent of all vessel tonnage and harvest more than half the global catch annually. However, they comprise only 1 percent of all fishing boats and 10 percent of all fishers. Below is a sampling of some of the results of their methods:

- Huge two-ton dredges with large chain bags are dragged along the ocean floor in search of scallops and other shellfish. In addition to their harvest, these dredges also scoop up large swaths of the sea floor, destroying plants, microorganisms, and other bottom-dwelling species (Lazaroff 2001).

- Giant sonar-directed drift nets, "with mouths wide enough to snare several 747 jumbo jets, . . . bring in up to 300,000 pounds at a time" (Helvarg 1997). "One fishing trip by 32 Japanese ships using drift nets resulted in the deaths of 50,000 sharks, over

1,000 small cetaceans [such as whales, dolphins, and porpoises], 52 fur seals and 22 turtles in the process of taking 3 million squid (McNeely et al. 1995:748).

- Longlines with up to three thousand one-hundred-foot branch lines indiscriminately catch thousands of nontargeted species— billfish, sharks, sea turtles, and sea birds, including endangered albatrosses (Australian Antarctic Division n.d.).

- The UN Food and Agricultural Organization estimates that between 18 and 40 million metric tonnes of marine species are killed annually as unwanted "bycatch" (World Wide Fund for Nature 1996).

- The *American Monarch*, a 340-foot $65 million super trawler, "can net and process about one million pounds of fish per day" (Helvarg 1997).

Obviously, these practices are extremely destructive of marine ecosystems and the species and organisms that live in them. Also, the industrial fishing fleet with its powerful technological capability and extremely wasteful practices is depleting global fish stocks faster than they can replenish themselves. Evidence is not hard to find: in 1989, the world catch peaked at 86 million tons; in 1990, a UN survey of the world fisheries reported that all commercial species were either "fully exploited, over-exploited, or depleted"; and in 1992, the world's most productive fishery (the Canadian Grand Banks) was closed due to depletion of cod stocks (King 1996).

The first "factory ship" was built in 1954, and by the late 1950s government-subsidized mass production of industrial stern-trawlers was well underway in most fishing nations (King 1996). These early vessels, while extremely productive and efficient in comparison to traditional fishing boats, are no match for today's super trawlers. In terms of vessel design, horsepower, fuel efficiency and capacity, electronics, remote sensing, hydraulics, and refrigeration, a vessel built in 1965 is only half as efficient as one built in 1980, which in turn is only half again as efficient as the 1995 model (Fitzpatrick and Newton 1998). Consequently, globalized fish extraction has ensued on a scale never before even imagined.

As the figures cited in the examples above would suggest, the extraordinarily equipped industrial fishing fleet is owned by large transnational corporations (King 1996). And similar to the agro/food sector (as a result of mergers and acquisitions in the past two decades), currently just three or four TNCs dominate the entire global fishing, processing, and retail industry.[3] Hampered by quota restrictions off the coasts of North America and Europe, these fleets have expanded their horizons to cover the entire globe—only to deplete still other fisheries and damage other ocean habitats.

Not only are the methods of the industrial fishing fleet seriously depleting world fisheries and badly damaging ocean habitats, eventually they could also represent a threat to human life itself. In 1998, more than 1,600 marine scientists and conservation biologists from sixty-five countries issued a warning of just such a threat (MCBI 1998). As well as depletion of marine species and damage to ocean ecosystems, the scientists stated that the 70 percent of the earth's surface that is covered by oceans is also under siege from pollution, alien species, and global atmospheric change—all the result of human agency. Because the oceans contain considerably more biodiversity than the land, their deterioration poses immediate danger for sustained human existence.

Consequently, it would appear that on land as well as on sea the forces of globalization—in this case, technologically enhanced transnational corporations motivated by economic dominance—are reducing the diversity of the global biosphere. As McNeely et al. (1995:733) conclude: "Biotic impoverishment is an almost inevitable consequence of the ways in which the human species has used and misused the environment in the course of its rise to dominance"—and, with ever more powerful technologies, we are increasing this biotic impoverishment at a potentially species-threatening rate.

## Pollution

The other side of the human resource extraction/production/consumption equation is waste elimination and/or pollution. "Pollution"—the act of contaminating or otherwise harming the environment—is neither an absolute nor a static concept. Simplistic though it may appear, pollution is a human construct that changes over time and circumstance. Consider the air that we expel. Is it pollution? The general consensus is that it is not. But what of other emissions that were not thought to be harmful, but now are? In some cases, such as DDT, either current knowledge and/or measurement was insufficient to evaluate these emissions adequately. In other cases, such as human sewage, there was not enough critical mass to render them harmful. And in still other cases, such as smog, the emissions

## BOX 4.2

## MANCHESTER, ENGLAND (2 JULY 1835)

". . . Thirty or forty factories rise on the tops of the hills. . . . Their six stories tower up; their huge enclosures give notice from afar of the centralisation of industry. The wretched dwellings of the poor are scattered haphazard around them. Round them stretches land uncultivated but without the charm of rustic nature, and still without the amenities of a town. The soil has been taken away, scratched and torn up in a thousand places, but it is not yet covered with the habitations of men. The land is given over to industry's use. The roads which connect the still-disjointed limbs of the great city, show like the rest, every sign of hurried and unfinished work; the incidental activity of a population bent on gain, which seeks to amass gold so as to have everything else all at once, and, in the interval, mistrusts all the niceties of life. Some of these roads are paved, but most of them are full of ruts and puddles into which foot or carriage wheel sinks deep. Heaps of dung, rubble from buildings, putrid, stagnant pools are found here and there among the houses and over the bumpy, pitted surfaces of the public places. No trace of surveyor's rod or spirit level. Amid this noisome labyrinth, this great sombre stretch of brickwork, from time to time one is astonished at the sight of fine stone buildings with Corinthian columns. It might be a medieval town with the marvels of the nineteenth century in the middle of it. But who could describe the interiors of these quarters set apart, home of vice and poverty, which surround the huge palaces of industry and clasp them in their hideous folds. On ground below the level of the river and overshadowed on every side by immense workshops, stretches marshy land which widely spaced ditches can neither drain nor cleanse. Narrow, twisting roads lead down to it. They are lined with one-story houses whose ill-fitting planks and broken windows show them up, even from a distance, as the last refuge a man might find between poverty and death. None-the-less the wretched people living in them can still inspire jealousy of their fellow-beings. Below some of their miserable dwellings is a row of cellars to which a sunken corridor leads. Twelve to fifteen human beings are crowded pell-mell into each of these damp repulsive holes.

The fetid muddy waters, stained with a thousand colours by the factories they pass, of one of the streams I mentioned before, wander slowly round this refuge of poverty. They are nowhere kept in place by quays: houses are built haphazard on their banks. Often from the top of one of their steep banks one sees an attempt at a road opening out through the debris of earth, and the foundations of some houses or the debris of others. It is the Styx of this new Hades. Look up and all around this place and you will see the huge palaces of industry. You will hear the noise of furnaces, the whistle of steam. These vast structures keep air and light out of the human habitations which they dominate; they envelop them in perpetual fog; here is the slave, there the master; there is the wealth of some, here the poverty of most; there the organised efforts of thousands produce, to the profit of one man, what society has not yet learnt to give. Here the weakness of the individual seems more feeble and helpless even than in the middle of a wilderness.

A sort of black smoke covers the city. The sun seen through it is a disc without rays. Under this half-daylight 300,000 human beings are ceaselessly at work. A thousand noises disturb this dark, damp labyrinth, but they are not at all the ordinary sounds one hears in great cities.

The footsteps of a *busy* crowd, the crunching wheels of machinery, the shriek of steam from boilers, the regular beat of the looms, the heavy rumble of carts, those are the noises from which you can never escape in the sombre half-light of these streets. . . .

From this foul drain the greatest stream of human industry flows out to fertilise the whole world. From this filthy sewer pure gold flows. Here humanity attains its most complete development and its most brutish; here civilisation makes its miracles, and civilised man is turned back almost into a savage."

*Source*: Tocqueville, 1957 [1835]:106–8.

did not occur in combination with other conditions that together made them harmful. In other words, as circumstances and their evaluation change, the definition of pollution also changes.

Although human beings have always created waste, it did not cause a major problem until they began to live in communities. And as these human settlements grew in size, so too did problems of waste elimination, including the spread of disease. Thus, urbanization or the increasing concentration of people in small areas first produced problems associated

**Table 4.3    U.S. Air Pollutant Emission Trends (thousand short tons)**

| POLLUTANTS | 1940 | 1950 | 1960 | 1970 | 1980 | 1990 | 1998 |
|---|---|---|---|---|---|---|---|
| Carbon monoxide | 93,616 | 102,609 | 109,745 | 129,444 | 117,434 | 98,523 | 89,455 |
| Nitrogen oxides | 7,374 | 10,093 | 14,140 | 20,928 | 24,384 | 24,049 | 24,454 |
| Volatile organic compounds | 17,161 | 20,936 | 24,459 | 30,982 | 26,336 | 20,936 | 17,917 |
| Sulfur dioxide | 19,952 | 22,357 | 22,227 | 31,161 | 25,905 | 23,660 | 19,647 |
| Directly emitted particulate matter[a] | 15,957 | 17,133 | 15,558 | 13,042 | 7,119 | 29,962 | 34,741 |
| Lead | – | – | – | 221 | 74 | 5 | 4 |

*Source*: Adapted from Environmental Protection Agency, 2000.
*Note*:
a. Less than 10 microns in aerodynamic diameter ($PM_{10}$).

with pollution. However, it was not until the industrial revolution that pollution became rampant, as industrial cities with their many coal-fired factories and hundreds of thousands of factory workers sprang up to supply the ever growing demand for manufactured goods. In order to appreciate fully what uncontrolled urban and industrial growth can produce in terms of soil, water, and air pollution, I have included a vivid 1835 eyewitness description of Manchester, England by the great political philosopher, Alexis de Tocqueville (see Box 4.2). Unfortunately, Tocqueville's description of Manchester in the early stages of the industrial revolution applies with equal force to contemporary unplanned urban sprawl in many developing countries.

At the outset of the industrial revolution, attempts at pollution control in both Europe and North America achieved mixed results. Although regulations on smoke abatement, sewage treatment, and water delivery were imposed, urban smog and outbreaks of cholera, tuberculosis, smallpox, typhus, and scarlet fever continued to kill hundreds of thousands of people, and acid rain and other forms of pollution posed additional challenges (Environmental History Timeline n.d.). It was not until after World War II that systematic identification and measurement of all types of known pollution were made and accompanying legislation introduced. As a result, during the past three decades some significant gains in pollution control have been achieved. For example, Table 4.3 presents data for the past fifty years in the United States on the emissions of six pollutants "for which ambient air standards have been set, based on established criteria for risk to human health and/or environmental degradation" (Environmental Protection Agency 2000). In other words, given our current state of knowledge, these six atmospheric pollutants are deemed to be among the most injurious to human health and environmental sustainability.

Four of these six pollutant emissions peaked in 1970, the year when the U.S. Environmental Protection Agency (EPA) was created, and subsequently amended the Clean Air Act and established other regulatory emissions standards. Similar to other industrial countries at this time, the United States targeted the environment as a priority concern. The reductions in emissions since 1970 are all the more significant when it is considered that in the United States between 1970 and 1995, the number of miles driven increased by 116 percent, the gross domestic product rose by 99 percent, and population expanded by 28 percent. Most noteworthy is the 98 percent reduction in lead emissions over this period, an accomplishment achieved by legislatively phasing out leaded gasoline. In other words, given sufficient political resolve, it is possible to reverse our destructive environmental record. However, the EPA (2000) cautions that "while progress has been made, it is important not to lose sight of the magnitude of the air pollution that still remains."

Besides examining the impact of pollution on various aspects of the environment such as soil, water, and air, it is instructive to consider how pollution takes place—the human activities that produce it. As I have already mentioned, waste elimination is a necessary and therefore deliberate feature of human existence, although sometimes it may also be unintentional, as I discuss later. If waste elimination is done without harm to the environment, which includes people, then by definition it is not pollution. In this sense, waste can be eliminated harmlessly, if the environment has sufficient capacity to absorb it naturally in its present form (for example, compostable materials), or if the waste is transformed into a substance such that the environment can then absorb it naturally (for example, sewage treatment). For most of human existence, waste elimination was generally of this type. In other words, it was not pollution in the sense of damaging the environment.

With increasing technological capability and thus the extraction and transformation of natural resources into manufactured goods, the nature of human waste began to change. No longer were many materials and substances able to be absorbed by the environment. It is at this point that waste became pollution in the broadest sense of the term. Examples of early human pollution are found at archeological sites which contain various human made artefacts of the particular period. A modern illustration of the relationship between technology and human waste comes from an examination of waste disposal in different parts of the world (UNESCAP 2000). Not only do people in technologically developed Northern countries have more waste per capita (from 2.75 to 4.0 kg/day) than those in the South (0.5 kg/day), what they dispose of also varies substantially. The majority of domestic waste in the North is comprised of non-biodegradable paper, metals, glass, and plastic, while over half of the waste in the South consists of more environmentally friendly food matter and ash. Moreover, although people in the North throw away between five and eight times more than Southerners, domestic municipal waste accounts for a much smaller proportion of all waste in the North than it does in the South. Most waste in developed countries is generated by technologically intensive primary and secondary industry.

The least harmful type of pollution, which has also been practiced for the longest period of time, is the *legal disposal of nonhazardous, non-biodegradable waste*. It comprises normal everyday garbage which is a byproduct of our many domestic, municipal, commercial, and industrial activities. Since the industrial revolution, as a result of our expanding technologies and growing population, we have quite literally built hundreds of thousands of mountains of non-toxic garbage that now form part of our environment. As I mentioned earlier, most of this non-biodegradable garbage has been produced in the North. Although the effects of nonhazardous legal pollution are generally not thought to cause damage to the environment, there have been reported incidents of landfill seepage contaminating drinking water (Bassis n.d.).

A more recent and growing form of pollution is the *legal disposal of hazardous waste*, which consists of substances that are currently defined as harmful to human health and/or the environment. Of the estimated 300 to 400 million tonnes of infectious, toxic, corrosive, flammable, explosive, and radioactive material discharged annually by industry worldwide, the overwhelming majority of it (90 percent) is generated in the North, especially by the United States (81 percent) (UNESCAP 2000).[4] Hazardous waste, most of it (50 to 70 percent) produced by the chemical and allied products industry, now accounts for approximately 10 to 15 percent of all industrial waste—a percentage that is increasing 2 to 5 percent yearly. Although strict measures are taken either to contain or treat toxic substances, no method is foolproof. For example, earthquakes have dislodged contaminants from sealed wells deep underground, and to date, "no satisfactory method has yet been demonstrated for disposing permanently of radioactive wastes" (Bassis n.d.).

In the developed countries, because of increasingly higher costs and tighter restrictions associated with disposing of hazardous waste legally, many corporations have resorted to illegal means. Box 4.3 describes two early infamous cases—the dumping of mercury into the sea by one company that resulted in widespread mercury poisoning of both people and marine life in Japan, and the dumping of toxic chemical waste by another company into the Love Canal in the United States. Other more common forms of *illegal hazardous waste disposal* include dumping bilge and other toxic substances at sea and exporting waste to countries that have less rigorous pollution regulations (usually in the South). In 1989, in an effort to control the unsafe disposal of harmful wastes, many nations formally agreed to place limits on "transboundary movements of hazardous wastes and their disposal" (UNEP 2000). However, notwithstanding these efforts, as I mentioned in Chapter 3 organized crime is now also heavily involved in dumping and exporting hazardous waste materials, earning an estimated $10 to $12 billion annually (ICTA 2000). Consequently, rather than attempting to control the disposal of these life-threatening materials, a better solution might lie in legislatively reducing the generation of these hazardous technological byproducts.

Of all the forms of deliberate pollution I have mentioned, one of the most potentially damaging is the *malevolent release of destructive biological, chemical, combustive/explosive, or radioactive materials* into the environment. Although historically more rare than the other types of pollution, the probability of widespread interactional devastation of both people and ecosystems cannot be discounted. War and terrorist acts are the major vehicles for this type of pollution, and with the increasing variety and sophistication of technologies available for delivering weapons of mass destruction, it is likely that this probability will increase. For example, following the terrorist attacks on New York and Washington, D.C., in September 2001, the bacterium anthrax was delivered anonymously via the U.S. Postal Service to various members of the U.S. Congress and media outlets. Although none of the intended recipients of the anthrax-tainted letters died from exposure to the bacillus, several people were infected and five postal workers were killed (U.S. Department of State 2002). In turn, the anthrax attacks have prompted government officials to prepare for other biological and chemical attacks, including possible use of the very deadly and highly contagious smallpox and plague bacteria (Kostoff 2001). Clearly, this form of pollution represents a growing threat to both people and their environment.

As well as deliberate forms of pollution, there is also *accidental pollution*. Human action or inaction, equipment malfunction, natural occurrences such as earthquakes, and other contingencies can all trigger accidental pollution. Although normally minor in impact, there are many documented cases of massive pollution resulting from accidents. Box 4.3 describes three of the most devastating of these (Bhopal, Chernobyl, and the *Exxon Valdez*), illustrating that even though exacting and rigorous precautionary measures may be followed, no procedure is fail-safe; over the long run accidents will occur. And given the increasing number, complexity, and interdependence of technological systems I described in Chapter 3, it is highly likely that both the rate and the severity of these accidents will increase.

Finally, over the course of the twentieth century and particularly in recent decades, governments, industry, and ordinary people have come to the horrible realization that what at first were thought to be safe practices and procedures later were identified as being extremely harmful to both people and the environment. The list of such *initially unknown pollutants* is relatively long, and some of their consequences for human sustainability are potentially catastrophic. For example, there is consensus within the scientific community that the growing and accumulating emissions of carbon dioxide by industry and vehicles is causing global temperatures to rise (see Box 2.1 and Figure 2.2). Should sufficient portions of the polar ice caps melt, not only would this cause massive coastal flooding throughout the world, it would also have direct impacts on the entire agro/food system and the eco-environment on which it depends.

Another initially unknown pollutant with devastating consequences is the emission of chemical chlorofluorocarbons (CFCs) used in manufacturing aerosol sprays, refrigerators, and air conditioners. Highly stable and long lasting CFCs directly attack the protective ozone layer in the stratosphere that shields us from the sun's ultraviolet rays. Exposure to these rays causes skin cancer and eye cataracts among humans, reduces crop yields, and kills phytoplankton—"ocean plants that are a food staple for squid, fish, seals, penguins, and whales" (Close and Playford 1997). Although an international agreement was signed in 1988 to phase out the use of CFCs, they are still being manufactured in some countries and

# BOX 4.3

# MAJOR INDUSTRIAL DISASTERS

Although the cumulative impact of industrialization since it first began 250 years ago has had far greater effects on the environment than any one industrial catastrophe, nevertheless a listing of some of the most damaging of these disasters does serve a useful purpose. It indicates in a most dramatic way the inevitability of unforeseen and unintended consequences, highlighting Ellul's point that at the outset of most technological ventures, we have very little idea of the long-term consequences. Imagine what someone might say about some of our current practices fifty years from now. Also, the list below makes us think of the thousands and thousands of much smaller accidents that occur on a daily basis. Note that for each of the cases described, the full extent of the environmental damages is never determined. More precise data are provided on the effects of these disasters on human populations, although again they are difficult to assess in their entirety.

### 1949: Minamata, Japan (Mercury poisoning or "Minamata disease")[5]

Minamata disease was not officially recognized until 1956, but its origins occurred much earlier.

The first signs that something was amiss in the seas near Minamata [a coastal town] appeared around 1949. Dead fish floated on the top of the bay and shellfish emitted a noxious odour when opened. Soon, catches began to decline. By 1953, local residents reported that cats "danced" in circles before collapsing into the bay; seabirds and crows were also observed spiralling unexpectedly into the sea. Shortly thereafter, the first cases of human sickness were noted (Maruyama 1996).

At first, it was thought that the residents of the fishing village had some kind of contagious disease; however, it was later discovered that the cause of the widespread pollution came from the nearby Chisso Company that was dumping methyl mercury into the sea as an unwanted byproduct of acetaldehyde. In 1957, the Minamata Fishermen's Cooperative demanded that Chisso stop dumping mercury into the sea, but it was not until 1968 that Chisso was ordered to cease operations. In 1987, the former President and Plant Manager were found guilty of professional negligence leading to involuntary manslaughter.

As of 1993, the Japanese government confirmed that 2,255 victims (both living and dead) had suffered mercury poisoning; 2,376 others were still seeking victim status. "Some physicians estimate that at least half of the 200,000 people who lived along the coast of the Shiranui Sea in the late 1950s were affected by some form of mercury poisoning" (Maruyama 1996). In addition, there was widespread and devastating—but undocumented—marine pollution.

### 1953: Love Canal, USA (Toxic chemicals)

Similar to the Minamata case, the presence of toxic waste at Love Canal, New York, was not officially declared until 1978, but the problem reached back to 1947 when Hooker Chemicals and Plastic Corp. bought an abandoned 15-acre canal site so that it could dump its chemical waste byproducts. In 1953, with the landfill full of thousands of tons of toxic chemicals, Hooker topped it off with dirt and sold it for one dollar to the Niagara Falls Board of Education. Included in the sale was a warning by Hooker that the site contained buried chemical waste and a disclaimer absolving the company of any liability. In the same year, the Board of Education built a school directly on the landfill and sold the surrounding property for residential housing. The Board did not mention the previous use of the land.

From the late 1950s through the mid-1970s, residents of Love Canal made "repeated complaints of odors and 'substances' surfacing in their yards" (Love Canal Collection 1998). Finally in 1978, after many studies and tests, the New York State Commissioner of Health declared a medical state of emergency and ordered the school to be closed. Following quickly was a similar declaration by the President of the United States, which resulted in the relocation of 236 families.

By 1995, two hundred tons of highly lethal dioxin and more than two hundred other chemical compounds had been uncovered, and the Environmental Protection Agency had reported that Love Canal residents had chromosome damage, which put them at a higher risk of cancer, reproductive problems, and genetic damage. These discoveries resulted in all nine hundred Love Canal families being relocated at federal expense, and the parent company of Hooker settling a $20 million suit with 1,328 residents and agreeing to pay an additional $227 million for state and federal cleanup costs.

## 1984: Bhopal, India (Chemical gas leak)

Triggered by a violent chemical chain reaction, forty-five tons of highly toxic and unstable methyl isocyanate (MIC) gas escaped from a Union Carbide pesticide plant in Bhopal, India. A blanket of gas covered the densely populated slum settlements located within five miles of the plant, killing more than 4,000 and affecting at least 300,000 more. Some 7,000 animals also perished. No environmental impact study was ever conducted, although trees and plants in the area became yellow and brittle. The leak was attributed to mechanical failure, poor maintenance, nonfunctioning safety devices, lack of contingency plans, and human error and negligence at both the operator and management levels. Lack of information and disaster relief preparedness in the city of Bhopal compounded the severity of the accident. Union Carbide closed the plant immediately after the accident, and in 1993, paid $700 million to the victims (Shrivastava 1996).

## 1986: Chernobyl, Ukraine (Nuclear power plant explosion)

A chemical explosion resulting from operator error in one of the nuclear reactors at Chernobyl was the precipitating cause of the Chernobyl disaster, but it was a disaster-in-waiting long before. Initial shoddy construction of the facility, unsound reactor design, and a minimal safety code—for example, no Geiger counters to monitor radiation—were also contributing factors. The explosion produced a large radioactive cloud that passed over most of Ukraine, Belarus, and parts of Russia and northern Europe. Most exposed to radiation were the 600 plant staff, 600,000 emergency cleanup workers, and 116,000 people living within a thirty-kilometer radius of the plant who were evacuated shortly after the explosion—an area that was never resettled. Victims received doses ranging from 32 to 500 times natural background radiation. However, remarkably few were killed (31) or suffered from acute radiation sickness (141), although the incidence of thyroid cancer among children increased significantly.

The impact of the accident on agricultural practices, food production and use and other aspects of the environment has been and continues to be much more widespread than the direct health impact on humans. Within the former Soviet Union, large areas of agricultural land are still excluded from use and are expected to continue to be so for a long time, and the monitoring of food produced in a much larger area continues (Nuclear Energy Agency 2001).

Northern areas of Finland, Sweden, and Scotland also monitor their food and animal production.

### 1989: Alaska, USA (Crude oil spill)

Due to a series of human errors, the oil tanker *Exxon Valdez* hit a reef off the coast of Alaska, spilling 11 million gallons of crude oil into Prince William Sound. Before cleanup efforts could be mounted, a storm carried the oil forty miles out to sea. In less than two months the oil slick had spread 470 miles, covering 1,300 miles of pristine coastline with black sludge. No human lives were lost, but the damage to wildlife and fragile Arctic ecosystems was staggering. Anywhere from 350,000 to 390,000 seabirds and 5,500 sea otters were killed. "At the height of clean-up activity in 1989 more than 11,000 workers, 1,400 vessels, and 80 aircraft were at work in the region" (Davis 1996). Cleanup efforts continued for more than three years, costing $900 million. Exxon paid one billion dollars to the State of Alaska and various federal agencies, and $302 million for 12,300 other claims. Scientists are still uncertain of the long-term effects of the spill.

smuggled illegally into others, thus adding to the continuing depletion of stratospheric ozone (*New Scientist* 1997).

Other initially unknown pollutants are listed in Table 4.4. The presence of so many harmful substances initially thought to have only benign effects on the biosphere has prompted many environmental scientists to propose what has been called "the precautionary principle." In other words, rather than wait until there is incontrovertible scientific evidence that some industrial product or process is harmful to human health or the environment, by which time it may be too late, actions should be based on the assessment of *threats* of harm. According to Ted Schettler, Science Director of the Science and Environmental Health Network:

We're talking about enormously complex interactions among a number of systems. Now we're starting to think that some of these things are probably unknowable and indeterminate. . . . the precautionary principle doesn't tell you what to do, but it does tell you [what] to look at (cited in Appell 2001).

Table 4.4    Types of Human Waste Elimination and Pollution

| TYPES | ILLUSTRATIONS |
| --- | --- |
| Deliberate waste elimination | Naturally absorbed compostable materials |
| Deliberate pollution | |
| Nonhazardous, lawful pollution | Non-biodegradable landfills |
| Hazardous, lawful pollution | Sealed landfills of toxic chemicals and radioactive material |
| Hazardous, unlawful pollution | Bilge dumping at sea; illegal hazardous waste disposal (e.g., Minamata, Love Canal); exporting hazardous waste |
| Hazardous, unlawful, malevolent pollution | War; terrorism (e.g., anthrax) |
| Accidental pollution | Bhopal gas leak; Chernobyl nuclear power plant explosion; *Exxon Valdez* oil spill |
| Initially unknown pollution | Acid rain; DDT; Agent Orange; asbestos; $CO_2$ emissions; chemical chlorofluorocarbons (CFCs) |

Because of the complex interdependencies involved and the potentially disastrous consequences that could result, the precautionary principle is increasingly being incorporated into government policy and legislation.

Table 4.4 summarizes all of the various forms of human waste elimination and pollution I have discussed. Central to this discussion is the role that technology plays. As human beings have developed more complex, interdependent, and "unnatural" ways to extract, transform, and consume the earth's resources, so too have they created more ecologically damaging forms of waste elimination. Moreover, although these eco-destructive technologies have been designed in and for the North, their impacts are global. Now, because of these technological impacts, for the first time in human history our relationship to the natural eco-environment has become increasingly precarious.

## Biotic Changes to the Environment

When human beings first lived together in agricultural communities, they began to make biotic changes to their environment. For example, early farmers, using trial and error methods over many generations, learned that some varieties of grains and vegetables grew better than others, and that some of their animals either produced more milk or were stronger than others. This realization led to selective breeding of plants and animals, as these farmers attempted to encourage the particular traits they sought to reproduce. However, as they became increasingly successful in accomplishing their objectives, they also decreased the diversity in the various species they were breeding. Throughout the world, particular species of plants and animals were bred that not only had desirable characteristics from the point of view of their breeders, but also were favorably adapted to their individual ecosystems.

Consequently, localized selective breeding has been practiced for thousands of years, generally without ill effects on the natural environment, except for some initial loss of biodiversity. However, problems began to arise in the sixteenth century when people first started migrating on a large scale to other world regions, taking with them, both deliberately and unknowingly, their native plants and animals—and thereby microorganisms. Suzuki and Dressel (1999:113–14) describe some of the effects of introducing alien species into different ecosystems:

We have ample evidence about the hazards of exotic organisms in a new environment. Rabbits in Australia, zebra mussels in the Great Lakes, cats on tropical islands, purple loosestrife spreading across North American waterways—all these species were benign or useful in the places in the world where they belonged, but out of the surroundings in which they evolved, where they existed along with other organisms to keep them in check, they have become pests that are devastating local native wildlife and costing billions of dollars a year in lost crops, eradication programs and restoration.

And with increases in the rate, speed, and destination of international travel, the probability of even more disruption to local ecosystems also increases.

Early explorers and settlers not only brought plants and animals to foreign climes, they also took with them another set of invasive organisms—their own idiosyncratic germs which had evolved in response to the particular ecological and cultural conditions of the places from which they came. For example, physiologist Jared Diamond (1999a:195–214) claims that the major reason that Europeans were able to conquer the Americas and other parts of the world was not so much their superior military might, but rather their "nastier germs." Because the Europeans had built up immunity to various epidemic diseases such as smallpox, measles, influenza, and typhus, originally transferred to them from their domesticated animals, and because hunting/gathering cultures did not have these same animals, the result was widespread eradication of these indigenous societies. The actual mortality statistics are staggering:

Far more Native Americans died in bed from Eurasian germs than on the battlefield from European guns and swords. Those germs undermined Indian resistance by killing most Indians and their leaders and by sapping the survivors' morale. For instance, in 1519 Cortés landed on the coast of Mexico with 600 Spaniards, to conquer the fiercely militaristic Aztec Empire with a population of many millions. That Cortés reached the Aztec capital of Tenochtitlán, escaped with the loss of "only" two-thirds of his force, and managed to fight his way back to the coast demonstrates both Spanish military advantages and the initial naïveté of the Aztecs. But when Cortés's next onslaught came, the Aztecs were no longer naive and fought street by street with the utmost tenacity. What gave the Spaniards a decisive advantage was smallpox, which reached Mexico in 1520 with one infected slave arriving from Spanish Cuba. The resulting epidemic proceeded to kill nearly half the Aztecs, including Emperor Cuitláhuac. Aztec survivors were demoralized by the mysterious illness that killed Indians and spared Spaniards, as if advertising the Spaniards' invincibility. By 1618, Mexico's initial population of about 20 million had plummeted to about 1.6 million (Diamond 1999a:210).

With increasing global migration, not only were diseases transmitted from human to human, but also to entire ecosystems. As the recent outbreaks of hoof and mouth and "mad cow" diseases have demonstrated, what was once a local problem can soon become global in its repercussions. (Mad cow disease, which is a form of transmissible spongiform encephalopathy [TSE], has a direct human analog in "variant Creutzfelt-Jakob disease" for which there is no known treatment [Orr and Powell 2001].) Modern transportation technologies and our affinity for them comprise the global conduit through which these diseases spread (see Box 1.4). Consequently, it is increasingly problematic to contain local problems within their places of origin. As Diamond (1999a:206) points out, "The explosive increase in world travel by Americans, and in immigration to the United States, is turning us into another melting pot—this time, of microbes that we previously dismissed as just causing exotic diseases in far-off countries." And as I mentioned in the previous section, deadly viruses can be deliberately employed to infect particular populations and their ecosystems. Of course, when these measures are taken, their effects are not limited only to targeted populations; they can radiate far beyond through a highly mobile population and many interdependent ecological networks.

A very recent and amazing development in our ability to make biotic changes is genetic engineering. This discipline either recombines or repositions genes in a particular organism or removes genes from one organism and inserts them into another organism of a different species, and even of a different kingdom. An example is the splicing of "spider genes into goats in an effort to create new, super-strong fibres that will be expressed by the genes in the milk" (Suzuki and Dressel 1999:100).

This technological ability to create new life forms is the subject of highly charged controversy and debate (UNDP 2001). On one side are the advocates who list the benefits of genetic engineering: increased production and productivity in agriculture, forestry, and fisheries; more reliable cross-breeding; improved vaccines against human and animal disease; increased production and new types of pharmaceuticals; and improved quality of food. On the other side are those who prescribe a precautionary approach, especially given the fact that much of the research on genetic engineering is sponsored by the very corporations that stand to profit from genetically modified organisms. Although tangible benefits may well come from genetic manipulation, what other consequences might it also yield for human beings and their ecological environment? Among the immediate concerns for human health are that novel genes could introduce toxins and allergens into food; and for the environment, "genetically modified organisms could displace existing species and change the ecosystem," or "transfer . . . into related species," or "have unintended harmful effects on non-target species" (UNDP 2001:67). Geneticist David Suzuki outlines the horns of the dilemma:

As a science that goes to the very heart of all life's forms and functions, genetics has enormous implications; it is full of promise to benefit and improve human lives, but equally heavy with potential to destroy and cause untold suffering. For those who care about the long-term flourishing of genetics, it is vital to raise questions and anticipate problems, as well as proclaiming the potential benefits (Suzuki and Dressel 1999:102).

Given the advantage of hindsight regarding other seemingly beneficial technologies, the complexity and interdependence of all living things, our current state of knowledge and understanding of these complexities and interdependencies, and the fact that we are exploring unchartered territory where any number of virtually inconceivable mishaps might occur, do we have any choice but to proceed with the utmost precaution?

## Exploitation of Wild Living Resources

Over the millennia, but particularly in the last half century, human-kind has created increasingly efficient, comprehensive, and novel technologies for harvesting the natural resources it desires. And as these technologies have expanded, so too have they revealed new desires, which in turn have required more natural resources. Consequently, not only can a now very large human population extract resources from nature more efficiently than it did fifty years ago, it also extracts a much greater proportional amount. For confirmation of this observation, see Table 4.1, and also examine the developments I listed in Box 1.5 that were not present in 1950.

The efficient and growing human exploitation of the earth's natural resources forms the basis for the scientific claim that the world is about to experience a mass extinction every bit as great as that which destroyed the dinosaurs 65 million years ago. Says world famous paleoanthropologist Richard Leakey, "Whatever way you look at it, we're destroying the Earth at a rate comparable with the impact of a giant asteroid slamming into the planet, or even a shower of vast heavenly bodies" (Leakey and Lewin 1995).

. . . today, humans consume 40 percent of net primary productivity (NPP) on land; that is, the total energy trapped in photosynthesis worldwide, minus that required by the plants themselves for their survival. In other words, of all the energy available to sustain all the species on Earth, Homo sapiens takes almost half. . . . For every extra 1 percent of global NPP commandeered by our species in the coming decades, a further 1 percent will become unavailable to the rest of nature. Eventually, primary productivity will fall, as space for the producers falls, and a downward spiral will eventually kick in. The world's biological diversity will plummet, including the productivity on which human survival depends. The future of human civilization therefore becomes threatened (Leakey and Lewin 1995).

Leakey is not alone. According to a survey of four hundred research scientists, all members of the prestigious American Institute of Biological Sciences—which represent the fields of biochemistry, botany, conservation biology, entomology, genetics, marine biology, microbiology, molecular biology, neuroscience, and physiology—70 percent "believe that we are in the midst of a mass extinction of living things, and that this loss of species will pose a major threat to human existence in the . . . [twenty-first] century" (American Museum of Natural History 1998).

Both Leakey and the four hundred scientists surveyed attribute the cause of this sixth major extinction in the history of the planet almost entirely to the actions of humankind. The increasing rate of population growth (from 1 billion to 6 billion in just 200 years) and the growing consumption of natural resources (see Table 4.1) is putting the biosphere under severe stress. Habitat loss and fragmentation, pollution, and biotic changes to the environment are collateral contributors to the massive loss of biodiversity that is occurring. Although scientists do not know how much biodiversity is actually required to support human life as we know it, they are adamant in their conviction that it represents the key to our continuing survival:

Among the findings revealed by the survey, scientists identified the maintenance of biodiversity—the variety of plant and animal species and their habitats—as critical to human well-being; they rate biodiversity loss as a more serious environmental problem than the depletion of the ozone layer, global warming, or pollution and contamination. The majority (70%) polled think that during the next thirty years as many as one-fifth of all species alive today will become extinct, and one-third think that as many as half of all species on the Earth will die out in that time (American Museum of Natural History 1998).

The evidence upon which Leakey bases his conclusion of a major extinction comes from surveys of the world's tropical rainforests, which cover 7 percent of the world's land surface, but contain approximately half of the world's known species. From yearly satellite images taken during the 1990s, average annual rainforest loss due to logging and land clearing was 80,000 square miles, which is 40 to 50 percent more than in the 1980s. Projecting this rate of loss would mean that only 10 percent of the original forested area will remain shortly after the turn of this century, and then just "a tiny remnant by 2050." Basing his calculations on "island biogeographic theory," Leakey predicts that should only 10 percent of the rainforests remain, then 50 percent of the species in them will become extinct. Similar extinctions that will occur elsewhere lead Leakey to conclude that "Homo sapiens is poised to become the greatest catastrophic agent since a giant asteroid collided with the Earth sixty-five million years ago, wiping out half the world's species in a geological instant."

Leakey acknowledges that although the total number of species is not known, thus accounting for the sometimes wide range in scientific predictions of just how many species are lost, nevertheless even the current lowest estimate of 17,000 species lost each year is still 68,000 times greater than the normal extinction rate of one every four years which has been established from fossil records. Extinction of this magnitude, says Leakey, "is easily comparable with the Big Five biological crises of geological history," except for the fact that this sixth major extinction is being caused by humans and their assumed technological dominance.

## OVERVIEW OF HUMAN ENCROACHMENT ON THE ENVIRONMENT

What drives all these harmful human intrusions upon the environment? Why can't we recognize these critical human-environment interfaces and take appropriate action? In our hunting-gathering days, we had no difficulty identifying critical human-environment interfaces, although we did not think of them in this way. For example, the water, food, and shelter we wrested from nature each day were critical human-environment interfaces. Are they today? Not for most of us: we get our water from the city or municipality, our food from the grocery store, and our shelter from a real estate agency. As Jacques Ellul reminds us, whereas our historical involvement with nature was direct (that is, we lived in a state of nature, and we were an integral part of it), nature is now mediated by social and technical structures (see Chapter 2). These structures comprise our real environment for us now. When we buy something in a store or on-line, how many of us actually think of the relationship of that purchase to the natural environment, to the natural processes that took place in order to fulfill our requirements? The environment is virtually opaque to us, except perhaps when we stop to smell the roses or go on vacation. Wackernagel and Rees (1996:4; italics in original) go so far as to say that "most writers on the . . . [environment]—even the good ones—treat the 'environment' as something *out there*, separate and detached from people and their works."

Especially for those of us in the urbanized North, our conception of and relationship to nature fundamentally changed as a result of the industrial revolution. As I mentioned at the beginning of Chapter 3, it was during this period that we began to think we could control nature. And as soon as we began thinking this way, we conceptually removed ourselves from nature. We developed an anthropocentric, superior orientation:

## BOX 4.4

## THE RHYTHM OF LIFE

We are obsessed with time—Greenwich mean time, daylight savings time, real time, timetable, on time, full-time, time off, closing time, record time, saving time, time and motion, time is money.

We weren't always this way. For most of our existence, we geared our activities pretty much to the natural rhythms of the earth as it spun and rotated on its axis. Only in the eighteenth century, when work became a separate activity performed away from home, did we begin to change our conception of time. Our real obsession with time began during the industrial revolution, as people began to adjust their activities to the pace of the machines they invented. For example, the steam engines used to power factories were expensive to run, and they were especially expensive to turn off and then on. The solution was to run them continuously, which resulted in shift work. (Think of how the electric light bulb changed our use of time.) In turn, this introduced a new form of payment. Instead of being paid by the job, or the month, or the day, workers began to be paid by the hour.

As well as factories, the railroad industry was an early convert to strict enforcement of and rigid adherence to a time schedule. Clocks and voluminous timetables allowed the railroad to transport both thousands of passengers and tons of freight at high speed through an extensive network of lines with safety and dependability. Time became the commandant of the railroad:

All those who have direct responsibility for the actual operations of trains must carry a fine timepiece which will gain or lose not more than forty seconds in two weeks and which must be cleaned and regulated twice a year by a railroad watch inspector. A delay of thirty seconds in leaving a terminal calls for explanation, five minutes' delay means investigation, and a half hour gives apoplexy to every official from the superintendent to the lowest foreman. On single track roads where trains meet at passing tracks, a thirty seconds' delay means that one of the trains will be almost a half mile from a passing track when the other reaches it, and that means delay of a second train, with possible misunderstanding and resultant disaster (Cottrell 1939:190–91).

The modern prophet of time was Frederick Winslow Taylor, who first introduced time and motion study to industry at the beginning of the twentieth century:

... his stop watch was his bible. If any such social upheaval can ever be attributed to one man, the logic of efficiency as a mode of life is due to him. With "scientific management," as enunciated by Taylor, we pass far beyond the old rough computations of the division of labor; we go into the division of time itself (Bell 1962:231–32).

Taylor, an engineer at the American Bethlehem Steel Company, converted the old rule-of-thumb procedures of workers into specific time-designated tasks and task elements, which then became standardized operating procedures dictated by management. Taylor was convinced that managers should become responsible for planning to the tiniest detail all the elements that comprised workers' jobs, establish a time limit for each task element, and then pay workers according to the actual number of work units completed—that is, piece work instead of day work. An application of Taylor's time and motion principles is contained in the collective agreement signed between the U.S. Steel Corporation and the CIO Steel Workers in 1946:

Material: River sand, moisture 5.5% approx., weight per cu. ft. 100–110 pounds.
Equipment: . . . 32" shovel, No. 2 furnace.
Working conditions: Under roof, smooth concrete floor, all other conditions normal.
Production rate: For shoveling sand from pile to box—average weight of sand on shovel—15 lbs; 12.5 shovelfuls per minute (Bell 1962:236).

We have come a long way in the computation of human activity since Taylor's division of it into minutes and seconds. Now, with the microelectronic revolution, we have moved to milliseconds (one thousandth of a second), used to measure sprinters and "packet travel time on the Internet"; microseconds (one millionth of a second or $10^{-6}$); nanoseconds (one billionth of a second or $10^{-9}$); picoseconds (one trillionth of a second or $10^{-12}$); femtoseconds ($10^{-15}$ of a second), used in laser technology; and even attoseconds (one quintillionth of a second or $10^{-18}$), used in photon research (Computing Fundamentals 2001).

As a result of our cumulative technological innovations, we are now in closer harmony with what we have created than with the natural rhythms of life that guide everything else on Earth.

nature was something to be used; it was a vast limitless resource for our consumption. We also physically removed ourselves from nature as increasingly we began to live in technological environments in which space and time became human rather than natural constructs (see Box 4.4).

These recently acquired attitudes toward nature form the principal basis of our ecological problems today. Our conceptual and physical separation from nature has resulted in our inability to discern adequately just what constitute critical human-environment interfaces. Instead, at least until very recently, we believed that human ingenuity would always prevail. Problems could be solved by science and technology. As a result, one of the most critical human-environment interfaces is how people perceive nature and its relationship to them. As Wackernagel and Rees (1996:xi) state, "The first step toward reducing our ecological impact is to recognize that the 'environmental crisis' is less an environmental and technical problem than it is a behavioral and social one." They present their argument in terms of system theory:

The premise that *human society is a subsystem of the ecosphere*, that human beings are embedded in nature, is so simple that it is generally overlooked or dismissed as too obvious to be relevant. However, taking this "obvious" insight seriously leads to some profound conclusions. The policy implications of this ecological reality run much deeper than pressing for improved pollution control and better environmental protection, both of which maintain the myth of separation. If humans are part of nature's fabric, the "environment" is no mere scenic backdrop but becomes the play itself. The ecosphere is where we live, humanity is dependent on nature, not the reverse. Sustainability requires that our emphasis shift from "managing resources" to managing *ourselves*, that we learn to live as part of nature (Wackernagel and Rees 1996:4; italics in original).

With respect to our current ecological crises, Boyden (1996) states that *we face one absolute certainty*, which should we ignore will mean our demise as a species: *there are definite ecological limits* to the amount of habitat we can convert entirely for human use, the tons of pollutants we can discharge into the environment, the number of biotic changes we can introduce, and the quantity of natural resources we can exploit. Boyden says that although scientists cannot pinpoint exactly "how much longer the biosphere can withstand the present trends," nor "predict which particular ecological change represents the biggest threat to the system," nevertheless the evidence I have presented in this chapter indicates we are nearing the ecological limits of the global biosphere on a number of fronts:

- we have hugely increased our exploitation of the earth's natural resources during the last fifty years (Table 4.1);

- we are presently using 30 percent more natural resources than are available on a sustainable basis (Box 4.1);

- our current technoenergy requirements are putting extreme pressure on the global ecosystem (Boyden 1996);

- 73 percent of the world's land surface is at least "partially disturbed" by humans, and more than a third is completely "human dominated" (McNeely et al. 1995:751);

- 1,600 marine scientists issued a warning that the oceans are under siege from depletion of marine life, damage to ecosystems, pollution, alien species, and global atmospheric change (MCBI 1998);

- there are widespread and increasing discharges of industrial pollution into the environment, at least 10 to 15 percent of it toxic (UNESCAP 2000);

- carbon dioxide and other human-produced emissions are causing global warming, which is melting the Arctic polar ice cap and disrupting many ecosystems (Box 2.1); and

- 70 percent of scientists of the American Institute of Biological Sciences believe we are in the midst of one of the largest human-induced mass extinctions of species in the history of the planet (American Museum of Natural History 1998).

If all of these facts were not evidence enough that we are nearing the ecological limits of the earth as far as our own survival is concerned, Box 4.5 contains a "warning to humanity" signed by 1,700 of the world's leading scientists, including the majority of Nobel laureates in the sciences. This warning was issued a decade ago; however, our activities over

# BOX 4.5

# WORLD SCIENTISTS' WARNING TO HUMANITY

*Some 1,700 of the world's leading scientists, including the majority of Nobel laureates in the sciences, issued this appeal in November 1992.*

## INTRODUCTION

Human beings and the natural world are on a collision course. Human activities inflict harsh and often irreversible damage on the environment and on critical resources. If not checked, many of our current practices put at serious risk the future that we wish for human society and the plant and animal kingdoms, and may so alter the living world that it will be unable to sustain life in the manner that we know. Fundamental changes are urgent if we are to avoid the collision our present course will bring about.

## THE ENVIRONMENT

The environment is suffering critical stress:

### The Atmosphere

Stratospheric ozone depletion threatens us with enhanced ultraviolet radiation at the earth's surface, which can be damaging or lethal to many life forms. Air pollution near ground level, and acid precipitation, are already causing widespread injury to humans, forests, and crops.

### Water Resources

Heedless exploitation of depletable ground water supplies endangers food production and other essential human systems. Heavy demands on the world's surface waters have resulted in serious shortages in some 80 countries, containing 40 percent of the world's population. Pollution of rivers, lakes, and ground water further limits the supply.

### Oceans

Destructive pressure on the oceans is severe, particularly in the coastal regions which produce most of the world's food fish. The total marine catch is now at or above the estimated maximum sustainable yield. Some fisheries have already shown signs of collapse. Rivers carrying heavy burdens of eroded soil into the seas also carry industrial, municipal, agricultural, and livestock waste—some of it toxic.

### Soil

Loss of soil productivity, which is causing extensive land abandonment, is a widespread by-product of current practices in agriculture and animal husbandry. Since 1945, 11 percent of the earth's vegetated surface has been degraded—an area larger than India and China combined—and per capita food production in many parts of the world is decreasing.

### Forests

Tropical rain forests, as well as tropical and temperate dry forests, are being destroyed rapidly. At present rates, some critical forest types will be gone in a few years, and most of the tropical rain forest will be gone before the end of the next century. With them will go large numbers of plant and animal species.

### Living Species

The irreversible loss of species, which by 2100 may reach one-third of all species now living, is especially serious. We are losing the potential they hold for providing medicinal and other benefits, and the contribution that genetic diversity of life forms gives to the robustness of the world's biological systems and to the astonishing beauty of the earth itself. Much of this damage is irreversible on a scale of centuries, or permanent. Other processes appear to pose additional threats. Increasing levels of gases in the atmosphere from human activities, including carbon dioxide released from fossil fuel burning and from deforestation, may alter climate on a global scale. Predictions of global warming are still uncertain—with projected effects ranging from tolerable to very severe—but the potential risks are very great.

Our massive tampering with the world's interdependent web of life—coupled with the environmental damage inflicted by deforestation, species loss, and climate change—could trigger widespread effects, including unpredictable collapses of critical biological systems whose interactions and dynamics we only imperfectly understand.

Uncertainty over the extent of these effects cannot excuse complacency or delay in facing the threats.

## POPULATION

The earth is finite. Its ability to absorb wastes and destructive efflu-ent is finite. Its ability to provide food and energy is finite. And we are fast approaching many of the earth's limits. Current economic practices which damage the environment, in both developed and underdeveloped nations, cannot be continued without the risk that vital global systems will be damaged beyond repair.

Pressures resulting from unrestrained population growth put de-mands on the natural world that can overwhelm any efforts to achieve a sustainable future. If we are to halt the destruction of our environment, we must accept limits to that growth. A World Bank estimate indicates that world population will not stabilize at less than 12.4 billion, while the United Nations concludes that the eventual total could reach 14 billion, a near tripling of today's 5.4 billion. But, even at this moment, one per-son in five lives in absolute poverty without enough to eat, and one in ten suffers serious malnutrition.

No more than one or a few decades remain before the chance to avert the threats we now confront will be lost and the prospects for humanity immeasurably diminished.

## WARNING

We the undersigned, senior members of the world's scientific com-munity, hereby warn all humanity of what lies ahead. A great change in our stewardship of the earth and the life on it is required, if vast human misery is to be avoided and our global home on this planet is not to be irretrievably mutilated.

## WHAT WE MUST DO

Five inextricably linked areas must be addressed simultaneously:

**We must bring environmentally damaging activities under con-trol to restore and protect the integrity of the earth's systems we depend on. . . .**

**We must manage resources crucial to human welfare more ef-fectively. . . .**

**We must stabilize population. . . .**

**We must reduce and eventually eliminate poverty.**

**We must ensure sexual equality, and guarantee women control over their own reproductive decisions.**

## DEVELOPED NATIONS MUST ACT NOW

The developed nations are the largest polluters in the world today. They must greatly reduce their overconsumption, if we are to reduce pressures on resources and the global environment. The developed nations have the obligation to provide aid and support to developing nations, because only the developed nations have the financial resources and the technical skills for these tasks.

Acting on this recognition is not altruism, but enlightened self-interest: whether industrialized or not, we all have but one lifeboat. No nation can escape from injury when global biological systems are damaged. No nation can escape from conflicts over increasingly scarce resources. In addition, environmental and economic instabilities will cause mass migrations with incalculable consequences for developed and undeveloped nations alike.

Developing nations must realize that environmental damage is one of the gravest threats they face, and that attempts to blunt it will be overwhelmed if their populations go unchecked. The greatest peril is to become trapped in spirals of environmental decline, poverty, and unrest, leading to social, economic, and environmental collapse.

Success in this global endeavor will require a great reduction in violence and war. Resources now devoted to the preparation and conduct of war—amounting to over $1 trillion annually—will be badly needed in the new tasks and should be diverted to the new challenges.

A new ethic is required—a new attitude towards discharging our responsibility for caring for ourselves and for the earth. We must recognize the earth's limited capacity to provide for us. We must recognize its fragility. We must no longer allow it to be ravaged. This ethic must motivate a great movement, convincing reluctant leaders and reluctant governments and reluctant peoples themselves to effect the needed changes.

The scientists issuing this warning hope that our message will reach and affect people everywhere. We need the help of many. . . .

**We call on all to join us in this task.**

*Source*: Union of Concerned Scientists, 2000.

the past decade suggest that humanity has not taken this warning as seriously as it must. The present scientific opinion, mentioned several times during this chapter, is that at most we have a window of opportunity of only two to three decades. In the following chapter, I offer a few strategies that hopefully we can put into effect during this extremely critical period.

The ecological crises that all the world's people now find themselves in have their origins in the North. Major habitat loss and fragmentation, pollution, biotic changes to the environment, and exploitation of the earth's natural resources not only originated in Northern industrialized countries, they continue to predominate mainly in the North, although the South is desperately trying to catch up. In other words, the cumulative processes of industrialization, including industrial technology, urbanization, international trade, economic expansion, and most importantly, the human motivations underlying these processes, are largely responsible for producing the cataclysmic estrangement of humankind from nature. Moreover, given the fact that these ecological crises have become especially fateful in the last fifty years (notwithstanding the significant addition of 3.4 billion people to the world's population during this same period), part of the responsibility must also be shared by the transnationally coordinated forces of globalized production, distribution/transmission, and consumption. In other words, global actions yield global outcomes, including a worsening of global environmental degradation. However, although it is possible to attribute probable specific cause and agency for the world's present ecological crises, their impacts are global. To paraphrase Buckminster Fuller, *all* of us are passengers on the spaceship, Earth.

## CHAPTER SUMMARY

4.1    Humankind represents one microsystem in the vast interdependent global ecological environment, yet its impact on this environment has been devastating in a variety of ways.

4.2    During the last fifty years, human population has more than doubled, while economic growth, spurred by giant transnational corporations, has multiplied more than six times. These two factors have exacted a very heavy toll on the environment in terms of exploitation of natural resources.

4.3    Over the course of human history, the impact of technology on the environment has increased to the point that now the overwhelming share of the energy devoted to human extraction, production, consumption, and pollution are used by the very technologies we have devised to control our life chances on planet Earth.

4.4 Virtually all human activity results in habitat loss and fragmentation, which in turn reduces biodiversity. Only 27 percent of the world's land surface remains undisturbed by humans. The greatest contributor to habitat loss and fragmentation is corporate enterprise.

4.5 As human beings have extracted, transformed, and consumed an ever increasing share of natural resources, so too have they polluted more and more of the environment with their waste. Industrial waste, produced mainly by developed countries, causes the most damage to the environment. Many hazardous pollutants such as $CO_2$ and CFCs were initially believed to have no ill effects on the global ecosphere.

4.6 People also make biotic changes to their environment: selective breeding of plants and animals, the introduction of alien species and microorganisms into new ecosystems, and most recently, genetic engineering. Because genetic engineering involves the creation of new life forms whose long-term effects are not known, many scientists urge a precautionary approach based on threats of harm to both people and ecosystems.

4.7 Because of the ever increasing exploitation of natural resources by Homo sapiens and the resulting loss of biodiversity, many scientists "believe that we are in the midst of a mass extinction of living things, and this loss of species will pose a major threat to human existence in the . . . [twenty-first] century" (American Museum of Natural History 1998).

4.8 A major reason underlying human abuse of the environment is that we have conceptually and physically detached ourselves from nature. Since the industrial revolution, people in developed countries have adopted an anthropocentric superior orientation, believing they have the technological capability to control nature. This orientation leads to the view that nature and everything that it comprises represent a vast, almost limitless resource for human consumption.

4.9 However, we now face *one absolute certainty*: there are definite ecological limits to the amount of habitat we can convert entirely for human use, the tons of pollutants we can discharge into the environment, the number of biotic changes we can introduce, and the quantity of natural resources we can exploit. The overwhelming evidence indicates that we are quickly nearing these limits in terms of our survival as a species.

4.10  The major sources of the ecological crises we face today are the technological and organizational forces of industrialization and globalization. These forces are responsible for commandeering large areas of the global biosphere for extraction and production, polluting the environment beyond its capability to absorb waste materials naturally, introducing alien species, microorganisms, and genes into new ecosystems, and harvesting natural resources at rates much faster than they can replenish themselves.

# 5

## CONTROL IN A GLOBALIZING WORLD: PROBLEMS AND PROSPECTS

*The only weapon we have to oppose the bad effects of technology is technology itself. There is no other. We can't retreat into a non-technological Eden which never existed. We can't look into ourselves, take comfort from any doctrine of individual salvation, and trust to our natural goodness to carry us through. Anyone who does that is afflicted by romantic illusions, in the worst sense, about what he sees within himself: he hasn't used reason to explore the irrational. The problems for humanity are altogether less innocent, more difficult and different in kind. It is only by the rational use of technology—to control and guide what technology is doing—that we can keep any hopes of a social life more desirable than our own: or in fact of a social life which is not appalling to imagine.*

—C. P. Snow, *Public Affairs*

**THIRTY YEARS AGO, WHEN C. P. SNOW** uttered these words, he identified three major global dangers, each of them "brought about by technology": overpopulation, the gap between the rich and poor countries of the world, and the possibility of thermonuclear war. Today, these dangers remain, and indeed the first two have intensified. Moreover, they have been joined by two additional dangers, also technologically derived: the collision between growing human demand and Earth's diminishing capacity to supply, and the vulnerability of the electronically interdependent global infrastructure. Of these two dangers, obviously the global ecosystem presents the more serious set of problems in that our very survival is at stake. However, the human global system, as it is presently conceived and operates, is exacerbating the problems we are having with the biosphere. In point of fact, both systems represent one immense inter-related problem.

In this final chapter, I assess how helpful the theories presented in Chapter 2 are in understanding the problems of control I have raised throughout the book. The actual question I want to address is: What are the specific effects of globalization on human control and how have they come about? However, because it is impossible to separate the specific effects of globalization from other processes and events occurring during the latter part of the twentieth century, I have described *all* significant changes in control over the past fifty years, and now will determine how well these changes can be incorporated into the theories I introduced in Chapter 2. In addition, I provide a summary of the major problems of control I have identified. This summary serves as the basis for my appraisal in the latter half of the chapter of how we can deal with these systemic problems, for as Nobel laureate Herbert Simon (1987:11) reminds us:

Technological revolutions are not something that "happen" to us. We make them, and we make them for better or for worse. Our task is not to peer into the future to see what . . . [technology] will bring us, but to shape the future that we want to have—a future that will create new possibilities for human learning, including, perhaps most important of all, new possibilities for learning to understand ourselves.

## CONTROL SYSTEMS IN THEORETICAL PERSPECTIVE

In reviewing the data presented in the book in terms of the theories reviewed in Chapter 2, I proceed by ranking the theories according to their ability (from least to most) to account for the changes in control we have witnessed during the past half century. Least valuable in making sense of control in a globalizing world are the two development theories (modernization and convergence) that predict greater world convergence, which obviously has not occurred for the world at large. Another reason why these theories have limited utility is that they view convergence as a desirable goal, whereas I have identified it as a serious obstacle to achieving control of both the human global system and the global ecological environment. The two underdevelopment theories (dependency and world-systems theory) occupy a middle ground in terms of their utility. Although they provide a sound theoretical rationale for modern globalization and specify its historical origins, they analyze only the *hierarchical* control of the core over the periphery, not the particular issues of control I have raised. However, I do develop a critique of these control issues that is consistent with the tenets of world-systems analysis. Most valuable for my purposes are the two technological development theories (cultural lag and technological system theory) because they deal directly with problems of control and also shed light on the momentous technological innovations that have permitted modern globalization to emerge. These theories provide a basis for theoretically elaborating upon the issues of control I have discussed.

## Development Theories

Although modernization and convergence theory predict worldwide industrialism, clearly industrialism has not occurred in most regions of the world, nor according to the material presented in Chapter 4 is industrialism sustainable on a worldwide basis. For example, Box 4.1, "Our Ecological Footprint" explicitly states: "If everyone on Earth lived like an average American [which according to modernization theory represents the highest stage of societal evolution], we would need six Earths to satisfy the aggregate material demand."

However, on a much more limited basis, convergent industrialism has materialized. Developed capitalist nations have achieved technological convergence through the establishment of an interdependent ICT global network that connects economic, political, and sociocultural systems by means of a common protocol—the Internet. The case study of General Motors described in Chapter 3 provides a prime example of this convergence. Not only did GM create an integrated worldwide infrastructure for all its business entities, in the process its suppliers and dealers adopted the same technical processes and systems, and by dint of its stature as a world-leading transnational corporation, many other companies adopted the same standards as GM. Indeed, even transnational criminal organizations have embraced convergent globalization through their adoption of new communications and transportation technologies which allow them to pursue global markets.

As convergence theory stipulates, techno-economic convergence causes structural adaptations that in turn have repercussions on other aspects of society until eventually all industrialized societies, no matter how dissimilar they were initially, converge in certain patterns of social organization and behavior. One example of such a structural adaptation I described in Chapter 3 is the convergence of urban and national infrastructures within developed capitalist countries. However, as I reported, these infrastructures not only provide essential services to citizens, in addition, because they are computerized and interdependent, they also create new vulnerabilities and are therefore subject to greater risks of being compromised, either deliberately or unintentionally.

Convergence is also evident in the global patterns and processes of extraction and production practiced by capitalist enterprise, which as I pointed out in Chapter 4 is the unequivocal leader in both these categories of human activity. By developing efficient technologies coupled with rational organizational expertise, capitalist enterprise has systematically increased output, at the same time that it has placed increasing demand upon the world's natural resources. Indeed, *a direct consequence of the success of technologically enhanced, free market enterprise has been the unrelenting exploitation of natural resources.*

A significant byproduct of global extraction and production is pollution. As technological processes have become more complex, so too has the nature of industrial waste. Increasingly since the industrial revolution, the unwanted remains of industry have become less easily absorbed by the natural environment, and are in growing proportion harmful to both people and the entire biosphere. Moreover, the continued expansion and variety of global extraction and production is resulting in even more hazardous pollutants being discharged into the land, sea, and air.

Finally, convergence is increasingly noticeable in global patterns of consumption. Not only are highly recognizable global brands readily available worldwide, but consumption for its own sake is continuously urged upon us, as the Western-controlled global media exhort us to buy products and services we "simply cannot do without." Table 4.1 provides an indication of just how much consumption has increased in the past fifty years. As Thorstein Veblen (1973 [1899]) informed us a century ago, "conspicuous consumption" (in the North) has become a measure of our status, our worth, and indeed, our very identity.[1] However, as the founding editor of *Scientific American* warns us: "Goods of necessity for which demand is finite, even at 10 billion population, can be had from the Earth's resources, [but] satisfaction in reward of other kinds must displace the hankering after goods of status for which demand is infinite" (Piel 1992:43).

Although modernization and convergence theory erred in their pre-

diction of *worldwide* industrialism, nevertheless convergence in technological, economic, political, and sociocultural structure and process has
certainly taken place among the rich developed nations, especially during
the past three decades. However, while proponents of this model of development view convergence as a desirable objective, I argue the opposite
case. First, from a systems perspective, convergence within and between
interconnected systems increases system vulnerability, while system diversity increases the odds of survivability. In other words, "variety within a
system must be at least as great as the environmental variety against which
it is attempting to regulate itself" (Buckley 1968:495). Second, from a
substantive point of view, the particular kinds of convergence practiced
by the developed countries are predicated on a model of economic growth—
growth in all aspects of human activity, including extraction, production,
consumption, and pollution. However, as I noted in Chapter 4, there are
definite ecological limits to the amount of habitat we can convert entirely
for human use, the tons of pollutants we can discharge into the environment, the number of biotic changes we can introduce, and the quantity of
natural resources we can exploit. And all the evidence available suggests
we are rapidly approaching these limits. Consequently, for these two reasons, modernization and convergence theory are no longer viable models
of human development.

## Underdevelopment Theories

As I mentioned in Chapter 2, dependency and world-systems theory
offer relatively valid portrayals of global development over the past half
century. Indeed, world-systems analysis has charted the evolution of core
and peripheral states toward modern integrated globalism for the past
four hundred years. According to Wallerstein (1974:350), the basis for
the organization of the world system is economic: development proceeds
through a series of unequal exchanges between core and periphery which
serves to perpetuate and "expand the economic and social gaps" between
them. Table 3.2 on major metropolitan infrastructure indicators in core,
semiperipheral, and peripheral world regions demonstrates the stark reality of what these "economic and social gaps" mean in terms of everyday
living. Box 4.1 on "Our Ecological Footprint" reveals these economic
and social gaps in a different, but equally striking way: "consumption by
the [most] affluent 1.1 billion people [that is, the richest 20 percent of the
world's population, most of whom live in core countries] alone claims

more than the entire carrying capacity of the planet" (Wackernagel and Rees 1996:102).

Although dependency and world-systems theory accurately portray the inequities that exist in the world and how they came about, they do not address problems of interdependence in a networked system, nor do they deal extensively with the cumulative exploitation by core countries of the natural environment. However, it is possible to develop a scenario consistent with these theoretical perspectives.

Recent interpretations of world-systems analysis (Chase-Dunn and Grimes 1995:403) talk of "ceilings" or "limits" to various world trends that have "the capacity to throw the modern capitalist world-economy into either acute crisis or systemic collapse." Identified as especially problematic are population growth (which taxes finite natural resources), increasing technological change (which causes sectoral dislocation, relies on non-renewable energy sources, and produces harmful pollutants), growing size of firms and concentration of capital (which diminishes the power of states to redistribute income), Western hegemony (which challenges indigenous languages, cultures, and currencies), displacement of labor by machinery (which creates greater economic and social inequities, and a restructuring of the world economy), and degradation of the natural environment (which is a direct consequence of all the activities of the capitalist global economy). These trends are provoking heightened tensions between core and periphery relating to issues of entitlement, which as I mentioned in Chapter 1 has led to backlash and active opposition by the periphery.

What forms does this opposition take, given that "all [world-systems analysts] agree that the core has more economic and political/military power than the periphery" (Chase-Dunn and Grimes 1995:397)? Protests by peripheral states, while constant, have been relatively ineffectual over the four hundred-year-strong history of the capitalist world-system. More recently, a host of various nongovernmental organizations, including the environmental movement, have actively opposed globalization and Western hegemony. Although these groups have met with more success, unless they garner massive public support, they also are unlikely to pose a serious challenge to the well-entrenched capitalist world-system.

Another avenue of opposition lies in the direct assault on the bases of economic and political/military power in the core, which is to say, "the concentration of innovations in new lead industries and in military and organizational technologies that affect the relative power and capacities of firms and states" (Chase-Dunn and Grimes 1995: 397). In other words, as I discussed in Chapter 3, because the "innovations in new lead industries and in military and organizational technologies" involve complex interdependent systems that rely upon a common protocol for communication, these systems are vulnerable to attack by any person or group with the requisite knowledge and intent to sabotage these systems. And since September 11, 2001, acknowledgement of the likelihood of these attacks has increased: "Knowing that . . . [terrorist groups] cannot match our military might with conventional weapons, . . . [they] see cyber-attacks as a way to hit America's [and other core countries'] Achilles heel—our growing dependence on technology" (Former FBI Director, Louis J. Freeh, cited in Laytner 2001).

Thirty years ago, a huge redistribution of global capital from core to periphery took place when the OPEC nations demanded and received a fair market price for their oil, the lifeblood and major energy source of the capitalist industrial economy. Today, *information* is the mainspring driving the global digital economy. A concerted attack on the integrated information systems that guide and control the provision of essential services such as energy, water, telecommunications, transportation, finance, and government and emergency services could cause a digital economy to crash in the same way that a denial of oil could cause an industrial economy to grind to a halt. According to U.S. Attorney-General John Ashcroft: "A criminal anywhere in the world armed with nothing more than a personal computer and a modem can victimize individuals and businesses worldwide" (cited in Laytner 2001).

In the pre-digital era, threat was physical—that is, material. To challenge a nation-state meant physical assault on some part of it—the fuel that drives it, its transportation and communication infrastructure, its armed forces, or even its head of state. But these could be replaced, and the state would endure: "The king is dead, long live the king!"

In the digital era, threat can also be symbolic or nonmaterial.[2] To challenge a state symbolically involves the manipulation and destruction of *ideas*, such as software. If access can be gained to one interactive computer that relies upon universal programs based on a common logic, the conceptual foundation of the entire system is at stake. As the author of the great classic, *Democracy in America*, remarked—albeit in a different context—more than 150 years ago, "the science of despotism, which was once so complex, is simplified, and reduced, as it were, to a single principle" (Tocqueville 1956 [1840]:301).

Consequently, the very information and communication infrastructure that has permitted core nations to assume real-time global dominion could also conceivably "throw the modern capitalist world-economy into either acute crisis or systemic collapse" (Chase-Dunn and Grimes 1995:403). If the tensions between core and periphery on issues of entitlement are not addressed, in a manner acceptable to both, then in all probability we may expect to experience escalating assaults on the bases of core economic and political/military power in the manner I have described. This form of opposition by the periphery to the core cannot be ignored. Indeed, this opposition could provoke a re-evaluation of dependency and world-systems theory.

## Technological Development Theories

Unlike each of the two development theories and the two underdevelopment theories, which provide similar interpretations of how global development unfolds, the two technological development theories offer unique perspectives with respect to control in a globalizing world. Consequently, I deal with each theory separately.

**Cultural Lag Theory**    Ogburn's main thesis is that changes in material culture (science and technology) occur at a faster rate than changes in nonmaterial culture (values, norms, and social institutions), thereby producing strain or cultural lag. As a consequence, Ogburn argues that our major adaptation now is to the technological environment we have created: "It is no wonder then that our society with its numerous institutions and organizations has an almost impossible task in adjusting to this whirling technological environment" (1964:85 [1956]). Ogburn is referring to the introduction by special interest groups of technical control that may be at odds with our overall sociocultural values. Because technical control precedes social control, owing primarily to its cumulative nature, certain groups may gain advantage at the expense of larger societal interests. In Chapters 3 and 4, I referred to several situations that conform to Ogburn's definition of cultural lag:

- a technologically integrated global economic network operating in parallel with an international political system comprised of many independent states permits transnational corporations to be not fully accountable to any political or social entity;

- border-straddling TNCs can maneuver national laws on tariffs, financing, competition, labor standards, environmental protection, consumer rights, taxation, and transfer of profits to their own advantage;

- the globalized mass media have the technological capacity to reduce competition and influence public opinion far beyond their legal mandate;

- covert, continuous electronic surveillance jeopardizes our legally enshrined civil liberties;

- genetic engineering, if not regulated adequately, has the potential to introduce toxins and allergens into food, displace existing species, and have harmful effects on other species (UNDP 2001:67);

- unregulated technological exploitation and degradation of the natural environment by capitalist enterprise threatens our existence as a species;

- hackers, including pranksters, criminals, political activists, and terrorists, can illegally breach public and private computer networks for their own purposes;

- the unlawful malevolent release of destructive biological, chemical, combustive/explosive, or radioactive materials into the environment can put many people and ecosystems at severe risk.

These cultural lags have introduced more instability into the world than would otherwise have been the case because they pit various constituencies against each other: TNC against nation-state, global business against local enterprise, North against South, Big Brother against individual citizen, profit against human welfare, hacker against behemoth, terrorist against injustice, humankind against nature. Later in the chapter, I offer suggestions as to how we might deal with some of these cultural lags. Suffice it to say here that, in addition to the tensions of entitlement identified by world-systems analysis, the theory of cultural lag allows us to highlight major technological-legal tensions that also figure prominently in the quest for control in a globalizing world.

**Technological System Theory**    Similar to Ogburn, Jacques Ellul identifies technology ("technique") as the principal problem directly confronting developed countries and indirectly affecting all humankind. Although technological milieus such as cities and modern urban infrastructures have become crucial in providing for our existence, they also put us in danger. According to Ellul, technique has the following properties:

- it is ever-expanding, irreversible, and cumulative;

- it proceeds without plan; it "exists only to utilize . . . technological capacity" (1980:318);

- it transforms "wants" into "needs";

- "all technical progress has three kinds of effects: the desired, the foreseen, and the unforeseen" (1990:61);

- "unpredictability is one of the general features of technical progress" (1990:60);

- "the greater the technical progress, the larger the number of unpredictable effects" (1990:70);

- "the more technique advances, the more serious the risk and the greater its probability" (1990:98);

- "the universality of the technological environment produces the image of a Nature" (1980:316);

- it mediates and modifies all human activity;

- it engenders "the most reassuring and innocent ordinariness" (1990:19);

- it produces within human beings an estrangement from themselves.

Because of these features of technique, Ellul warns that we should incorporate "foresight" into our ideas of technical progress. In other words, we should "develop attitudes and institutions and instruction based on the constant possibility of a serious accident . . . [in that] the worst [case scenario] has become much more probable" (1990:98). In our evaluations of technique, we should attempt to stand outside the technological system; we should develop an independent "intellectual, moral, or spiritual reference point for judging and criticizing technology" (1980:318).

Throughout my discussion of the global system in Chapter 3, I noted many of Ellul's defining features of technique, particularly cumulative expansion, unpredictability, and risk. In fact, the major conclusion of Chapter 3 is that although the many technological innovations in transportation, communication, and information processing over the past three or four decades have enabled modern global economic integration to occur, the desired effects of greater predictability and control have been marred by the unforeseen effects of the complexity, interdependence, and standardization of these technologies which have introduced unparalleled systemic risks. For example, one of the original architects of the Internet—the central nervous system of the global system—recently concluded that "an attack designed to flood the [World Wide] Web's master directory servers with traffic 'is capable of bringing down the Internet'" (*New York Times*, 2001). Should this collapse occur, its effects would reverberate throughout the entire global system, ultimately disrupting all communication. In other words, the technological structure that supports globalization is itself vulnerable.

Concerning Ellul's claim that technique transforms wants into needs, consider some of the ramifications of the ICT revolution. Thirty years ago, we had not even heard of—let alone wanted—the microelectronic products such as personal computers, printers, scanners, copiers, fax machines, and cell phones that now represent "necessary" equipment in any modern home or office. In 1943, the President of IBM predicted that "there just might be a world market for five computers" (Horton 2000). In 2000, the actual number of computers in use worldwide was 557 million, of which 65 percent were in North America, the European Union, and Japan (*Electronics Industry Yearbook* 2000). Not only do these statistics reveal how wants turn into needs, they also demonstrate another of Ellul's assertions: "unpredictability is one of the general features of technological progress"[3] (1990:60).

Another unpredicted outcome of the ICT revolution I mentioned in Chapter 3 is the rise of transnational organized crime, "an unfortunate by-product of globalization" (CSIS n.d.). Moreover, not only was this outcome not predicted, it poses a much greater risk than what it replaced: in the next decade international criminal organizations will become increasingly adept at "exploiting computer networks upon which all modern government, public, private, and financial services will depend" (ICTA 2000). Consequently, "many countries are likely to be at risk of organized crime groups gaining significant leverage or even control over political and economic systems."

Also unpredictable and potentially full of risk is what will happen when humans direct "computers to look into our world and observe the world on our behalf" (Goode 2000)—that is, from a human perspective. For "the moment we ask [computers] to observe the world on our behalf, we are [further] going to ask them to manipulate it on our behalf." Although there may well be obvious "desired effects" that could be achieved in pursuing this venture, there are also more than likely many "unforeseen effects" that could significantly diminish rather than augment human control.

Ellul also helps to make sense of my discussion of the global ecological environment. For example, the ever-expanding, cumulative technologies we have developed since the industrial revolution, and particularly in the past fifty years, are largely responsible for the extremely well documented conclusion that we are nearing the ecological limits of the global biosphere, and thus, our existence as a species. In order to satisfy the ever-growing needs of a rapidly increasing population, humankind has created progressively efficient and comprehensive technologies in its systematic assault on Earth. Barely one-quarter of the world's land surface has escaped some form of human encroachment, and "of all the energy available to sustain all the species on Earth, Homo sapiens takes almost half" (Leakey and Lewin 1995).

Yet the assault on Earth has not been uniform. Major habitat loss and fragmentation, pollution, biotic changes to the environment, and exploitation of the earth's natural resources originated and still predominate in the technologically developed countries of the North. These countries account for only 15 percent of the global population, yet consume nearly all the carrying capacity of the planet. According to Ellul (1980:325), part of the explanation for this disproportionate using up of the planet's resources lies in the fact that those in the North have succumbed to "the technological imperative":

The human being who acts and thinks today is not situated as an independent subject with respect to a technological object. He is inside the technological system, he is himself modified by the technological factor. The human being who uses technology today is by that very fact the human being who serves it.

Consequently, unless those in the North develop an independent "intellectual, moral, or spiritual reference point for judging and criticizing technology" (1980:318), we may continue to expect even greater exploitation of the earth's resources in the future.

The technological imperative also helps us to understand our modern attitude toward nature. Living completely and totally within a technological system distorts our perceptions of reality: "the universality of the technological environment produces the image of a Nature" (1980:316). For those of us ensconced in this system, technology has become reality, and it, not nature, provides our daily requirements. Nature is the "scenic backdrop" (Wackernagel and Rees 1996:4). Because technology mediates and modifies all human activity, it produces within us an estrangement from ourselves. Instead of realizing that we are creatures of nature and totally dependent upon it for our survival, we believe that technology will prevail—no matter what.

Ellul's analysis offers a sweeping indictment of our slavish, uncritical attachment to technique. Immersed as we are in a technological milieu, we are adamant in our conviction that we can achieve ultimate control, that we can control nature itself. We are convinced by our technical accomplishments: planning birth, splitting atoms, walking on the Moon, inventing intelligence, creating life, and forestalling death. But in our drive to design even more powerful technical systems, we lose our human capacity for thinking outside of these systems. We become programmed to the technological imperative. We lose touch with reality beyond technique. Ellul (1990:411) argues that only by "recognizing our nonfreedom" in this technological imperative can we then begin to evaluate technique critically and independently, thus revealing the technological tensions that impede human and social development in a globalizing, but finite, world.

## SUMMARY OF THEORETICAL PERSPECTIVES ON CONTROL

Each of the theories of social change I have reviewed offers unique insight into major problems of control in the modern global era. A summary of these problems serves as the foundation for my discussion in the remainder of the chapter of how we might develop programmatic solutions for them. Although there is much overlap, I categorize these problems according to the major dimensions of the human global system and the overall global eco-environment. Each of these problems represents an unparalleled challenge for humankind at the beginning of the twenty-first century.

## Technical Problems

Convergence as a system objective is flawed. The standardization and interdependence of the electronic global system increases the risk of total system failure and ensuing loss of control, either as a result of deliberate attack or unforeseen circumstance, such as accidents, technical malfunction, or natural causes. The desired effects of information and communications technology—greater predictability and control of the global system—are being subverted by mounting risks stemming from its unforeseen effects.

## Economic Problems

The application by capitalist enterprise and criminal organizations of revolutionary innovations in science and technology permits these forces to remain beyond the effective control of various social institutions whose mandate it has been to regulate them.

## Political Problems

Due to various ceilings or limits of the world-system such as population growth, technological change, consolidation and concentration of capital, Western hegemony, displacement of labor, and environmental degradation, the world is becoming increasingly unstable. At issue are growing concerns of entitlement as a diminishing core population consumes an ever growing proportion of the world's depleting resources at the expense of the expanding peripheral nations.

## Sociocultural Problems

Ever-expanding and cumulative technologies are continually inflating human needs, such that we are nearing the ecological limits of the global biosphere. Because people from developed countries are totally immersed in technological systems, they have a systemic incapacity to comprehend adequately the dangers inherent in these systems and to realize they are ultimately bound by laws of nature.

## Environmental Problems

The global structure and processes of extraction, production, consumption, and pollution are causing an unsustainable loss of biodiversity and incremental environmental degradation. Compounded by increases in both human population *and* demand, this deterioration of the global eco-environment is so far resistant to effective regulatory control.

All of these problems of control are exacerbated by the effects of cumulative technology. If we don't deal with them, especially the environmental problems, at best we face a rapidly deteriorating quality of life; at worst we could drive ourselves into extinction. These problems will only get worse—unless we engage in decisive collective action to reverse their effects.

## PROSPECTS FOR REGAINING CONTROL

Obviously, as C. P. Snow has indicated, there are no perfect solutions to the problems I have outlined, no quick fixes for the dilemmas we face. However, again citing Snow (1971:10), "we now have enough experience to see how some follies can be avoided." As the technological, social, and natural systems in which we live have experienced radical change over the course of human history, so too must our coping strategies change. The limiting constraints we now confront in a globalized world are vastly different from those we faced in the past. We must realize that our behavior, both individually and collectively, has repercussions far beyond what on the surface may appear to be isolated acts.

In this section, I selectively describe some promising strategies and solutions that various individuals and organizations have initiated to deal with these problems. My treatment of these strategies is not exhaustive; rather it can only be suggestive of some of the options we have available to reverse humankind's self-destructive course. However, I am optimistic that these strategies will prompt additional ideas and suggestions for constructively dealing with these issues.

Central to the search for resolution are strategies that appeal to our *enlightened self-interest*. In other words, because all of us are passengers on spaceship Earth, strategies that harm some can eventually harm all. Whether it be the perils of an interdependent electronic system, the unregulated activities of transnational corporations, the grossly inequitable distribution of the world's resources, unbridled human wants, or the systematic assault on the global biosphere, all these actions reverberate throughout the entire human community. Only by considering options that work in the long-term interests of humankind as a whole can we hope to realize our own individual dreams and aspirations, as well as those of our grandchildren's children.

Although co-operation cannot supply all the answers to the problems we face, no solution will work without it. Either we pursue our own self-interest against a background of growing inequality, insecurity and degradation, or we embark on a new era of collective action (Edwards 1999:11).

## Technical Dimension

As I indicated in Chapter 3 (see especially Figure 3.1), intelligent, complex, interdependent electronic control systems, responsible for monitoring a vast range and number of activities, now span the globe. The Internet is the integrative linchpin that connects this constellation of systems, including individually connected personal computers. Although the desired effects of achieving greater scale, access, speed, and efficiency have in some cases surpassed our imagination, and are still continuing, the unforeseen effect of cascading system failure diminishes overall system reliability, and indeed could produce grave as well as costly consequences. Paradoxically, interdependence, the very feature that produces the desired effects, also causes the unforeseen effect. Although recent efforts in software design (specifically, "distributed control" and "survivability") increase system security and dependability, they do not solve the logical problem that interdependence poses. Neither do other undertakings such as constructing fire walls, installing encryption devices, integrating security into system design, or introducing redundant lines of communication to increase connectivity. The *only* way to solve the problem that interdependence poses is to "decouple," or separate, the overall system at various strategic points (Brinsmead 1999).

Recent work on the simultaneous operation of the Internet in conjunction with *intra*nets and *extra*nets may hold one decoupling solution (Internet Chicago 2002). An intranet is an internally secure version of the Internet; it is a local or wide area network that is restricted to an explicitly defined group of users, usually employees of public or private organizations. Information exchanged in an intranet is not available for public viewing, nor can an intranet be easily breached from outside the system. It is decoupled from the Internet. In a similar fashion, an extranet is a slightly less secure, but still "controlled access" network that limits entry to registered users outside (such as suppliers and clients) as well as those within the intranet. An extranet is a protected portion of the Internet, decoupled from it by passwords and encryption.[4] Although not a perfect solution, the creation of intranets and extranets does address many of the problems associated with a globally interdependent Internet.

Other notable efforts to increase the reliability and security of the global information and communications infrastructure include the following:

- The formation of the Internet Society (2001), an organization of both individual and public and private organizational members in more than one hundred countries, which facilitates "global coordination and cooperation on the Internet." Its activities focus "on the Internet's development, availability, and associated technologies."

- The establishment of the World Information Technology and Services Alliance (WITSA 2001), a worldwide consortium of forty-one information technology industry associations, which in October 2001, inaugurated a Global Information Security Summit.

- The presence of many public and private, national and international organizations whose sole purpose it is to enhance information and communications security, especially as it applies to the Internet.

- Research, profiling, and intelligence analysis of past security breaches to determine trends and patterns in order to issue warning advisories and increase Internet security (Williams et al. n.d.).

- Basic long-term research on interdependence of critical infrastructures, security, and system design (Williams et al. n.d.), including analysis of the effects of common, standardized elements such as Microsoft operating systems[5] and Intel PC microprocessors (Schwartz 2001).

- International collaboration to introduce or modify national laws in a globally consistent manner to reduce the cultural lag between legislation and the new cyber-reality[6]. Significant in this regard is the Council of Europe's "Convention on Cybercrime." Signed by twenty-eight European states, plus the United States, Canada, and Japan in November 2001, "its main objective . . . is to pursue a common criminal policy aimed at the protection of society against cybercrime, especially by adopting appropriate legislation and fostering international co-operation" (Council of Europe 2002).

- Education and training of individual users, system administrators, network managers, chief information officers, technicians, and others responsible for the global information and communications infrastructure to raise the level of security awareness (Cross 2000).

Most significant in drawing widespread and urgent attention to the technical problems of control in an age of integrated globalism have been the tragic events of September 11, 2001. As the U.S. House of Representatives' Committee on Science stated one month after the attacks:

The terrorist attacks of September 11, 2001 brought into stark relief the nation's physical and economic vulnerability to attack within our borders. The relative ease with which terrorists were able to implement their plans serves as a pointed reminder of the need to identify critical "soft spots" in the nation's defenses. Among the nation's vulnerabilities are our computer and communications networks, on which the country's economic and critical infrastructures for finance, transportation, energy and water distribution, and health and emergency services depend. The existence of these vulnerabilities has called into question the extent to which the nation's technological research programs, educational system, and interconnected operations are able to meet the challenge of cyber warfare in the 21st century (Committee on Science 2001).

Not only are these concerns being raised in the United States, they are also attracting serious attention in all developed countries which rely on these integrated electronic systems. *For the first time in history, due to their technological dependence on interconnected global systems, the richest and most powerful nations in the world are vulnerable to decisive attacks by nations, groups, and even individuals armed with little more than a computer, a modem, and the requisite skills.* As a result, according to experts in intelligence analysis:

. . . the advent of computer warfare has the potential to significantly change the balance of power in a world increasingly dependent on sophisticated technologies. Nations that would never consider themselves players in the arena of global power strategies may now be considering their place in a different kind of world. . . . In the world of Information Warfare, technological capability, rather than the size of kinetic weapons arsenals or standing armies, is the primary factor in determining the balance of power. And *because of the constantly expanding interdependencies inherent in today's cyber environment*, there is a growing possibility of wide-ranging unintended effects associated with any sort of malicious operations against a network (Williams et al. n.d; italics added).

If these potentially widespread, devastating, and imminent threats don't serve as a sufficient stimulus for solving the technical problems of control I have raised, it is unlikely that anything will. Hopefully, something constructive may yet come from this American tragedy.

## Economic Dimension

In Chapter 2, I noted that the problem of a "growing lack of congruence between the 'world economy,' with its tendencies to promote ever-greater levels of economic integration, and an 'international political system' comprised of many rival states" (Gill and Law 1988:364–65) was an instance of a global cultural lag, and in Chapter 3, I discussed how transnational investment may be seen as a logical and rational extension on the part of business enterprises to adapt to and control their environment. I explained that because of between-nation variability in laws and regulations, transnational corporations can selectively choose where in the world it is most profitable for them to operate, with the consequence that the balance of power between corporation and state has shifted in favor of corporations.

An obvious solution to this dilemma for nation-states is to adopt a strategy similar to that of transnational corporations—that is, to form standard supranational agreements for the purpose of regulating TNC activity (Hedley 1999). Although attempts have been made along these lines over the past few decades, little success has been achieved. The main stumbling block appears to be the presumed loss of national sovereignty that would be entailed in such a move, in which nations would have to yield some of their regulatory authority to an international tribunal. However, it may well be argued that nation-states have given up even more of their sovereign rights by doing nothing. For example, in the United States, which is by far the most popular foreign investment location, the Internal Revenue Service (IRS) expressed "fears that multinational corporate groups might attempt to shift income, deductions, and other items among related entities to avoid paying its fair share of taxes in the United States" (OECD 1993:9). In a 1992 report, the IRS noted that "while many foreign controlled corporations have reported sizeable profits and paid substantial taxes, nevertheless *on average such companies report less than half as much income as similar corporations that are United States controlled"*[7] (OECD 1993:9, italics added). However, if the United States entered into a multilateral agreement with other countries, then it could impose a common set of regulations to which TNCs would have to comply if they wanted to conduct business in any of these countries.

Just such an agreement with respect to both trade and foreign investment has been adopted by the fifteen member countries that form the European Union (EU). A supranational European Commission has established a level playing field upon which all the activities of TNCs within the EU are legally monitored and regulated. Although each member country has had to yield some of its national authority over trade and foreign investment policy, the overall regulatory framework provides more political control over corporate activity than any one country could achieve on its own. Instead of involving itself in direct competition for foreign investment, the EU cooperatively establishes policy in line with the broad social, economic, and environmental objectives of all its member countries, thus in large part eliminating the cultural lag between the technologically enhanced activities of transnational corporations and jurisdictional control of these activities[8] (European Union 2001). Although the history of the EU has been long and sometimes stormy, its success can be attributed to the fact that its regulatory structure more closely parallels transnational corporate activity than any devised to date. In other words, global problems require global solutions.

The EU model raises an additional point: *economic* objectives are not the only criteria by which TNCs are evaluated. In addition, the EU also considers *social* and *environmental* issues in its formulation of regulatory policy, thus providing a more comprehensive and balanced framework for its citizens. Indeed, this model could be formally expanded to include input from all legitimate stakeholders such as unions and professional associations, as well as NGOs representing consumers, the environment, and other "authorized" concerns. Although the addition of these groups at the bargaining table would make the proceedings exceedingly complex, the resulting "social contract" would be much more reflective of broader societal interests and concerns.

Finally, in formulating economic policy, not only should non-financial issues be taken into consideration, so also should plans encompass a time frame much longer than is often the case, such as with corporations fixated on quarterly and annual revenues, and governments with limited terms of office. Especially when contemplated actions will have a direct impact on the environment, decision makers should carefully examine the long-term implications of these actions.[9]

In sum, in governing the activities of TNCs and other global entities, national governments, as representatives of all citizens, should themselves join together in global agreements that are broadly reflective of all stakeholders and that adopt a long-range sustainable perspective. However, like the European Union, the path to such global agreements can only occur one step at a time. Obviously, given so many competing interests, it is difficult to frame these agreements, or we would have more of them in place. Rather, a good starting point would be first to negotiate issues on which there appear to be general consensus among a certain coalition of nations (Edwards 1999:184–85). From these initial cooperative successes, other issues and other nations could be added in an attempt to build a more comprehensive set of agreements that would incorporate the interests of the many, as opposed to the will of a few.

## Political Dimension

At a conference on "Creating Digital Dividends," Microsoft founder Bill Gates challenged the claim that being connected to the Internet could yield immediate benefits for the entire world population (Verhovek 2000). With almost half the world's 6 billion people living on less than $2 a day, and 1.2 billion people living on less than $1 a day (World Bank 2001:3), Gates asserted that the overwhelming priority for these people is just trying to stay alive: "I mean, do people have a clear view of what it means to live on $1 a day? There's no electricity in that house. None."

At least one other person at the conference, James F. Moore, Chairman of GeoPartners Research Inc., defended Gates: "He's right, and I'd emphatically support him on this, that other divides are more important than the digital divide: the divide on health care, the human rights divide, the education divide."

In October 2001, following the terrorist attacks on the United States and the response by President Bush and his advisors to launch a bombing campaign in Afghanistan, the Washington, D.C.-based Worldwatch Institute suggested a different course of action: "The United States and other industrial nations should launch a global 'Marshall Plan' to provide everyone on earth with a decent standard of living" (Bell and Renner). Based on the economic support that the United States provided war-torn Europe following World War II, Worldwatch argues that a new Marshall Plan represents perhaps the most viable means possible for "advancing human security and controlling terrorism":

Globalization has raised expectations, even as modern communications make the rising inequality between a rich, powerful, imposing West and the rest of the world visible to all. Poverty and deprivation do not automatically translate into hatred. But people whose hopes have worn thin, whose aspirations have been thwarted, and whose discontent is rising, are far more likely to succumb to the siren song of extremism. This is particularly true for the swelling ranks of young people whose prospects for the future are bleak. Some 34 percent of the developing world's population is under 15 years of age.

On the issue of how much such a plan would cost, Worldwatch reports that it would require only 5 percent of the $780 billion now being spent annually on worldwide military expenditures[10]:

A 1998 report by the United Nations Development Programme estimated the annual cost to achieve universal access to a number of basic social services in all developing countries:

- $9 billion would provide water and sanitation for all;
- $12 billion would cover reproductive health for all women;
- $13 billion would give every person on Earth basic health and nutrition; and
- $6 billion would provide basic education for all (cited in Bell and Renner).

The Worldwatch Institute concludes its proposal for a global Marshall Plan by stating that "we must all understand that in the end, weapons alone cannot buy us a lasting peace in a world of extreme inequality, injustice, and deprivation for billions of our fellow human beings."

In 1947, when U.S. Secretary of State George C. Marshall first proposed the European Recovery Program, he stated that it was directed "against hunger, poverty, desperation, and chaos" (1997 [1947]). Credited with rebuilding the economic infrastructure of Europe, restoring agricultural and industrial productivity, and preventing famine and political chaos (as well as earning Marshall a Nobel Peace Prize), the

Marshall Plan drew immediate support from around the world (National Archives 1997).

Why couldn't a new Marshall Plan be equally successful? In many ways, current global conditions mirror the "hunger, poverty, desperation, and chaos" of the post-war years. As the present U.S. Secretary of State Colin L. Powell remarked at a conference in February 2002: "terrorism really flourishes in areas of poverty, despair and hopelessness, where people see no future" (cited in Purdum and Sanger 2002).

No doubt there are many who would say that world poverty is not *their* problem. It is easy to imagine many people saying, "If I had to work hard to provide a decent living for myself and my family, why shouldn't they?" Aside from the fact that it is we in the core nations who are responsible for having created such an extremely inequitable world-system (Wallerstein 1974), consider the alternative of doing nothing. September 11 provided a glimpse of what can occur. If we do not take responsibility for our fellow human beings, the probability of world disorder will increase enormously. Only by acting in our own enlightened self-interest can we hope to minimize our very real vulnerabilities to apparent acts of terror. As former world statesman Lester Pearson warned us decades ago: "Before long, in our affluent, industrial computerized jet society, we shall feel the wrath of the wretched people of the world. There will be no peace" (cited in Tinbergen 1976:59).

It is important to note that those in the South do not want charity from the North; rather they seek more of a voice in their own self-determination. In a report broadly reflective of the needs and desires of those living in developing countries, the South Commission (1990) identified both internal and external obstacles to the development of the South, and charted its own development priorities.[11] Central to its development objectives is acceptance by the North not only of the legitimacy of Southern perspectives, but also of the South's right to be an active participant both in determining and achieving its development agenda. No longer is the South willing to play a peripheral and passive role in matters that directly affect it.

As I mentioned in Chapter 1, for many nations, cultures, institutions, organizations, and individuals in the world, modern globalism represents an elitist, Western-dominated form of economic and cultural imperialism over which they have little or no control. Increasingly, important decisions affecting crucial aspects of millions and millions of people's lives are made, not by democratically elected political representatives, but by transnational corporations and international agencies such as the World Bank, International Monetary Fund, and World Trade Organization that do not have the mandate of the people. Especially during the 1990s, many different counterforces to globalization protested against this de facto form of global governance, demanding that their concerns also be addressed. Leading these protests have been grassroots and international nongovernmental organizations of every stripe and hue. By their very presence, they are challenging the legitimacy of this transnational hegemony to dictate the terms of the global order. According to Brown et al. (2000:283), NGOs have broadened the terms of reference of this new global order by:

- Identifying problematic globalization consequences that might otherwise be ignored;

- Articulating new values and norms to guide and constrain international practice;

- Building transnational alliances that advocate for otherwise ignored alternatives;

- Altering international institutions to respond to unmet needs;

- Disseminating social innovations that have international applications;

- Negotiating resolutions to transnational conflicts and disagreements; and

- Mobilizing resources and acting directly on important public problems.

In all these endeavors, NGOs are introducing social and environmental concerns that hitherto have not been considered important enough to be on the global agenda. Whether at the bargaining table, on the Internet, or in the streets, these new global forces for *civil society* are definitely having an impact. (See Box 5.1 on how a cooperative campaign by several NGOs successfully challenged a World Trade Organization ruling and forced Northern-based pharmaceutical corporations to accept substantially less than their list price on patented life-saving drugs for people at risk in the South.) Only time will tell if their efforts will yield a more inclusive and sustainable world order.

## Sociocultural Dimension

In the introduction to this section on "Prospects for Regaining Control," I suggested that as the various systems in which we live have changed over time, so also must our coping strategies, particularly in regard to social and ecological sustainability. In addition, I stated that enlightened self-interest is a necessary ingredient in how we may resolve the urgent problems facing us. In other words, rather than another technological revolution, what we need now is *a revolution in human values*.

In a thought-provoking article on "Places to intervene in a system," Donella Meadows (1997) provides a rank-ordered list of how it is possible to regulate, control, and even change complex systems such as corporations, economies, societies, ecosystems, *and* individuals. At the top of her list is "the mindset or paradigm out of which a system arises," and just below this entry is "the goals of the system." Both of these points of system leverage involve the *values* that drive systems in particular ways, but as Meadows points out, it is extremely difficult to intervene successfully in systems at these levels. Ogburn (1922:143–96) provides the reasons why: there is resistance to change or cultural inertia operating in the form of vested interests preserving the status quo; predispositions toward familiar routines, habits, custom, and tradition; social pressures to con-

---

## BOX 5.1

## HEALTH BEFORE WEALTH

Every day 37,000 people, mostly from developing countries, die from treatable, often infectious diseases. Nearly half these victims are children under the age of five. Although drugs are available, they are priced far beyond the reach of the world's poor. These drugs could be produced much more cheaply, but the World Trade Organization (WTO) through its Agreement on Trade Related Intellectual Property Rights (TRIPS) has granted exclusive proprietary rights for at least twenty years to the large Northern-based pharmaceutical corporations that originally patented them. Consequently, "at a time when millions of lives are at risk from newly-virulent diseases, and from increasing drug resistance to old killers, trade rules threaten to make basic medicines even less affordable to the poor."

In an effort to provide cheap generic (that is, non-patented) drugs to those at risk, Oxfam, Health Gap, and Third World Network, with the support of Médecins Sans Frontières, Consumer Project on Technology, Consumers International, Health Action International, and The Network, launched an Internet campaign to collect signatures on a "Health before Wealth" petition asking the WTO to allow "governments of developing countries greater freedom to take the necessary measures to protect public health."

On November 14, 2001, at the WTO conference in Qatar, Oxfam International Media Officer Ian Bray presented the Health before Wealth petition to the Director General of the WTO. Signed by more than 32,000 people from 163 countries and territories, the petition convinced the WTO to modify "the potentially lethal side-effects of the TRIPS agreement." Governments of developing countries now have "the right to grant compulsory licenses (overriding patents) and the freedom to determine the grounds upon which such licenses are granted."

For Oxfam's Ian Bray, the outcome of the WTO conference "was a salutary lesson, if one was needed, that politicians and officials do listen when enough people genuinely express their concern. Those 32,000 people who did take the time to care and sign the petition made a difference and helped the developing countries get the deal they fought for in Qatar."

*Source:* Adapted from http://oxfam.org.uk/cutthecost/index.html and related Oxfam links.

form; and anxiety regarding uncertainty and change that provokes a conservative reaction.

How then is it possible to *change* human values?

Ronald Inglehart (1990:68) provides a conceivably useful answer: "one's basic values reflect the conditions that prevailed during one's pre-adult years." In other words, although *individual* values change little over a lifetime, value adaptation to one's environment (or "culture shift" as Inglehart calls it) occurs en masse through the process of generational replacement, whereby *a succeeding generation assumes values more in keeping with its present circumstances* than the generation it is replacing.

Inglehart's thesis may be seen as a special case of cultural lag, such that nonmaterial human values catch up or adjust to changed material circumstances on a generational basis. If Inglehart's thesis is correct, given the revolutionary changes in our material circumstances over the past fifty years (that is, two generations), then there should be evidence of changes in values among the young over this same period. What evidence is there for Inglehart's thesis of generational value change?

Perhaps the first beginnings of cultural adjustment to a new material reality may be found in the 1960s when President John F. Kennedy issued a call to the young people of America: "Ask not what your country can do for you, ask what you can do for your country." With these words, he established the Peace Corps "to promote world peace and friendship" (Peace Corps, n.d.). "Since 1961, more than 163,000 Americans have joined the Peace Corps, working to bring clean water to communities, teach children, help start new small businesses, and stop the spread of AIDS." Although a small beginning, nevertheless joining the Peace Corps was a radical alternative to joining the armed forces.

Shortly after the founding of the Peace Corps, the first of ten United World Colleges was opened in Wales in 1962. Its purpose was to bring youth between the ages of 16 and 19 together from all over the world "to gain a knowledge and understanding of a variety of races and cultures" in an environment that "fosters peace, cooperation, and personal challenge" (United World Colleges n.d.). Later, other colleges were set up in Canada, the United States, Italy, Swaziland, Singapore, Venezuela, Hong Kong, Norway, and India.

While the global impacts of these and similar ventures were small at the outset, it may be argued that their contributions have been cumulative and have helped to create a new awareness and understanding of humanity in a globalizing world. Another new awareness also began to take hold with the publication in 1962 of Rachel Carson's *Silent Spring*, a book that revealed to many for the first time the dangers of the indiscriminate use of poisonous and biologically potent chemical pesticides. Carson's book, now translated into more than a dozen languages, is credited with spawning the environmental movement, establishing courses and programs in environmental studies, and the founding of the U.S. government's Environmental Protection Agency (Rachel Carson Council 2001). Very definitely, her work has prompted a sea change in the attitudes of the generations that followed her, for it was her conviction that "the more clearly we can focus our attention on the wonders and realities of the universe about us, the less taste we shall have for destruction" (1954).

From these beginnings, over the past two generations literally millions of organizations, projects, and programs have arisen whose core values are attuned more closely to our present global circumstances, such that humankind may *possibly* evolve in a sustainable manner. For example, many of the nongovernmental organizations I have mentioned throughout this book, as well as educational and training programs and books and articles, reflect the new reality of how an expanding human population with seemingly insatiable needs is having devastating and irreversible impacts in a finite world.

There is also some support for Inglehart's thesis that the young may have a better grip on this new reality than older generations. For example, a 1993 nationally representative survey of American adults (18 years and older) asked respondents if they agreed or disagreed with a number of statements about the environment (Steel 2000). Particularly with regard to two of these statements, younger age cohorts reflect a far less anthropocentric perspective than their older counterparts. Whereas more than four-fifths of those aged 18 to 29 disagreed with the statement, "Plants and animals exist primarily for human use," the corresponding percentages of disagreement among older cohorts was successively lower: 30 to 45 years = 63 percent, 46 to 60 years = 52 percent, and for those over 60, only 33 percent disagreed. Similarly, nearly two-thirds of the youngest respondents disagreed with the statement, "Humankind was created to rule over the rest of nature," compared to slightly more than one-third among the oldest respondents. These findings provide striking, although limited, support for Inglehart's predicted paradigm shift in values. As younger generations replace older ones, the growing view appears to be that human beings are just one of millions of interdependent species inhabiting the planet, rather than some kind of god-like stewards. While this is good news, nevertheless it must be evaluated within the context of the data presented in Table 4.1, which reveal a far greater proportional use of the world's resources over the past fifty years than can be accounted for by population growth alone. That is, *words* alone are insufficient for a paradigm shift to take place; they must be accompanied by a corresponding change in *behavior*.

Similar words of encouragement come from a 1992 twenty-four-nation *Health of the Planet* survey (Dunlap 1994). "Covering a greater number and wider range of nations than have ever been included in an environmental opinion survey" (1994:115), one question asked nationally representative respondents to "rate the quality of the environment in the world as a whole." The overwhelming majority in 21 of the 24 rated it as "very" or "fairly bad." Although the respondents from developing countries were a little less likely to hold this opinion, nevertheless more than half of them in six out of the nine developing countries included in the poll came to this conclusion. However, again it is necessary to evaluate these findings within a broader context. As I mentioned in the previous subsection ("Political Dimension"), almost half the world's population is barely surviving, let alone plundering the planet's natural resources. What these people aspire to is "a decent standard of living" (Cantril 1965) that, while not nearly as luxurious as that enjoyed by Northerners, could nevertheless, due to the numbers involved, have widespread environmental impacts on this and future generations. Consequently, while there are encouraging signs of value change among all humankind, these signs have yet to be translated into decisive and comprehensive actions that will arrest and reverse the harmful trends in human activity recorded over the last half-century.

## Global Eco-environment

The principal human stressors on the global eco-environment are Northern-based cumulative technology, a capitalist enterprise system predicated on economic growth, rising material demand, and Southern-based population growth. Although Southern population growth is now in decline, the globally integrated Northern system of extraction, production, consumption, and pollution shows few signs of slowing down. In fact, this system is now being increasingly emulated in the South. As I mentioned in Chapter 4, these stressors are responsible for the finding that present human requirements are almost 30 percent more than the productive land available to satisfy them (Wackernagel and Rees 1996). In other words, we are using up natural capital, thus depriving future generations of the benefits we take for granted.

In Chapter 1, I reported that as a result of satellite technology, we now have "an international Earth-observing capability" that is able to monitor, measure, and assess the interaction of all the various environmental elements—including human beings and what they do—that comprise the very complex global ecosystem. From this and other less comprehensive ecological surveys, scientists have established an immense database of ecological statistics that can inform global socioeconomic and

environmental policy.[12] Consequently, although we have sufficient information, we lack the necessary resolve to take appropriate action, or do we?

Similar to my discussion of establishing a supranational tribunal to
monitor and regulate transnational economic enterprise, a major problem with instituting appropriate global environmental safeguards lies in
the fact that currently there is no international agency with the necessary
regulatory capability. Without such an agency or at least a comprehensive
international framework agreement involving all nations, it is virtually
impossible to address the interdependent global environmental problems
that threaten each of us, no matter where in the world we live.

How much support is there for such an international environmental
protection agency? In the 1992 *Health of the Planet* survey mentioned
earlier (Dunlap 1994:124: italics added), this very issue was raised:

1. "Would you favour or oppose our government contributing
   *money* to an international agency to work on solving global
   environmental problems—strongly favour, somewhat favour,
   somewhat oppose, strongly oppose?"

2. "Would you favour or oppose giving an international agency the
   *authority* to influence our government's policy in environmentally
   important areas—strongly favour, somewhat favour, somewhat
   oppose, strongly oppose?"

Table 5.1 presents the results for the representative samples in the
twenty-four countries polled who either strongly or somewhat favored
both of these actions. As may be seen, the majority in all nations were in
favor of both contributing money and giving authority to a supranational
environmental agency, with greater endorsement being given to financial
support. On average, more than three-quarters of the people in each country
surveyed favored a financial contribution, while two-thirds favored as-
signing authority to such an international agency. Slightly greater support
for these actions was evidenced in developed countries compared to developing countries. These data indicate that regardless of what official
government stances are toward the financial support of an international
regulatory environmental agency (see Box 2.1), in most of the countries
surveyed, there is overwhelming *popular* support for such an undertak-
ing. Consequently, at the grassroots level there appears to be the resolve
necessary to take appropriate action, at least in word.

An important indirect stressor on the global eco-environment is the

**Table 5.1     Percentage of Popular Support for an International
Environmental Agency**

| NATION | Favor Contributing Money to Agency (%) | Favor Giving Authority to Agency (%) |
|---|---|---|
| Finland | 90 | 74 |
| Netherlands | 89 | 75 |
| Great Britain | 89 | 73 |
| Hungary | 84 | 72 |
| Portugal | 83 | 74 |
| Korea (Rep.) | 83 | 74 |
| Norway | 83 | 65 |
| Germany (West) | 82 | 78 |
| Russia | 79 | 76 |
| Switzerland | 79 | 71 |
| Ireland | 79 | 70 |
| Poland | 78 | 70 |
| Japan | 78 | 65 |
| Denmark | 78 | 52 |
| Canada | 77 | 70 |
| Mexico | 77 | 61 |
| Philippines | 75 | 64 |
| Turkey | 75 | 60 |
| India | 75 | 57 |
| United States | 74 | 63 |
| Nigeria | 73 | 70 |
| Chile | 68 | 54 |
| Uruguay | 61 | 54 |
| Brazil | 56 | 62 |
| Average 24-nation support | 78 | 67 |

*Source*: Adapted from Dunlap, 1994:124.
*Note*: National sample sizes ranged from 770 to 4,984 with a mean size of 1,238. "Samples in this size range should be accurate within approximately plus-or-minus 3 percentage points of the national populations" (Dunlap 1994:116).

manner in which the international financial system measures human progress. In various parts of this book, I have referred to gross national product (GNP) and gross domestic product (GDP). These are two slightly different measures of the total monetary value of goods and services produced by the citizens or residents of a country over a certain period of time, usually a year. Every time money changes hands and is formally recorded, "progress" is made. However, let us consider the 11-million-gallon *Exxon Valdez* crude oil spill off the coast of Alaska in 1989 (see Box 4.3). Was that progress? Yes, according to how the GNP and GDP are computed. Consider the costs of the cleanup ($900 million) and the lawsuits that were filed ($1.3 billion). These huge sums were *added* to the American GNP and GDP, which means that the United States had a higher GNP/GDP during that time than it would have had if the *Exxon Valdez* had made it safely to port.

Does this illustration of how GNP and GDP are computed sound preposterous? Yes, say thousands of critics who are advocating for new measures of progress based on whether human activities are productive or destructive, sustainable or unsustainable. According to these critics, a "nation's central measure of well-being works like a calculating machine that adds but cannot subtract. It treats everything that happens in the market as a gain for humanity, while ignoring everything that happens outside the realm of monetized exchange, regardless of the importance to well-being" (Cobb et al. 1995:65). These critics propose a "genuine progress indicator" (GPI) or an "index of sustainable economic welfare" (ISEW) that is sensitive to, among other things, "resource depletion and degradation of the habitat" (1995:72). To the extent that these dimensions are factored into nations' "progress accounts," citizens *and their governments* can become more aware of both the benefits *and* the costs of various activities. As it is now, "when measured by the GDP, . . . [a] nation's most desirable habitat is a multibillion dollar, toxic Superfund site" (Baker 1999).

Consider the slogan promoted by the U.S. Environmental Protection Agency (2001): "Reduce, Reuse, and Recycle." What if all consumers in a country were to eat 10 percent less than they do now, and not purchase a new car until their present one was at least ten years old, thereby systematically reducing their consumption? What effects would this behavior have on the nation's gross domestic product, and how would it affect the genuine progress indicator? While the GDP would drop, the GPI would rise. Which of these measures provides information absolutely essential for human survival? Given the current fact that total human demand exceeds global ecological supply by 30 percent, we have no alternative but to reduce aggregate demand—sooner or later. And we need to know on a continuing basis how well (or poorly) we are doing in achieving this crucial objective.[13] Consequently, all countries should be developing genuine progress indicators so they can adjust their policies accordingly. In fact, *this is precisely the kind of information that transnational banks are now seeking in determining which countries represent sound investment opportunities* (Baker 1999). They are commissioning "ecological footprint" surveys to find out countries' ecological capacities and whether or not they have "ecological deficits" or are "overspending" their natural capacities. Not only is this kind of information *now* deemed to be extremely useful to transnational business, it is also without a doubt *fundamental* for the preservation of humankind.

Another indirect stressor on the global eco-environment is the traditional system of government taxation, which does not take into account conservation and sustainability. However, during the last decade, based on the principle that "we use less of what is taxed and more of what is not" (Friends of the Earth 1998), many national and local governments have enacted "green taxes" or ecological tax reforms. These new laws not only change behavior (of both corporations and ordinary individuals) in the direction of environmental sustainability, they also provide governments with revenue to engage in environmental restitution. Below is a sampling of some of the accomplishments to date (Friends of the Earth 1998):

- Through a system of both tax levies and refunds, Sweden established measurable environmental criteria "so that money moves from heavier polluters to lighter polluters." During the first year of implementing the new taxation measures, nitrogen oxide and nitrogen dioxide emissions, which contribute to acid rain, fell by 35 percent.

- As a result of industrial water-effluent taxes based on both the amount and toxicity of discharges, Germany has reduced its overall level of harmful water pollution.

- In the United States, the Washington state government instituted a tax credit system for workers participating in a ride-sharing program. Not only did the program result in less vehicle pollution, it also saved money that would otherwise have been necessary for building new roads. Washington also charges a $1 fee on new tires, which is earmarked for its tire recycling program.

- Britain has established a national tax credit system for materials that can be recycled in order to reduce its solid waste disposal.

These and many other ecological tax reforms are slowly having an effect in terms of reducing the systematic impacts of humans on their environment.

As I mentioned in Chapter 4, although we are nearing the ecological limits of the earth in terms of our own survival, there are heartening signs that many of us are, at long last, finally getting the message. Even industry, traditionally one of the worst offenders, is slowly changing its practices as increasingly it realizes the full meaning of *sustainable economic development.* Quite simply, if economic practices are not sustainable, there can be no long-term development; consequently, everyone loses. In this realization, industry is being "helped" by a growing number of NGOs, watchdogs, and ordinary people who are providing highly vocal reinforcement of this emerging mindset. For example, biologist, avid bird watcher, and environmentalist Jared Diamond (1999b) describes an extensive oil-drilling and natural gas field operating in Papua New Guinea. He found that rather than clearing the land and drilling wells in the traditional manner, this Chevron-managed consortium of transnational oil companies had kept the oil lease zone, "biologically one of the richest environments on Earth," in a "pristine" state. Because the joint venture had instituted very strict controls on both company operations and its employees, Diamond was able to observe very close to the oil camp "every single one of the . . . large, threatened bird species of the New Guinea lowlands."

Intrigued as to why this drilling operation adopted such unconventional procedures, which effectively tied sustainable development ideas to profit-making, Diamond asked a Chevron executive, and received the following response: "Bhopal, *Exxon Valdez,* and the North Sea [Shell] oil rig." In other words, it is beginning to make more sense in terms of the bottom line for corporations to conduct business in ecologically sustainable ways than it is to pay out *billions* of dollars in cleanup costs and legal settlement fees. And should industry worldwide have to comply with standards mandated by an international environmental protection agency, these procedures could represent the wave of the future.

## GLOBAL SCENARIOS

The strategies I have outlined are only a sampling of various options available to alleviate the problems I have raised in this book. The main reason for presenting them is to demonstrate that we do indeed have choices. It is only if we choose to do nothing that these problems then become intractable. Although some of the options I suggested may be unpalatable, such as significantly reducing our resource demands on the environment, in some cases we have no other choice if we are to continue as a species. In this final section of the book, I describe a number of global scenarios that various analysts and planners have proposed to try to anticipate problems before they occur.

Scenario planning is based on the selection of key parameters thought to be crucial for future development. One such parameter involves the *structure of international relations*. For example, if the world becomes even more globally integrated than it already is, how would this integration likely occur, and what are its implications? On the other hand, what might be expected if the reverse should take place—if an increasing emphasis were placed on local and regional spheres of influence? How would this type of global structure potentially emerge?

An equally important cross-cutting parameter involves the evaluation of whether various activities contribute to or detract from both *global human welfare and the biosphere*. What activities are likely to be beneficial, which would be destructive, and how might they come about?

Using these two parameters, let us now examine some possible global scenarios.

Allen Hammond (n.d.) offers one global scenario that its proponents argue is both globally integrated and contributes to overall human welfare:

*Market World* reflects a vision of the future that is widely held today. It assumes that free markets, private enterprise, and global market integration are the best way to increase prosperity and improve human welfare. Economic reform, privatization, and deregulation are, in this view, the key to the future.

The *Market World* scenario is consistent with a highly optimistic report commissioned by the Rand Institute (Antón et al. 2001). Although the report does acknowledge certain "concerns and tensions" such as increased class disparities within and between nations, reduced privacy, and threats to indigenous cultures, nevertheless it maintains that a broad, multidisciplinary technology revolution in "Bio/Nano/Material Trends and their Synergies with Information Technology" will promote greater global integration and "significant improvements in human quality of life." "Technology's promise is here today and will march forward."

However, according to another report issued by the Center for Economic and Policy Research (Weisbrot et al. 2001), this positive globally integrated scenario does not square with what globalization has achieved to date, not at least for human welfare. Examining data for all countries in the world, the researchers compared the last twenty years of globalization (1980–2000) to the previous twenty "pre-globalization" years (1960–80) with respect to income growth per capita, life expectancy, infant, child, and adult mortality, literacy, and education. They found that "for economic growth and almost all of the other indicators, the last 20 years have shown a very clear decline in progress as compared with the previous two decades." Although the authors of "The Scorecard on Globalization" acknowledge that these data do not prove that globalization has caused these decreases, they do "present a very strong *prima facie* case that some structural and policy changes implemented during the last two decades [such as the removal of trade barriers and restrictions on foreign direct investment] are at least partially responsible for these declines."

Wendell Berry (2001), writing in the aftermath of the September 11 tragedy, foresees an additional set of problems for globalization relating to control. Given the new reality of a post-September 11 world, globalism may now be characterized as being "held together by long and highly vulnerable lines of communication and supply." In order to protect this global system, an exorbitantly expensive worldwide police force—both physical and virtual—will be required that can only "be effective precisely to the extent that it oversways the freedom and privacy of the citizens of every nation." Because of this new reality, Berry opts for "a decentralized world economy which would have the aim of assuring to every nation and region a local self-sufficiency in life-supporting goods."

Samuel Huntington (1996) also envisions a more decentralized world system, but with more ominous overtones. He maintains that the world and its people will be organized and identified along major "cultural fault lines": Western, Confucian, Japanese, Islamic, Hindu, Slavic-Orthodox, Latin American, and African. Due largely to the effects of globalization such as increasing human interaction among different peoples, the weakening of the nation state as a source of identity, reactions against Western hegemony, and economic regionalism, the world is increasingly being divided into cultural enclaves based on common ethnicity, history, language, tradition, and, says Huntington, "most important, religion." The global vacuum left by the demise of communism and the end of the Cold War is being filled by civilizational sources of conflict. A similar "Fortress World" scenario is projected by Hammond (n.d.), although his model is predicated on the growing gap between rich and poor both between and within nations.

On a more positive note is a "postmaterialist" global scenario. Based on an examination of recent global trends and attitude surveys, Elgin and Le Drew (1997) find emerging support for the postmaterialist scenario as manifested by greater interaction and communication among all peoples, a reduction in materialist values, an evolving spirituality, more global ecological awareness, and a shift toward sustainable ways of living. Although the researchers state that this scenario is not representative of the mainstream, they do maintain that "a new global culture and consciousness have taken root and are beginning to grow in the world."

Which of these scenarios is most likely? Probably none of them. Rather, considered as a whole, they represent *multiple future possibilities*. That is, the structure of human relations worldwide will continue to exhibit signs of both greater integration and an emphasis on local autonomy, and similarly, some human activities will be *con*structive and some *de*structive. What these scenarios do highlight is the importance of these two parameters in assessing social change and planning future policy. For example, while it may be virtually impossible to halt or reverse the trend toward integrated globalism, we *can* modify it in ways that facilitate *balanced* human development, respect for cultural diversity, and environmental sustainability. Indeed, our very survival is contingent upon taking these actions. At the same time, maintaining strong local communities allows us to participate at an individual human level in achieving these same objectives.

The importance of local community cannot be overestimated, for it is at this level that we relate not only to technological systems, but also more importantly to each other and to the natural environment of which we are a part. Although we must take measures at the global level to ensure sustainable development, *it is at the community level that we have the opportunity to reflect upon our own humanness, apart from the technological systems we have created.* And to the extent that we can develop a human reference point for evaluating technology, just perhaps we can regain control over our own development.

## CHAPTER SUMMARY

5.1 Although modernization and convergence theory erred in their prediction of worldwide industrialism, nevertheless convergent industrialism has taken place in the rich developed nations, with the consequence that its cumulative effects on the eco-environment have severely diminished biodiversity which is essential for human survival.

5.2 According to world-systems analysis, various world trends have "the capacity to throw the modern capitalist world-economy into either acute crisis or systemic collapse" (Chase-Dunn and Grimes 1995:403). At issue are growing tensions between core and periphery on matters of entitlement. Should the core nations not heed and deal with these concerns in an equitable manner, certain factions within the periphery have demonstrated that they have both the capability and the resolve to attack the integrated electronic systems of the core that provide essential services, such as energy, water, telecommunications, transportation, finance, and government and emergency services.

5.3 Ogburn's theory of cultural lag identifies technology as the principal problem directly confronting developed countries and indirectly affecting all humankind. Important cultural lags identified in this book are: the inability to control adequately the activities of TNCs; the lack of sufficient controls to stop unauthorized bodies from breaching interdependent electronic systems; technological encroachment upon legally enshrined civil liberties; the impossibility of regulating the *unforeseen* effects of new technologies such as genetic engineering; the absence of an appropriate international agency to regulate the technological exploitation and degradation of the global eco-environment; and the difficulty of curtailing the malevolent release of technologically sophisticated weapons of mass destruction.

5.4 Ellul's technological system theory asserts that the technical structure that supports globalization is not under effective human control and is itself at serious risk of being compromised, either deliberately or unintentionally. In addition, ever expanding, cumulative technology is responsible for turning human wants into needs, such that we are now nearing the ecological limits of the global biosphere. Ellul maintains that technology produces its own imperatives, resulting in humans being unable to evaluate its effects critically and independently.

5.5   Central to the search for resolution of the problems identified above are strategies that appeal to our enlightened self-interest. With regard to the technical problems posed by an interdependent global electronic infrastructure, the only logical solution available is to decouple the overall system at various strategic points. Although this strategy would decrease the desired effects of achieving greater scale, access, speed, and efficiency, it would confine destructive incursions to the locations at which they penetrated the system.

5.6   To ensure that TNCs act in socially and ecologically responsible ways, it would be necessary for all nations to agree on establishing a supranational body to monitor and regulate their activities. Although this strategy would entail an initial loss of sovereignty for nation-states, it could achieve the kind of broad, long-term controls that are being sought. The European Union has successfully adopted this strategy through its formation of a supranational European Commission.

5.7   To deal with the problems of growing global inequality, insecurity, and degradation, the Wordwatch Institute offers a bold proposal: "The United States and other industrial nations should launch a global 'Marshall Plan' to provide everyone on earth with a decent standard of living" (Bell and Renner 2001). Worldwatch estimates that such a plan would cost only 5 percent of the $780 billion now being spent annually on worldwide military expenditures, and would go a long way to countering the growing view that modern globalism represents an elitist, Western-dominated form of economic and cultural imperialism over which most people in the world have little or no control. Many NGOs are advancing related proposals to achieve a more inclusive and sustainable world order.

5.8   Inglehart (1990) maintains that we are experiencing a human values revolution through the process of intergenerational replacement that is realigning human activities more in balance with present global social and ecological reality. Although the evidence is episodic and often limited to verbal declarations rather than overt actions, nevertheless there are notable substantive indications that such a values revolution is having positive impacts on human behavior.

5.9    One encouraging sign of this values revolution is the massive world-wide popular support for an international environmental protection agency that would have the authority to establish global policy on important environmental matters. Other strongly supported proposals include the revision of traditional indicators of human progress, such as GNP and GDP, to include measures of resource depletion and degradation of the habitat, and the institution of ecological tax reform.

5.10   Although, as Ellul states, "unpredictability is one of the general features of technical progress," nevertheless it is possible, and indeed necessary, to evaluate critically the impacts of human activity in terms of broad human welfare and environmental sustainability. Global scenario planning is one such strategy for assessing the possible outcomes of various courses of action. Important in this kind of endeavor is the ability of planners to remove themselves conceptually from the systems they are evaluating in order that they may arrive at policies that are in the best overall interests of the continuing evolution of humankind on planet Earth.

# NOTES

## Chapter 1

1. As the love bug virus story illustrates, there are other methods of attack which are most effective against an interlinked network.
2. Foreign direct investment is "net inflows of investment to acquire a lasting management interest (10 percent or more of voting stock) in an enterprise operating in an economy other than that of the investor" (World Bank 2001:330).
3. Although the number of international migrants now is greater than it ever has been, the massive transatlantic migration from Europe to North America at the turn of the twentieth century was greater as a proportion of the world's population.
4. In point of fact, Mandarin is spoken by more people in the world (885 million) than any other language, followed by Spanish (332 million) and then English (322 million) (*Ethnologue* 1999).
5. Firebaugh (2000) contests these findings. By factoring in countries' population size in cross-national comparisons of income inequality rather than simply comparing individual nations, Firebaugh (2000:334) asserts that the income gap between developed and developing countries "has been relatively stable over recent decades."
6. These data are based on an Internet survey of computer host domains, most of which are country codes. The Internet Software Consortium states that "there is not necessarily any correlation between a host's domain name and where it is actually located," particularly with respect to hosts with the generic domains of .net (47.761 million host computers), .com (44.520 million), .edu (7.754 million), .org (1.321 million), and .gov (0.793 million). However, it is generally acknowledged that virtually all of the hosts with a particular country code are resident in that

country and that the generic domains are in fact U.S. domains (see UNDP 1999:61–66).

## Chapter 2

1. This quotation was originally in French: "Plus ça change, plus c'est la même chose."
2. Life expectancy is "the average number of additional years a person would live if current mortality trends were to continue." It is most often cited as life expectancy at birth. Life span is "the maximum age that human beings could reach under optimum conditions. The human life span appears to be about 100 years" (Haupt and Kane 1980:9).
3. The survey was conducted in Argentina, Chile, East Pakistan (now Bangladesh), India, Israel, and Nigeria.
4. According to the World Bank (2000:291), the per capita gross national products of Singapore, Hong Kong, and Taiwan now place them among the "high-income" economies of the world. Wallerstein (1999) does offer an ex post facto analysis of "The Rise of East Asia."
5. The fifth permanent member of the UN Security Council is China.
6. Note, however, my discussion earlier in Chapter 2 of convergence in world structure: a transformation of the world from many diverse independent nations to one overall interconnected and interdependent global system.
7. In order to minimize the effects of anomalous short-term fluctuations, one subfield of economics known as "long wave theory" analyzes economic activities and events by placing them in as long a historical period as possible. See, for example, Kondratieff, 1984.

## Chapter 3

1. Given the tragic events of September 11, 2001, U.S. Customs may now very well increase its inspection of goods entering the United States.

## Chapter 4

1. One megajoule equals one billion joules. A "joule is the physical measurement for work. One joule corresponds to the work of lifting one kilogram ten centimetres off the ground. It can also be used to measure heat energy" (Wackernagel and Rees 1996:159).

2. The largest global food retailers are: Wal-Mart Stores (USA), Carrefour (France), Kroger (USA), Ahold (Netherlands), Metro (Germany), Albertson's (USA), and Tesco (UK) (Supermarket News n.d.).

3. King (1996) lists the three corporate leaders in the global seafood industry: Resource Group International (Norway), Tyson Seafoods (USA), and Dutch Sea Frozen Fish Foundation (Netherlands).

4. According to the U.S. Environmental Protection Agency, 850,000 industrial plants routinely use hazardous chemicals. In 1999, the EPA reported that these facilities "released 7.7 billion pounds of toxic chemicals during production and disposal into the air and water" (McGinn 2001).

5. Factual information about all the disasters comes from the authors cited in each case.

## Chapter 5

1. A search of Google.com revealed 16,200 Web sites associated with "shop till you drop" and 18,800 related to "shopping + compulsion."

2. In the digital era, threat can be both symbolic and physical. Examples of physical threats are conventional, chemical, and biological weaponry.

3. In 1977, the president of Digital Equipment Corporation stated: "There is no reason anyone would want a computer in their home" (Horton 2000). In 1981, the founder of Microsoft, Bill Gates, said: "640K ought to be enough for anybody." Yet when MS Windows 2000 was introduced two decades later, it required 128,000K to run (Horton 2000).

4. Box 1.1 on the FedEx tracking system is an example of an extranet. Customers who have recently shipped a package via FedEx can gain entry to the controlled access, secure FedEx extranet by entering their unique "tracking number" at the FedEx Web site. Limited only to people with legitimate and verifiable tracking numbers, the FedEx extranet permits customers to determine where en route their particular package is in the FedEx system.

5. For example, the pervasiveness of Microsoft products throughout all electronic information and communications systems contributed to the ability of the love bug virus to infect so many computers worldwide and cause as much damage as it did (see Chapter 1).

6. The alleged perpetrator of the love bug virus was not placed on trial in the Philippines because at the time there were no existent laws against "computer intrusions" (Williams et al. n.d.).

7. Note also the additional point I made in Chapter 3 about corporate taxation in the United States: in 1957, the corporate share of local property tax revenues was 45 percent; thirty years later its share had dropped to 16 percent (Reich 1992:281).

8. A common legal framework would also be effective in curtailing the activities of transnational criminal organizations.

9. The people of the Iroquois Nation took long-term planning extremely seriously: "In our every deliberation, we must consider the impact of our decisions on the next seven generations" (LaDuke 1997). Some activists are presently advocating for a "Seventh-Generation Amendment to the U.S. Constitution" such that "The right of citizens of the United States to use and enjoy air, water, sunlight and other renewable resources determined by the Congress to be common property shall not be impaired, nor shall such use impair their availability for future generations" (LaDuke 1997).

10. Of this $780 billion, 44 percent or $343 billion is the U.S. share.

11. The South Commission was composed of twenty-eight representatives from twenty-six developing countries that together constitute the majority of the world's population.

12. Although this ecological database is now relatively comprehensive, it only extends a few decades into the past, thus hampering both scientific interpretation and the ability to make reliable projections. While it is possible to obtain ecological measurements that extend hundreds and even thousands of years into the past, obviously these data are less complete than what we have now. However, they do provide a better basis for interpretation. Environmental scientist Thomas Sisk (2000) provides an example: "concerns over increasing concentrations of carbon dioxide in the atmosphere, and the implications this has for climate change, have led scientists to examine air trapped in rock and ice thousands of years ago. Analyses of the 'ancient air' have allowed scientists to reconstruct a record of atmospheric $CO_2$ concentrations reaching back 160,000 years. This history has demonstrated that the build-up of $CO_2$ and other greenhouse gases since the industrial revolution is unprecedented, at least since the last ice age."

13. On the issue of citizens and governments being more or less aware of the environmental costs of their activities, Donella Meadows (1997) tells the following story: "There was this subdivision of identical houses, . . . except that the electric meter in some of the houses was installed in the

basement and in others it was installed in the front hall, where the residents could see it constantly, going round faster or slower as they used more or less electricity. Electricity consumption was 30 percent lower in the houses where the meter was in the front hall."

# BIBLIOGRAPHY

American Civil Liberties Union. n.d. Answers to frequently asked questions about Echelon. Accessed 08/05/01 at www.aclu.org/echelonwatch/echfaq3.htm.

American Museum of Natural History. 1998. National survey reveals biodiversity crisis. Accessed 10/01/01 at www.well.com/user/davidu/amnh.html.

Amos, Jonathan. 2000. Questioning global warming. Accessed 11/30/00 at http://news.bbc.co.uk/hi/english/in_depth/sci_tech/2000/climate_change/newsid_1017000/1017204.stm.

Antón, Philip S., Richard Silberglitt, and James Schneider. 2001. *The global technology revolution: Bio/nano/materials trends and their synergies with information technology by 2015.* Accessed 06/07/01 at www.rand.org/publications/MR/MR1307/.

AOL Time Warner. 2001. About us. Accessed 06/27/01 at www.aoltimewarner.com/about/index.html.

Appel, David. 2001. The new uncertainty principle. Accessed 06/22/01 at www.biotech-info.net/uncertainty.html.

Armer, J. Michael and John Katsillis. 1992. Modernization theory. Pp. 1299–1304 in Edgar F. Borgatta and Marie L. Borgatta, eds. *Encyclopedia of sociology*, vol. 3. New York: Macmillan.

Australian Antarctic Division. n.d. Seabird mortality in longline fisheries. Accessed 08/30/01 at www.aad.gov.au/science/AntarcticResearch/AMLR/seabird_bycatch/default_print.asp.

Baker, Linda. 1999. Real wealth: The genuine progress indicator could provide an environmental measure of the planet's health. Accessed 01/06/02 at www.emagazine.com/may-june_1999/0599feat2.html.

Bassis, Luke. n.d. Waste disposal. Accessed 09/17/01 at www.umich.edu/ ~gs265/society/wastedisposal.htm.

Bell, Daniel. 1962. *The end of ideology.* New York: Free Press.

Bell, Dick and Michael Renner. 2001. A new Marshall Plan? Advancing human security and controlling terrorism. Accessed 12/23/01 at www.world watch.org/alerts/011009.html.

Bell Labs. 1999. Wireless Milestones. Accessed 08/23/00 at www.lucent.com/ minds/trends/trends_v4n1/timeline.html.

Berry, Wendell. 2001. Thoughts in the presence of fear. Accessed 12/05/01 at www.oriononline.org/pages/oo/sidebars/America/Berry.html.

Biersteker, Thomas J. 1978. *Distortion of development? Contending perspectives on the multinational corporation.* Cambridge, Mass.: MIT Press.

Biodiversity Unit, Commonwealth of Australia. 1993. Biodiversity Series, Paper No. 1. Accessed 05/29/00 at http://kaos.erin.gov.au/life/general_info/ op1.html.

Bliss, Frank W. 1996. The C4 Program at General Motors. Pp. 309–20 in Carl Machover, ed., *The CAD/CAM handbook.* New York: McGraw-Hill.

Boyden, Stephen. 1996. The need to change our consumption habits. Accessed 02/20/02 at www.ea.gov.au/pcd/economics/consumption.

Brandt Report. 1980. *North-South: A program for survival. Report of the Independent Commission on International Development Issues.* Cambridge, Mass.: MIT Press.

Brinkhoff, Thomas. 2001. The principal agglomerations of the world. Accessed 05/28/01 at www.citypopulation.de/World_j.html?E.

Brinsmead, Thomas S. 1999. How far can we go? The limits of feedback. Accessed 05/02/01 at www.syseng.anu.edu.au/~thomasee/ScienceEssay.html.

*Britannica.* 1999. Earth. Accessed 10/02/00 at www.britannica.com/bcom/ eb/arti.../0,5716,32267+1+31726,00.html.

Brown, L. David, Sanjeev Khagram, Mark H. Moore, and Peter Frumkin. 2000. Globalization, NGOs, and multisectoral relations. Pp. 271–96 in Joseph S. Nye and John D. Donahue, eds., *Governance in a globalizing world.* Cambridge, Mass.: Visions of Governance for the 21st Century.

Brown, Lester R. 2001. Paving the planet: Cars and crops competing for land. Accessed 08/15/01 at www.earth-policy.org/Alerts/Alert12.htm.

Brown, Lester R., Michael Renner, and Brian Halweil. 2000. *Vital Signs 2000:*

*The environmental trends that are shaping our future.* New York: W. W. Norton.

Brundtland Commission. 1987. *Our common future: World Commission on Environment and Development.* Oxford: Oxford University Press.

Buckley, Peter J. 1985. Testing theories of the multinational enterprise. In Peter J. Buckley and Mark Casson, *The economic theory of the multinational enterprise.* London: Macmillan.

Buckley, Walter. 1968. Society as a complex adaptive system. Pp. 490–513 in Walter Buckley, ed. *Modern systems research for the behavioral scientist.* Chicago: Aldine.

Business Environmental Leadership Council. 2000. Joint statement of the Business Environmental Leadership Council. Accessed 11/30/00 at www.pew climate.org/belc/statement.cfm.

Campbell, Duncan. 2000. Echelon: World under watch. Accessed 08/05/01 at www.zdnet.co.uk/news/2000/25/ns-16204.html.

Cantrill, Hadley. 1965. *The pattern of human concerns.* New Brunswick, N.J.: Rutgers University Press.

Carbon Dioxide Information Analysis Center. 2001. Global change data and information system. Accessed 02/20/02 at http://cdiac.esd.ornl.gov/about/intro.html.

Cardoso, F. H. and E. Faletto. 1979 [1969]. *Dependency and development in Latin America.* Berkeley, Calif.: University of California Press.

Carlin, George. n.d. The planet is fine. Accessed 06/26/01 at http://home.onestop.net/agnostic/text.html.

Carson, Rachel. 1954. Home page. Accessed 12/30/01 at www.rachelcarson.org/

CERT. 2001. CERT/CC Statistics 1988–2001. Accessed 05/17/01 at www.cert.org/stats/cert_stats.html.

Chandler, Alfred D., Jr. 1962. *Strategy and structure: Chapters in the history of industrial enterprise.* Cambridge, Mass.: MIT Press.

Chase-Dunn, Christopher and Peter Grimes. 1995. World-systems analysis. *Annual Review of Sociology* 21:387–417.

Clarke, Charles. 2001. A mighty challenge. Accessed 05/17/01 at www.cadcam-magazine.co.uk/htm/_features/090001.htm.

Class Technology. 2001. Holonic systems. Accessed 05/25/01 at www.class.com.au/library/aplss/holonicSystems.html.

Close, James and Greg Playford. 1997. Ozone: the pollution paradox. Accessed 09/24/01 at www.dec.state.ny.us/website/dar/bts/ozone/ozrpt.html.

CNN. 1998. CEOs hear the unpleasant truth about computer security. Accessed 05/17/01 at www.cnn.com/TECH/computing/9804/06/computer.security.pm/.

————. 2000a. "ILOVEYOU" computer bug bites hard, spreads fast. Accessed 08/14/00 at www.cnn.com/2000/TECH/computing/05/04/iloveyou.01/index.html.

————. 2000b. Clues lead to ILOVEYOU writer's older, cruder work. Accessed 08/14/00 at www.cnn.com/2000/TECH/computing/05/06/iloveyou.02/index.html.

————. 2000c. Hackers attack Microsoft network. Accessed 05/17/01 at www.cnn.com/2000/WORLD/europe/10/27/usa.microsoft/.

————. 2000d. False sense of cybersecurity a costly problem for U.S. Accessed 05/25/01 at www.cnn.com/2000/TECH/computing/06/20/false.cybersecurity.idg/index.html.

————. 2001. Pentagon says it is under daily computer attack. Accessed 05/25/01 at www.cnn.com/2001/TECH/internet/05/18/pentagon.reut/index.html.

Cobb, Clifford, Ted Halstead, and Jonathan Rowe. 1995. If the GDP is up, why is America down? *Atlantic Monthly* 276(4), October, pp. 59–78.

Collins, Keith. 2001. Statement before the U.S. Senate Committee on Appropriations. Accessed 09/02/01 at www.usda.gov/oce/speeches/051701co.html.

CommerceNet. 2000. Worldwide Internet Population. Accessed 10/05/00 at www.commerce.net/research/stats/wwstats.html.

Committee on Science. 2001. Cyber security—How can we protect American computers from attack? Accessed 12/03/01 at www.house.gov/science/full/oct10/full_charter_101001.htm.

Computer Associates. 2000. Virus Information Center. Accessed 05/17/00 at www.cai.com/virusinfo/virusalert.htm.

Computer Security Institute. 2002. Cyber crime bleeds U.S. organizations, survey shows. Accessed 04/18/02 at www.gosci.com/press/20020907.html.

Computing Fundamentals. 2001. General computing terms. Accessed 08/17/01 at http://whatis.techtarget.com/definition/0,289893,sid9_gci212620,00.html.

Corporate Watch. 1998. OECD Says: No MAI in April. Accessed 10/12/00 at www.corpwatch.org/trac/corner/worldnews/other/other110.html.

Cottrell, W. F. 1939. Of time and the railroader. *American Sociological Review* 4:190–98.

Council of Canadians. 1998. An update on MAI negotiations: October 14, 1998. Accessed 10/12/00 at www.canadians.org/campaigns/campaigns-maipub04.html.

Council of Europe. 2002. Convention on Cybercrime. Accessed 02/21/02 at http://conventions.coe.int/treaty/en/summaries/html/185.html.

Cross, Stephen E. 2000. The vulnerability of the Internet. Accessed 12/03/01 at http://usinfo.state.gov/topical/global/ecom/0051807.htm.

CSIS. n.d. Global Organized Crime Project. Accessed 06/01/01 at www.csis.org/goc/.

DARPA. 1998. Survivability of information systems. Accessed 05/31/01 at www.darpa.mil/ito/Solicitations/CBD_9804.html.

Davis, Kingsley. 1974. The migration of human populations. Pp. 53–65 in *The human population*. San Francisco: W. H. Freeman.

Davis, Nancy Y. 1996. The *Exxon Valdez* oil spill, Alaska. Accessed 08/25/01 at www.unu.edu/unupress/unupbooks/uu211e/uu211e01.htm.

Diamond, Jared. 1999a. *Guns, germs, and steel*. New York: W. W. Norton.

———. 1999b. Paradise and oil. *Discover* 20(3):94–112. Acceessed 01/09/02 at EBSCO Host (www.ebsco.com).

Diebold, John. 1990. *The innovators: The discoveries, inventions, and breakthroughs of our time*. New York: Truman Talley Books/Plume.

Dore, Ronald. 1973. *British factory – Japanese factory: The origins of national diversity in industrial relations*. Berkeley, Calif.: University of California Press.

Dunlap, Riley E. 1994. International attitudes towards environment and development. Pp. 115–26 in Helge Ole Bergesen and Georg Parmann, eds., *Green Globe yearbook of international co-operation on environment and development*. Oxford: Oxford University Press.

*Economist*. 2000. No hothouse deal. Accessed 11/29/00 at www.economist.com/agenda/displayStory.cfm?Story_ID=435994.

Edwards, John. 2001. Government—help or hindrance to deployment of teleworking? Accessed 01/18/02 at www.cefrio.qc.ca/allocutions/presentations/johnedwards.ppt.

Edwards, Michael. 1999. *Future positive: International cooperation in the 21st century*. London: Earthscan.

Einstein, Albert. 1936. Physics and reality. *Journal of the Franklin Institute* 221(3). Reprinted in Carl Seelig, ed. 1954. *Ideas and opinions by Albert Einstein*. New York: Wings Books, pp. 290–323.

———. 1954 (1941). The common language of science. Pp. 335–37 in Carl Seelig, ed., *Ideas and opinions by Albert Einstein*. New York: Wing Books.

*Electronics Industry Yearbook*. 2000. Numbers of computers in use worldwide, 1991–2000. Accessed 11/14/01 at www.e-insite.net/contents/pdf/cominuse.pdf.

El-Farra, Narmeen. 1996. Arabs and the media. Accessed 06/28/01 at www.calstatela.edu/faculty/sfischo/Arabs.html.

Elgin, Duane and Coleen LeDrew. 1997. *Global consciousness change: Indicators of an emerging paradigm*. Accessed 12/31/01 at www.awakeningearth.org/reports/gcc/gcnine.html.

Ellul, Jacques. 1973 (1964). *The technological society*. New York: Alfred A. Knopf.

———. 1980 (1977). *The technological system*. New York: Continuum.

———. 1981. *Perspectives on our age*. Toronto: Canadian Broadcasting Corporation.

———. 1990. *The technological bluff*. Grand Rapids, Mich.: William B. Eerdmans.

Environmental History Timeline. n.d. Accessed 09/09/01 at www.runet.edu/~wkovarik/hist1/timeline.new.html.

Environmental Protection Agency. 2000. *National air pollutant emission trends, 1900–1998*. Accessed 09/10/01 at www.epa.gov/ttn/chief/trends98/browse.html.

———. 2001. Produce less waste by practicing the 3 Rs. Accessed 01/04/02 at www.epa.gov/epaoswer/non-hw/muncpl/reduce.htm.

*Ethnologue*. 1996. Geographic distribution of living languages, 1996. Accessed 06/16/00 at www.sil.org/ethnologue/distribution.html.

———. 1999. Top 100 languages by population. Accessed 06/16/00 at www.sil.org/ethnologue/top100.html.

European Commission. 2000. Dependability initiative. Accessed 05/30/01 at http://dsa-isis.jrc.it/EDI-Hub/.

European Parliament. 1998. An appraisal of the technologies of political control. Accessed 08/05/01 at www.europarl.eu.int/stoa/publi/166499/execsum_en.htm?redirected=1.

European Union. 2001. Internal market. Accessed 12/21/01 at http://europa.eu.int/scadplus/leg/en/lvb/170000.htm.

*Eurotimes*. 2000a. EU history. Accessed 09/29/00 at www.ireland.com/eurotimes/history/fifties.htm.

———. 2000b. The Council of the European Union. Accessed 09/29/00 at www.ireland.com/eurotimes/guide/council.htm.

Evans, Peter B. 1992. Global systems analysis. Pp. 772–78 in Edgar F. Borgatta and Marie L. Borgatta, eds., *Encyclopedia of sociology*, vol. 2. New York: Macmillan.

Evans, Peter B. and John D. Stephens. 1988. Development and the world economy. Pp. 739–73 in Neil J. Smelser, ed., *Handbook of sociology*. Newbury Park, Calif.: Sage.

FAIR. 2000. AOL-Time Warner: Dawn of a golden age, or a blow to media diversity? Accessed 06/29/01 at http:www.fair.org/reports/aol-time-warner.html.

Firebaugh, Glenn. 2000. The trend in between-nation income inequality. *Annual Review of Sociology* 26:323–39.

Fisher, Julie. 1993. *The road from Rio: Sustainable development and the nongovernmental movement in the third world*. Westport, Conn.: Praeger.

———. 1998. *Nongovernments: NGOs and the political development of the third world*. West Hartford, Conn.: Kumarian Press.

Fitzpatrick, John and Chris Newton. 1998. Assessment of the world's fishing fleet. Accessed 08/30/01 at www.greenpeace.org/~oceans/globaloverfishing/assessmentfishingfleet.html.

Flower, Joe. 1997. The future of the Internet: an overview. Pp. 10–17 in David Bender et al., eds., *The future of the Internet*. San Diego, Calif.: Greenhaven.

Fligstein, Neil. 1990. *The transformation of corporate control*. Cambridge, Mass.: Harvard University Press.

Form, William. 1979. Comparative industrial sociology and the convergence hypothesis. *Annual Review of Sociology* 5:1–25.

*Fortune*. 2000. The *Fortune* Global 500. *Fortune* 142(3):227–F–24.

————. 2001. The *Fortune* Global 500. *Fortune*, 23 July:144–F–24.

Friends of the Earth. 1998. Citizens' guide to environmental tax shifting. Accessed 02/08/02 at www.foe.org/envirotax/taxbooklet/.

Furukawa, Shun'ichi. 2000. An institutional framework for Japanese crisis management. *Journal of Contingencies and Crisis Management* 8(1):3–14.

Gereffi, Gary. 1994. The international economy and economic development. Pp. 206–33 in Neil J. Smelser and Richard Swedberg, eds., *The handbook of economic sociology*. Princeton, N.J.: Princeton University Press.

Gerth, H. H. and C. Wright Mills, eds. 1958. *From Max Weber: Essays in sociology*. New York: Oxford University Press.

Gibbs, Jack P. 1994. *A theory about control*. Boulder, Colo.: Westview.

Gilder, George. 1989. *Microcosm: The quantum revolution in economics and technology*. New York: Simon & Schuster.

Gill, Stephen and David Law. 1988. *The global political economy*. Baltimore, Md.: Johns Hopkins University Press.

Gilman, Sidney. 1983. *The competitive dynamics of container shipping*. Aldershot, U.K.: Gower.

Global Climate Coalition. 2000. Collapse signals need for new direction in climate policy. Accessed 11/30/00 at www.globalclimate.org/index.htm.

GM. 2001. Company profile. Accessed 05/17/01 at www.gm.com/company/corp_info/profiles/.

Goode, Barbara G. 2000. Ground zero of the next big thing. Accessed 05/01/01 at www.sensorsmag.com/articles/1100/4/main.shtml.

Hagedorn, Robert and R. Alan Hedley. 1994. Social research. Pp. 23–52 in Robert Hagedorn, ed., *Sociology*. Toronto: Harcourt Brace.

Hall, A. D. and R. E. Fagen. 1968. Definition of system. Pp. 81–92 in Walter Buckley, ed., *Modern systems research for the behavioral scientist*. Chicago: Aldine.

Hammond, Allen. n.d. *Which world? Scenarios for the 21st century*. Accessed 01/10/02 at http://mars3.gps.caltech.edu/whichworld/explore/scenarios_top.html.

Haupt, Arthur and T. T. Kane. 1980. *Population handbook: International edition*. Washington, D.C.: Population Reference Bureau.

Hedley, R. Alan. 1978. Measurement: Social research strategies and their relevance to grading. *Teaching Sociology* 6(1):21–29.

————. 1992. *Making a living: Technology and change.* New York: HarperCollins.

————. 1994. How do you know? Epistemological aspects of sociology. *The annals of the international institute of sociology* 4:117–33.

————. 1999. Transnational corporations and their regulation: Issues and strategies. *International Journal of Comparative Sociology* 40:215–30.

————. 2000. Convergence in natural, social, and technical systems: A critique. *Current Science* 79(5):592–601.

Helvarg, David. 1997. Full nets—empty seas. Accessed 08/30/01 at www.thirdworldtraveler.com/Environment/FullNets_EmptySeas.html.

Hendrickson, Mary, William D. Heffernan, Philip H. Howard, and Judith B. Heffernan. 2001. Consolidation in food retailing and dairy. Accessed 08/30/01 at www.nfu.org/images/heffernan.pdf.

Herman, Amos. 1983. *Shipping conferences.* Deventer, Neth.: Kluwer, Law and Taxation.

Heylighen, F. 1991. The principle of selective variety. Accessed 08/13/01 at http://pespmc1.vub.ac.be/SELVAR.html.

Heywood, V. H. and I. Baste. 1995. Pp. 1–19 in V. H. Heywood and R. T. Watson, eds., *Global biodiversity assessment.* Cambridge: Cambridge University Press.

Hofstede, Geert. 1980. *Culture's consequences: International differences in work-related values.* Beverly Hills, Calif.: Sage.

Horton, William. 2000. Horseless-carriage thinking. Accessed 11/15/01 at www.asis.org/Conferences/Summit2000/horton/Horton.pdf.

Hudack, Mike. 1999. Explosive growth next six years. Accessed 05/23/01 at www.nwo.net/osall/News/Old_News/Industry_Growth/industry_growth.html.

Huntington, Samuel P. 1996. *The clash of civilizations and the remaking of world order.* New York: Simon and Schuster.

IBOY. 2001. International Biodiversity Observation Year 2001–2002. Accessed 06/24/01 at www.nrel.colostate.edu/IBOY/index2.html.

ICAO. 2001. Growth in air traffic projected to continue. Access 06/24/01 at www.icao.org/icao/en/pio200106.htm.

ICTA. 2000. *International crime threat assessment.* Accessed 05/23/01 at www.terrorism.com/documents/pub45270/pub45270index.html.

Idealist. 2000. Accessed 10/02/00 at www.idealist.org/.

IISDnet. 2000. Accessed 10/02/00 at http://iisd1.iisd.ca/about/default.htm.

Inglehart, Ronald. 1990. *Culture shift in advanced industrial society*. Princeton, N.J.: Princeton University Press.

Inkeles, Alex and D. H. Smith. 1974. *Becoming modern: Individual change in six developing countries*. Cambridge, Mass.: Harvard University Press.

InterAction. 2000. Accessed 09/29/00 at www.interaction.org/.

International Telework Association. 2001. Telework America 2001. Accessed 01/18/02 at www.telecommute.org/twa/twa2001/newsrelease.htm.

Internet Chicago. 2002. Intranets/extranets. Accessed 02/04/02 at http://home.icsp.net/internetchicago/intraextra.htm.

Internet Society. 2001. All about the Internet Society. Accessed 12/17/01 at www.isoc.org/isoc/.

Internet Software Consortium. 2002. Internet Domain Survey, January 2002. Accessed 02/25/02 at www.isc.org/ds/WWW-200201/index.html.

IPCC. 2001. Climate change 2001: The scientific basis. Summary for policymakers. Accessed 01/27/02 at www.ipcc.ch/.

ITU. 2000. ITU Telecommunication Indicators Update. Accessed 10/10/00 at www.itu.int/journal/200006/E/html/indicat.htm.

Kahn, Robert E. 1999. Evolution of the Internet. Pp. 157–64 in *World communication and information report 1999–2000*. Paris: UNESCO.

Karr, Alphonse. 1849. *Les guêpes*. Cited in John Bartlett. 1980. *Familiar quotations*. Boston: Little, Brown, p. 514.

Keister, Lisa A. and Stephanie Moller. 2000. Wealth inequality in the United States. *Annual review of sociology* 26:63–81.

Keniston, Kenneth. 1998. Politics, culture and software. Accessed 06/13/00 at http://web.mit.edu/kken/Public/papers2.htm.

Kentor, Jeffrey. 1998. The long-term effects of foreign investment dependence on economic growth, 1940–1990. *American Journal of Sociology* 103:1024–46.

Kerr, Clark, John T. Dunlop, Frederick H. Harbison, and Charles A. Myers. 1964 (1960). *Industrialism and industrial man*. New York: Oxford University Press.

King, Rob. 1996. Sinking fast: how factory trawlers are destroying U.S. fisheries. Accessed 08/30/01 at www.greenpeace.org/~oceans/globaloverfishing/

sinkingfast.html.

Kondratieff, Nikolai. 1984. *The long wave cycle.* New York: Richardson & Snyder.

Korten, David C. 2001. *When corporations rule the world.* Bloomfield, Conn., and San Francisco: Kumarian Press and Berrett-Koehler.

Kostoff, Ronald L. 2001. Predicting biowarfare agents takes on priority. Accessed 11/26/01 at www.the-scientist.com/yr2001/nov/comm_011126.html.

LaDuke, Winona. 1997. We need a seventh generation amendment. Accessed 01/07/02 at www.semcosh.org/7th.htm.

Laytner, Lance. 2001. Killer keystrokes. *South China Morning Post,* 3 November, p. 3.

Lazaroff, Cat. 2001. Lawsuit targets damaging dredges in scallop fishery. Accessed 08/30/01 at http://ens.lycos.com/ens/jun2001/2001L-06-06-06.html.

Leakey, Richard and Roger Lewin. 1995. *The sixth extinction.* Accessed 10/01/01 at www.well.com/user/davidu/sixthextinction.html.

Leiner, Barry M. et al. 2000. A brief history of the Internet. Accessed 05/11/02 at www.isoc.org/internet/history/brief.shtml.

Lenski, Gerhard and Jean Lenski. 1982. *Human societies: An introduction to macrosociology.* New York: McGraw-Hill.

Leuprecht, Peter. 1998. Canadian language model: Thoughts of a European. Accessed 06/16/00 at www.tbs-sct.gc.ca/ollo/symposium/english/conferencier/dis_leuprecht.html.

Libicki, Martin C. 1995. *Information technology standards: Quest for the common byte.* Accessed 05/22/01 at www/pirp.harvard.edu/pubs_pdf/libicki/libicki_quest/quest.htm.

Love Canal Collection. 1998. Background on the Love Canal. Accessed 08/24/01 at http://ublib.buffalo.edu/libraries/projects/lovecanal/background_lovecanal.html.

Machover, Carl, ed. 1996. *The CAD/CAM handbook.* New York: McGraw-Hill.

MacKeen, Dawn. 2000. U.S. clash on global warming. Accessed 11/29/00 at www.salon.com/news/feature/2000/11/17/emissions/index.html.

Marshall, George C. 1997 (1947). Against hunger, poverty, desperation and chaos. *Foreign Affairs* 76(3):160.

Maruyama, Sadami. 1996. Responses to Minamata disease. Accessed 08/24/01 at www.unu.edu/unupress/unupbooks/uu211e/uu211e05.htm.

MCBI. 1998. Troubled waters: A call for action. Accessed 10/01/01 at www.mcbi.org/twaters/release.html.

McGinn, Anne Plant. 2001. Detoxifying terrorism. Received from wwnews@crest.org on 11/19/01.

McNeely, J. A. et al. 1995. Human influences on biodiversity. Pp. 711–821 in V. H. Heywood and R. T. Watson, eds., *Global biodiversity assessment.* Cambridge: Cambridge University Press.

Meadows, Donella H. 1997. Places to intervene in a system. Accessed 01/14/02 at www.wholeearthmag.com/ArticleBin/109.html.

Merton, Robert K. 1949. *Social theory and social structure.* Glencoe, Ill.: Free Press.

———. 1973. Foreword. Pp. v–viii in Jacques Ellul, *The technological society.* New York: Alfred A. Knopf.

Microsoft. 2001. Microsoft Security Bulletin MS01-023. Accessed 05/30/01 at www.microsoft.com/technet/security/bulletin/MS01-023.asp.

Miyawaki, Raisuke. 1999. International cooperation to combat cybercrime and cyberterrorism. Accessed 06/01/01 at www.oas.org/juridico/english/miyawaki.htm.

Moore, Wilbert E. 1963. *Social change.* Englewood Cliffs, N.J.: Prentice-Hall.

Morgan, Fiona. 2000. Europe to U.S.: No deal on global warming. Accessed 11/29/00 at www.salon.com/news/feature/2000/11/28/kyoto_protocol/index.html?CP=YAH&DN=110.

Morris, Martina and Bruce Western. 1999. Inequality in earnings at the close of the twentieth century. *Annual Review of Sociology* 25:623–57.

Mowlana, Hamid. 1996. *Global communication in transition: The end of diversity?* Thousand Oaks, Calif.: Sage.

MSNBC. 2000. What next after climate talks fail? Accessed 11/29/00 at www.msnbc.com/news/491989.asp?cp1=1.

Multichannel Video Compliance Guide. 2000. Consumer, public interest groups oppose AOL Time Warner merger. Accessed 06/29/01 at www.dc.thompson.com/tpg/info/tube/tubejune.html.

Murdoch, William W. 1980. *The poverty of nations: The political economy of hunger and population.* Baltimore, Md.: Johns Hopkins University Press.

Naisbitt, John. 1982. *Megatrends: Ten new directions transforming our lives.* New York: Warner.

Nakamura, Akira. 2000. Different contingencies and shortage of crisis management in public administration: An introduction to Japan's crisis management. *Journal of Contingencies and Crisis Management* 8(1):1–2.

*Nando Times.* 2001. Technology: Defense Department taking greater steps to protect computers. Accessed 05/18/01 at www.nandotimes.com/technology/story/10401p-236854c.html.

NASA. 1996. The Earth Observing System: Understanding planet Earth. Accessed 09/27/00 at http://pao.gsfc.nasa.gov/gsfc/service/gallery/fact_sheets/earthsci/fs-96(06)-009.htm.

NASA. 2000. Sputnik and the dawn of the space age. Accessed 09/27/00 at www.hq.nasa.gov/office/pao/History/sputnik/.

National Archives and Records Administration. 1997. The Marshall Plan. Accessed 12/23/01 at www.nara.gov/exhall/featured-document/marshall/marshall.html.

*New Scientist.* 1997. The hole that will not mend. Accessed 09/24/01 at http://dhushara.tripod.com/book/diversit/extra/cfcr.htm.

*New York Times.* 2001. Experts say key Internet servers vulnerable to attack. Accessed 11/14/01 at www.nytimes.com/reuters/technology/tech-tech-icann-security.html?todaysheadlines.

NGO-NET. 2000. Accessed 10/02/00 at www.ngo-net.org/main/index-us.html.

NIPC. n.d. National Infrastructure Protection Center. Accessed 05/30/01 at www.nipc.gov/.

———. 2001. Advisory 01-011. Accessed 05/30/01 at www.nipc.gov/warnings/advisories/2001/01-011.htm.

Nua Internet Surveys. 2001. How many online? Accessed 01/18/02 at www.nua.ie/surveys/how_many_online/index.html.

Nuclear Energy Agency. 2001. Chernobyl fifteen years on. Accessed 08/25/01 at www.nea.fr/html/rp/chernobyl/chernobyl.html.

OECD. 1993. *Tax aspects of transfer pricing within multinational enterprises: The United States' proposed regulations.* Paris: Author.

———. 1995. Multilateral Agreement on Investment. Accessed 05/11/02 at www.oecd.org/daf/investment/fdi/mai/mairap95.htm.

———. 2000a. Membership. Accessed 09/29/00 at www.oecd.org/about/general/member-countries.htm.

―――. 2000b. OECD themes. Accessed 09/29/00 at www.oecd.org/activities/.

―――. 2000c. *OECD in figures*. Paris: Author.

Ogburn, William Fielding. 1922. *Social change with respect to culture and original nature*. New York: B.W. Huebsch.

―――. 1964 (1956). Technology as environment. Pp. 78–85 in Otis Dudley Duncan, ed., *William F. Ogburn on culture and social change*. Chicago: University of Chicago Press.

―――. 1964 (1957). Cultural lag as theory. Pp. 86–95 in Otis Dudley Duncan, ed., *William F. Ogburn on culture and social change*. Chicago: University of Chicago Press.

Ohmae, Kenichi. 1991. *The borderless world: Power and strategy in the interlinked economy*. Hammersmith, U.K.: Fontana.

Open Doors. 1999a. Fast facts. Accessed 10/05/00 at www.opendoorsweb.org/Press/fast_facts.htm.

―――. 1999b. 113,959 U.S. students have studied abroad this year. Accessed 10/05/00 at www.opendoorsweb.org/Lead%20Stories/stab1.htm.

Orr, Rena and Douglas Powell. 2001. BSE summary and fact sheet. Accessed 05/11/02 at www.foodsafetynetwork.ca/animal/bse-summary.htm.

Parenti, Michael. 1993. *Inventing the politics of news media reality*. New York: St. Martin's Press.

PBS. 2001. Notable hacks. Accessed 06/05/01 at www.pbs.org/wgbh/pages/frontline/shows/hackers/whoare/notable.html.

Peace Corps. n.d. About Peace Corps. Accessed 12/28/01 at www.peacecorps.gov/about/index.cfm.

Pearson, Roy and John Fossey. 1983. *World deep-sea container shipping: A geographical, economic and statistical analysis*. Aldershot, U.K.: Gower.

Phillips, Prasad. 1996. *Jules Verne, around the world in eighty days*. Accessed 09/26/00 at www.people.virginia.edu/~mtp0f/flips/review3.html.

Pianin, Eric. 2001. U.S. aims to pull out of warming treaty. Accessed 01/27/02 at www.washingtonpost.com/ac2/wp-dyn?pagename=articles&node=&contentId=A2354-2001 Mar27.

Piel, Gerard. 1992. *Only one world: Our own to make and to keep*. New York: W. H. Freeman.

Prabhu, Vitall. n.d. Distributed control systems. Accessed 05/25/01 at www.ie.psu.edu/people/faculty/prabhu/dcon/distcon.htm.

Public Citizen. 1998a. MAI provisions and proposals: An analysis of the April 1998 text. Accessed 10/12/00 at www.citizen.org/pctrade/MAI/What%20is/ ANALYSIS.htm.

———. 1998b. Joint NGO statement. Accessed 10/12/00 at www.citizen.org/ pctrade/MAI/Sign-ons/mai600ngo.htm.

Purdum, Todd S. and David E. Sanger. 2002. Two top officials offer stern talk on U.S. policy. Accessed 02/04/02 at www.nytimes.com/2002/02/02/international/02DIPL.html?todaysheadlines.

Rachel Carson Council. 2001. Home page. Accessed 12/30/01 at http:// members.aol.com/rccouncil/ourpage/.

Reich, Robert B. 1992. *The work of nations: Preparing ourselves for 21st century capitalism*. New York: Vintage.

Reichenbach, Hans. 1964. *The rise of scientific philosophy*. Berkeley, Calif.: University of California Press.

Schwartz, John. 2001. The land of monopolies. Accessed 02/28/02 at www.nytimes.com/2001/07/01/weekinreview/01SCHW.html?todays headlines.

Scott, W. Richard. 1998. *Organizations: Rational, natural, and open systems*. Upper Saddle River, N.J.: Prentice-Hall.

Sen, Amartya. 1999. *Development as freedom*. New York: Alfred A. Knopf.

Serling, Robert J. 1982. *The jet age*. Alexandria, Va.: Time-Life.

Shrivastava, Paul. 1996. Long-term recovery from Bhopal crisis. Accessed 08/24/01 at www.unu.edu/unupress/unupbooks/uu211e/uu211e0c.htm.

Simon, Herbert A. 1987. The steam engine and the computer: What makes technology revolutionary? *Computers and People* (11–12):7–11.

Sisk, Thomas D. 2000. Toward a land-use history of North America: A context for understanding environmental change. Accessed 01/04/02 at http:// biology.usgs.gov/luhna/chap1.html.

Snow, C. P. 1971. *Public Affairs*. London: Macmillan.

South Commission. 1990. *The Challenge to the South: The report of the South Commission*. New York: Oxford University Press.

Steel, Brent S. 2000. Competing natural resource paradigms in the West. Accessed 31/12/01 at http://osu.orst.edu/dept/pol_sci/fac/steel/cl/ps507/

read1.htm.

Supermarket News. n.d. SN global top 25. Accessed 02/01/02 at www.super marketnews.com/sntop25.htm.

Suzuki, David and Holly Dressel. 1999. *From naked ape to superspecies.* Toronto: Stoddart.

Sweet, Lois. 2000. Room to live: Healthy cities for the urban century. Accessed 05/29/01 at www.idrc.ca/Media/Urbanization_e.html.

Third World Network. 2000. Accessed 10/02/00 at www.twnside.org.sg.

Tinbergen, Jan. 1976. *Reshaping the international order.* New York: Dutton.

de Tocqueville, Alexis. 1956 [1840]. *Democracy in America.* New York: Mentor.

———. 1957 [1835]. *Journeys to England and Ireland.* London: Faber and Faber.

TV Free America. 1998. TV statistics. Accessed 07/31/01 at www.oc-profamnet.org/media/tv_statistics.htm.

UN. 1948. *Universal declaration of human rights.* Accessed 10/17/00 at www.un.org/Overview/rights.html.

———. 1998. Press Release: POP/656. Accessed 06/21/01 at http://srch1.un.org/plweb-cgi/fastweb?state_id=993154325&view=unsearch& docrank=1&.

———. 2000a. The UN in brief. Accessed 09/25/00 at www.un.org/Overview/brief.html.

———. 2000b. Security Council. Accessed 11/24/00 at www.un.org/documents/scinfo.htm.

UN Commission on Human Settlements. 2001. Global urban observatory databases. Accessed 01/29/02 at www.unchs.org/guo/gui/analysis.htm.

UNCTAD. 1998. *World investment report 1998.* New York: United Nations Conference on Trade and Development.

———. 1999. *World investment report 1999.* New York: United Nations Conference on Trade and Development.

———. 2000. *World investment report 2000.* New York: United Nations Conference on Trade and Development.

UNCTC. 1990. *The new code environment.* New York: Series A, No. 16, United Nations Centre on Transnational Corporations.

UNDP. 1998. *Human development report 1998*. New York: Oxford University Press.

———. 1999. *Human development report 1999*. New York: Oxford University Press.

———. 2000. *Human development report 2000*. New York: Oxford University Press.

———. 2001. Human development report 2001. New York: Oxford University Press.

UNEP. 2000. Basel basics. Accessed 09/17/01 at www.basel.int/pub/basics.html

UNESCAP. 2000. Solid waste. Accessed 09/05/01 at www.unescap.org/stat/meet/envir/stwes2-2waste.02.pdf.

Union of Concerned Scientists. 2000. World scientists' warning to humanity. Accessed 06/12/01 at www.ucsusa.org/about/warning.html.

United World Colleges. n.d. United World Colleges overview. Accessed 12/28/01 at www.uwc.org/uwcoverview.html.

*USA Today*. 1999. Security on trial in case of online Citibank heist. Accessed 12/07/00 at www.usatoday.com/life/cyber/tech/ctb284.htm.

U.S. Department of State. 2002. Anthrax. Accessed 02/02/02 at http://usinfo.state.gov/topical/hiv/anthrax.htm.

UVic International. 2000. Accessed 10/04/00 at www.uvic.ca/international.html.

Veblen, Thorstein. 1973 [1899]. *The theory of the leisure class*. Boston: Houghton Mifflin.

Verhovek, Sam Howe. 2000. Bill Gates turns skeptical on digital solution's scope. Accessed 11/03/00 at www.nytimes.com/2000/11/03/technology/03GATE.html.

Virus Bulletin. 2000. VBS/Love Let. Accessed 05/17/00 at www.virusbtn.com/VirusInformation/lovelet.html.

———. 2001. WildList index. Accessed 05/18/01 at www.virusbtn.com/WildLists/.

Wackernagel, Mathis and William E. Rees. 1996. *Our ecological footprint*. Gabriola Island, B.C.: New Society.

Wackernagel, Mathis et al. 2001. Ecological footprint of nations: December 2001 update. Accessed 02/02/02 at www.rprogress.org/.

Wallerstein, Immanuel. 1974. *The modern world-system: Capitalist agricul-*

*ture and the origins of the European world-economy in the sixteenth century.* New York: Academic Press.

————. 1999. The rise of East Asia, or the world-system in the twenty-first century. Pp. 34–48 in Immanuel Wallerstein, *The end of the world as we know it: Social science for the twenty-first century.* Minneapolis, Mn.: University of Minnesota Press.

Weber, Max. 1947. *The theory of social and economic organization.* New York: Oxford University Press.

Weier, John. 2000. Reaping what we sow. Accessed 08/27/01 at http://earthobservatory.nasa.gov/Study/Lights2/.

Weisbrot, Mark et al. 2001. The scorecard on globalization 1980-2000: Twenty years of diminished progress. Accessed 09/20/01 at www.cepr.net/globalization/scorecard_on_globalization.htm.

WHAT. 2000. Accessed 10/02/00 at www.what.org.uk/index.htm.

Whitehouse, David. 2000. Sun's warming influence "under-estimated". Accessed 11/30/00 at http://news.bbc.co.uk/hi/english/sci/tech/newsid_1045000/1045327.stm.

Wilikens, Marc and Tom Jackson. 1997. Survivability of networked information systems and infrastructures. Accessed 05/30/01 at http://dsa-isis.jrc.it/EDI-Hub/pdf/survivability.pdf.

Williams, Phil, Casey Dunlevy, and Tim Shimeall. n.d. Intelligence analysis for Internet security. Accessed 12/03/01 at www.cert.org/archive/html/Analysis10a.html.

Wilson, Charles Erwin. 1952. Statement to the Senate Armed Forces Committee. In John Bartlett, ed., *Familiar quotations.* Boston: Little, Brown, 1980:817.

Wilson, Edward O. 1999. The final countdown. Accessed 08/14/01 at http://magazine.audubon.org/biodiversity.html.

WINS. 1998. Wireless Integrated Network Sensors. Accessed 05/02/01 at www.janet.ucla.edu/WINS/wins_intro.htm.

WITSA. 1999. Critical information protection: A framework for government/industry dialogue. Accessed 06/01/01 at www.witsa.org/papers/cip.htm.

————. 2001. About WITSA. Accessed 12/17/01 at www.witsa.org/about/.

Wolfensohn, James D. 1997. *The challenge of inclusion.* Address to the Board of Governors of The World Bank Group, Hong Kong, China.

World Bank. 1987. *World Development Report 1987*. New York: Oxford University Press.

―――. 1998. Implications of the year 2000 problem. Accessed 05/24/01 at www.worldbank.org/infodev/y2k/toolkit/Implications.htm.

―――. 2000. *World development report 1999/2000*. Oxford: Oxford University Press.

―――. 2001. *World development report 2000/2001*. Oxford: Oxford University Press.

World Resources Institute. 2000. WRI conference explores new businesses to transform global digital divide into dividends. Accessed 10/17/00 at www.igc.org/wri/press/dd_transform.html.

World Tourism Organization. 2000. Tourism highlights 2000. Accessed 10/05/00 at www.world-tourism.org/esta/monograf/highligh/HL_MK.htm.

Worldwatch Institute. 1999. Plant losses threaten future food supplies and health care. Accessed 08/26/01 at www.worldwatch.org/alerts/990916.html.

World Wide Fund for Nature. 1996. The rise and fall of modern fisheries. Accessed 08/30/01at www.panda.org/resources/publications/water/fishfile2/fish33.htm.

Woytinsky, W. S. and E. S. Woytinski. 1955. *World commerce and governments: Trends and outlook*. New York: Twentieth Century Fund.

WTO. 2000. The WTO in brief. Accessed 10/11/00 at www.wto.org/english/thewto_e/whatis_e/inbrief_e/inbr00_e.htm.

ZDNet. 1999. Microsoft on trial: MS "crossed the line" says economist. Accessed 05/17/00 at www.zdnet.co.uk/news/1999/0/ns-6525.html.

# INDEX

# ABOUT THE AUTHOR

**ALAN HEDLEY,** Professor of Sociology at the University of Victoria in Canada, has published extensively in the areas of technology, social change, and development. His previous book, *Making a Living: Technology and Change*, involved a historical analysis of industrialization in Britain, the United States, and Japan. In 1995, as Vice-President of the International Institute of Sociology, he initiated the Dialogue Graduate Scholarship Program for Women in Developing Countries.

Also from Kumarian Press...

*Global Issues*

**Capitalism and Justice:** Envisioning Social and Economic Fairness
John Isbister

**The Cuban Way:** Capitalism, Communism and Confrontation
Named 'Outstanding Academic Title' by CHOICE Magazine, Ana Julia Jatar-Hausmann

**Inequity in the Global Village:** Recycled Rhetoric and Disposable People
Jan Knippers Black

**The Hidden Assembly Line:**
Gender Dynamics of Subcontracted Work in a Global Economy
Edited by Radhika Balakrishnan

**Promises Not Kept:** The Betrayal of Social Change in the Third World
FIFTH EDITION
John Isbister

**Sustainable Livelihoods:** Building on the Wealth of the Poor
Kristin Helmore and Naresh Singh

*Conflict Resolution, Environment, Gender Studies, Globalization, International Development, Microfinance, Political Economy*

**Advocacy for Social Justice:** A Global Action and Reflection Guide
David Cohen, Rosa de la Vega, Gabrielle Watson for Oxfam America and the Advocacy Institute

**Bound:** Living in the Globalized World
Scott Sernau

**The Humanitarian Enterprise:** Dilemmas and Discoveries
Larry Minear

**Shifting Burdens:** Gender and Agrarian Change under Neoliberalism
Edited by Shahra Razavi

**The Spaces of Neoliberalism:** Land, Place and Family in Latin America
Edited by Jacquelyn Chase

**War's Offensive on Women:**
The Humanitarian Challenge in Bosnia, Kosovo, and Afghanistan
Julie A. Mertus for the Humanitarianism and War Project

Visit Kumarian Press at **www.kpbooks.com** or call **toll-free 800.289.2664** for a complete catalog.

 *Kumarian Press, located in Bloomfield, Connecticut, is a forward-looking, scholarly press that promotes active international engagement and an awareness of global connectedness.*

# DATE DUE

| | | | |
|---|---|---|---|
| | | | |
| | | | |
| | | | |
| | | | |
| | | | |
| | | | |
| | | | |
| | | | |
| | | | |
| | | | |
| | | | |
| | | | |
| | | | |
| | | | |
| | | | |
| | | | |
| | | | |

Demco, Inc. 38-293